COVID-19 AND THE VOLUNTARY AND COMMUNITY SECTOR IN THE UK

Responses, Impacts and Adaptation

Edited by
James Rees, Rob Macmillan, Chris Dayson,
Chris Damm and Claire Bynner

First published in Great Britain in 2023 by

Policy Press, an imprint of
Bristol University Press
University of Bristol
1-9 Old Park Hill
Bristol
BS2 8BB
UK
t: +44 (0)117 374 6645
e: bup-info@bristol.ac.uk

Details of international sales and distribution partners are available at
policy.bristoluniversitypress.co.uk

© Bristol University Press 2023

British Library Cataloguing in Publication Data
A catalogue record for this book is available from the British Library

ISBN 978-1-4473-6550-1 hardcover
ISBN 978-1-4473-6551-8 paperback
ISBN 978-1-4473-6552-5 ePub
ISBN 978-1-4473-6553-2 ePdf

The right of James Rees, Rob Macmillan, Chris Dayson, Chris Damm and Claire Bynner to be identified as editors of this work has been asserted by them in accordance with the Copyright, Designs and Patents Act 1988.

All rights reserved: no part of this publication may be reproduced, stored in a retrieval system, or transmitted in any form or by any means, electronic, mechanical, photocopying, recording, or otherwise without the prior permission of Bristol University Press.

Every reasonable effort has been made to obtain permission to reproduce copyrighted material. If, however, anyone knows of an oversight, please contact the publisher.

The statements and opinions contained within this publication are solely those of the editors and contributors and not of the University of Bristol or Bristol University Press. The University of Bristol and Bristol University Press disclaim responsibility for any injury to persons or property resulting from any material published in this publication.

Bristol University Press and Policy Press work to counter discrimination on grounds of gender, race, disability, age and sexuality.

Cover design: Hayes Design and Advertising
Front cover image: Shutterstock / GoodStudio

Contents

List of figures and tables		v
Notes on contributors		vi
Acknowledgements		xiv

1	Introduction James Rees, Rob Macmillan, Chris Dayson, Chris Damm and Claire Bynner	1

PART I Experience, impacts and lessons for the voluntary community sector

2	Mobilising the voluntary sector: critical reflections from across the four UK nations Nick Acheson, Laura Crawford, Jurgen Grotz, Irene Hardill, Denise Hayward, Eddy Hogg, Rhys Dafydd Jones, Matthew Linning, Sally Rees, Alasdair Rutherford, Ewen Speed, Amy McGarvey, Catherine Goodall, Joanna Stuart and Debbie Maltman	17
3	Bouncing back: the employment of sector attributes to recover from crises Tony Chapman	30
4	The impact of COVID-19 on the formation and dissolution of charitable organisations Diarmuid McDonnell, Alasdair Rutherford and John Mohan	45
5	Paying the price of 'doing good' in the face of crisis Sarah Smith, Tracey M. Coule and Daniel King	61

PART II Key policy fields and inequalities

6	Shifting sands: challenges and opportunities for the voluntary sector during the COVID-19 pandemic Jon Burchell, Joanne Cook, Harriet Thiery, Erica Ballantyne, Fiona Walkley and Silviya Nikolova	77
7	At the COVID-19 frontlines: voluntary sector support for refugee and migrant families in Glasgow Maureen McBride, Elaine Feeney, Clara Pirie and Jane Cullingworth	91
8	The value and contribution of BAME-led organisations during and beyond COVID-19 Abigail Woodward, Beth Patmore, Gilli Cliff and Chris Dayson	104
9	The impact of the COVID-19 pandemic on advocacy work of voluntary sector organisations in Wales Elizabeth Cookingham Bailey, E. Katharina Sarter and Vita Terry	118

10	Community ownership of physical assets in changing times: the context of opportunities in the pandemic *Carina Skropke*	130
11	The impact and effect of COVID-19 on BAME-led voluntary sector organisations: resilience and new ways of working *Karl Murray*	143
12	Voluntary sector organisations, older people and healthy ageing during the COVID-19 pandemic *Chris Dayson, Emma Bimpson, Angela Ellis Paine, Joseph Chambers, Jan Gilbertson and Helen Kara*	156

PART III Perspectives from practice and policy

13	Emotions in the VCSE sector during the pandemic *Vita Terry, Houda Davis and Marilyn Taylor*	173
14	The experience of community-led businesses during the COVID-19 pandemic *Sophie Reid*	186
15	The response of voluntary community sports clubs to COVID-19 *Geoff Nichols, Lindsay Findlay-King and Fiona Reid*	199
16	The latent strength of community ties: how voluntary sector infrastructure organisations utilised their local networks in response to COVID-19 *Lucy Smith*	211
17	How many of us had pandemic in our risk register? A snapshot of experiences of community buildings during the first lockdown of 2020 *Ann Hindley and John Wilson*	225
18	Leading through a pandemic *Patricia Armstrong with Jayne Stuart*	237
19	Afterword *Margaret Harris*	249

Index	258

List of figures and tables

Figures

3.1	Continuity and change in the third sector	31
3.2	Fluctuations in the income of medium-sized TSOs in north-east England and Cumbria, 2004–20	36
3.3	Relative importance of income sources to TSOs (Third Sector Trends, north-east England and Cumbria, 2010–19)	38
3.4	Mismatch between expectations and reality on rising income, 2009–21	41
4.1	Deviation from average level of formations for seven charity jurisdictions, 2015–21	51
4.2	Deviation from average level of dissolutions for seven charity jurisdictions, 2015–21	51
4.3a	Trends in the formation of charities in England and Wales	52
4.3b	Trends in the formation of charities in Scotland	53
4.4a	Trends in the dissolution of charities in England and Wales	54
4.4b	Trends in the dissolution of charities in Scotland	55
4.5	Trends over time in the insolvencies of charitable companies in England and Wales	56
16.1	Diffusion model between the NCL CCG, Voluntary Action Camden and GoodGym	217
16.2	Diffusion model between Croydon Voluntary Action, London Plus, the Emergency Committee and its donors	220

Tables

12.1	LNN support for health ageing prior to the COVID-19 pandemic	159
12.2	How the LNNs supported healthy ageing during the COVID-19 pandemic	164
14.1	Overview of studies included	188
17.1	Levels of reserves at the two periods	232

Notes on contributors

Editors

Claire Bynner is Lecturer in Social Justice and Community Action at the Moray House School of Education and Sport, University of Edinburgh. She leads the research team for Children's Neighbourhoods Scotland, a place-based approach to reducing child poverty in Scotland. Her recent research examines family wellbeing, service responses and collaboration during the COVID-19 pandemic.

Chris Damm is Research Fellow at the Centre for Regional Economic and Social Research, Sheffield Hallam University, where he leads the Voluntary Sector Research Cluster. His research focuses on data and theory relating to the role and funding of the voluntary sector in the provision of welfare services.

Chris Dayson is Professor of Voluntary Action, Health and Wellbeing, Sheffield Hallam University. His research focuses on the contribution of local voluntary and community organisations to health and wellbeing, and he has led a number of major research projects exploring their response to and the impact of the COVID-19 pandemic.

Rob Macmillan is Principal Research Fellow at the Centre for Regional Economic and Social Research at Sheffield Hallam University.

James Rees is Reader and Deputy Director of the Institute for Community Research and Development at the University of Wolverhampton. He is a Co-Editor of *Voluntary Sector Review* and has published widely on aspects of the voluntary sector, particularly in relation to public service delivery and leadership.

Chapter authors

Nick Acheson is an independent researcher and was formally a Lecturer in Social Policy at Ulster University and a Visiting Research Fellow at the Centre for Social Innovation, Business School, Trinity College Dublin. He was formally Editor of *Voluntary Sector Review*.

Patricia Armstrong is CEO of ACOSVO (the Association of Chief Officers of Scottish Voluntary Organisations) and a DBA Research student

Notes on contributors

with Edinburgh Napier University. Pat is also a board member of the Charity Regulator in Scotland, OSCR, and has over 30 years' experience of leadership roles in the sector.

Erica Ballantyne is Director of the Operations Management and Decision Sciences Research Centre at the University of Sheffield Management School. Her research interests include: sustainable logistics and freight transport operations, particularly last mile contexts, and electrified transport applications; and reverse logistics and retail returns management.

Emma Bimpson is Research Associate at the Centre for Regional Economic and Social Research, Sheffield Hallam University.

Jon Burchell is Senior Lecturer at Sheffield University Management School and was the Principal Investigator on the ESRC-funded MoVE project, investigating community responses to the COVID-19 pandemic. His research focuses on cross-sectoral dialogue and collaboration and social action.

Joseph Chambers is former Research Associate at the Centre for Regional Economic and Social Research, Sheffield Hallam University.

Tony Chapman is Professor and Director of Research, Policy and Practice at St Chad's College, Durham University. He has been working on the Third Sector Trends Study, which was initiated by Northern Rock Foundation, since 2008. The current round of the research will continue until 2023.

Gilli Cliff is an Age Better learning officer on the Age Better in Sheffield programme at South Yorkshire Housing Association.

Joanne Cook is Chair in Organisational Behaviour and Human Resource Management at Hull University Business School. Jo's training is multidisciplinary and her research interests include public, private and third sectors alongside expertise in gender, migration and ageing. She is currently the Principal Investigator on the NIHR-funded project investigating local area coordination as a preventative approach.

Elizabeth Cookingham Bailey is Lecturer in Public Service Management at the University of South Wales. Her research focuses on the role of voluntary sector organisations in the creation and delivery of social policy, the privatisation of education and the development of education policy, and the history of social policy.

Tracey M. Coule is Professor of Non-profit Work and Organization in the Department of Management at Sheffield Hallam University. She was formerly Programme Leader of Sheffield Business School's Doctorate in Business Administration (DBA) and a member of SHU's Voluntary Action Research Group (VARG).

Laura Crawford is Teaching Fellow at the University of Birmingham. Her research and teaching expertise is in social, cultural and historical geography, specifically focusing on disability, care, research methods and voluntary action.

Jane Cullingworth is Research Associate at the University of Glasgow and the University of Strathclyde. Her research explores the involvement of civil society actors in democratic governance and the resulting challenges for non-state actors in maintaining both autonomy from the state and legitimacy with civil society.

Houda Davis is Senior Researcher at the Institute for Voluntary Action Research, with experience working across the voluntary, funding and public sectors. Houda's research interests include health and wellbeing in place-based partnerships, learning and evaluation in trusts and foundations, and community-led responses to climate change.

Angela Ellis Paine is Research Fellow at the Third Sector Research Centre, University of Birmingham. Her research explores different aspects of the role of voluntary action and the relationships between volunteers, voluntary organisations, the state and society.

Elaine Feeney is a PhD researcher in Urban Studies at the University of Glasgow.

Lindsay Findlay-King is Principal Lecturer in Sport Management at Northumbria University. She is the Chair of the UK Sports Volunteering Research Network and has researched and published across various areas of sport volunteering, particularly in relation to two key areas: community-run sport facilities and diversity in volunteering.

Jan Gilbertson is Senior Research Fellow at the Centre for Regional Economic and Social Research, Sheffield Hallam University.

Catherine Goodall is a senior policy and influencing advisor at the National Council for Voluntary Organisations. Catherine leads on volunteering policy, engaging with a wide range of issues for volunteering. She has a background in supporting system change in local authorities, research and policy, primarily for children's social care.

Jurgen Grotz is Director of the Institute for Volunteering Research at the University of East Anglia, UK. He is a social scientist and examines the difference volunteering makes to individuals and communities.

Irene Hardill is Professor of Public Policy in the Department of Social Sciences at Northumbria University. She was formerly Director of the Northumbria Centre for Citizenship and Civil Society, and has a particular expertise in volunteering and the voluntary and community sector.

Margaret Harris is Emeritus Professor at Aston University, and a Visiting Professor at Birkbeck, University of London.

Denise Hayward is Chief Executive of Volunteer Now, the regional volunteering support organisation for Northern Ireland. She has extensive experience in organisational and public volunteering policy development, creating good-quality volunteer opportunities and involving volunteers. She has expertise in third sector governance gained over her career in the voluntary sector.

Ann Hindley is an independent researcher/consultant with a background in community development. She was Regional Co-Ordinator for Community Matters in Yorkshire and the Humber for three years and continued working for them as an associate on community asset transfer until their closure.

Eddy Hogg is Senior Lecturer in Social Policy at the University of Kent. His research looks at volunteering, charitable giving and public attitudes to the voluntary sector. Recently, he has worked on research on youth volunteering, volunteering in public services, voluntary action for schools, and charity and fundraising regulation.

Rhys Dafydd Jones is a social geographer based at Aberystwyth University. He is interested in faith, migration and participation in civil society.

Helen Kara is an independent researcher who operates as We Research It Ltd.

Daniel King is Professor of Organisational Studies and Co-Director of the Centre for People, Work and Organisational Practice. He led the project 'Respond, recover, reset: the voluntary sector and COVID-19', funded by the ESRC, and has published widely on the voluntary sector and alternative forms of organising.

Matthew Linning is Head of Research and Evaluation at Volunteer Scotland. He has published widely on the impact of volunteering participation in society, including the historic environment, youth volunteering, and volunteering health and wellbeing benefits. Formerly, he was a Director of DTZ plc, heading up its UK Economics Team.

Debbie Maltman is a research officer at Volunteer Scotland. She has published several reports on volunteering in Scotland, primarily focusing on qualitative analysis and considering different measures of volunteer participation. Prior to joining Volunteering Scotland Debbie undertook a Master's in Data Science at Stirling University.

Maureen McBride is Research Associate at the School of Education at the University of Glasgow. She is a sociologist interested in inequalities, with a particular focus on class and race. Her current research focuses on child poverty, communities and youth activism.

Diarmuid McDonnell is Lecturer in Social Sciences at the University of the West of Scotland. His research examines a number of topics concerning nonprofit organisations: funding sources and networks; measuring and modelling organisational and financial risk; evaluating regulatory interventions; and estimating geographical distribution of charitable activity.

Amy McGarvey is Research Manager at NCVO. Amy leads on a range of research programmes, including the Time Well Spent series. She has a background in developing and evaluating educational programmes, and spent several years providing research and consultancy to UK policy makers as a researcher at TNS BMRB (now Kantar Public).

John Mohan is Professor of Social Policy at the Third Sector Research Centre, University of Birmingham. His research is currently focused on the distinctive contribution of the third sector to society and health in contemporary Britain.

Karl Murray is a freelance researcher, evaluator and trainer with a focus on the voluntary and community sector. He has worked on a range of projects with The Ubele Initiative and Action for Race Equality (formerly BTEG), and internationally, with a focus on research and consultation within the Black, Asian and Minority Ethnic communities.

Notes on contributors

Geoff Nichols is Honorary Senior Lecturer with Sheffield University Management School. He has researched volunteers in sport since 1993 and written books and papers on this subject. He retired from university teaching in 2020, but continues his research interests.

Silviya Nikolova is Lecturer in Health Economics at the Academic Unit of Health Economics. Her current research focuses on economic evaluation and economics of frailty and ageing. Silviya also undertakes research in health and social care services evaluation. Her research uses quantitative methods applied to large data sets including routine NHS data.

Beth Patmore is Senior University Teacher in Innovation and Entrepreneurship at the Sheffield University Management School, University of Sheffield.

Clara Pirie is Widening Participation Tutor at the University of Glasgow.

Sally Rees is Health and Social Care Manager at WCVA (Wales Council for Voluntary Action) and is currently on a two-year secondment to the Welsh government as Head of Evaluation and New Models of Care. Her research background is in social policy.

Fiona Reid is an independent researcher and Director of Bayfirth Research. Her research focuses on sport volunteers and voluntary sport clubs. She is Vice-Chair of the UK Sports Volunteering Research Network and a member of the Research Advisory Group of the Observatory for Sport in Scotland.

Sophie Reid is a freelance social researcher and a Research Associate at Power to Change. Her work includes supporting organisations to measure and improve social impact, research on food systems and community business, and facilitating public dialogue on major social questions.

Alasdair Rutherford is Professor of Social Statistics at the University of Stirling. His research focus is the analysis of administrative and survey data in the fields of health, social care and the third sector. He has also been involved in a number of initiatives to build data analysis skills among third sector practitioners.

E. Katharina Sarter is Senior Lecturer in Social Policy and Public Service Management at the South Wales Business School, University of South Wales. Her research focuses on public policies and regulation, including employment and the regulation of labour, multi-level governance and comparative research.

Carina Skropke is a doctoral researcher at CRESR, Sheffield Hallam University. She is interested in social transformation and alternative approaches to urgent social challenges. Her research is co-funded by Power to Change and focuses on potential community solutions through asset ownership.

Lucy Smith is a London School of Economics alumna, an independent researcher and a sociologist who works with London's voluntary sector on a variety of research and capacity-building projects.

Sarah Smith is Research Fellow with the Centre for People, Work and Organisational Practice. She worked on the project 'Respond, recover, reset: the voluntary sector and COVID-19', funded by the ESRC.

Ewen Speed is Professor of Medical Sociology in the School of Health and Social Care at the University of Essex. He has published on the politics and governance of the English NHS and wider comparative analyses of international health policy. He is Associate Editor of the journal *Critical Public Health*.

Jayne Stuart is Head of Sustainability at ACOSVO. Jayne is a charity trustee and a former chief executive with over 25 years' experience in voluntary sector leadership.

Joanna Stuart is an independent researcher specialising in volunteering and the voluntary sector. Recent work includes research on volunteer wellbeing and the impacts of COVID-19 on voluntary and community organisations. She is a Research Associate at NCVO and a Visiting Research Fellow at Nottingham Trent University.

Marilyn Taylor is Visiting Research Fellow at the Institute for Voluntary Action Research and has published widely in the field of community policy and practice.

Vita Terry is Principal Researcher at the Institute for Voluntary Action Research, whose research interests are small and medium-sized voluntary organisations, emotions and wellbeing in voluntary sector work, and community engagement. She has previously researched organisational change in asylum seeker and refugee voluntary sector organisations.

Harriet Thiery is Research Associate at Hull University Business School and was the Primary Researcher on the MoVE project, investigating community responses to the COVID-19 pandemic. Her research interests include localism, civil society, social policy and the interactive relationships between power, policy and discourse.

Fiona Walkley is Lecturer in Marketing at Hull University Business School. Fiona brings senior marketing expertise from a 15-year career in international marketing, managing well-known consumer brands, to the university. Her research has focused on applying marketing concepts in the context of public policy, specifically social action and government work to build community capacity and mobilise volunteers.

John Wilson is a project manager for Community Matters, a charity that offers support to organisations managing community buildings.

Abigail Woodward is Research Fellow at the Centre for Ageing Population Studies, University College London. Her research focuses on the lived experiences of underserved populations including ethnic minority groups. She is currently working on a project looking at the self-management of long-term health conditions among people experiencing socioeconomic deprivation.

Acknowledgements

The editors would like to thank Sarah Ward at Sheffield Hallam University for her careful proofreading and assistance with formatting. We also thank colleagues at the Voluntary Sector Studies Network (VSSN) who constructed and contributed to the research repository from which several of the chapters originated.

1

Introduction

James Rees, Rob Macmillan, Chris Dayson, Chris Damm and Claire Bynner

Introduction

The COVID-19 pandemic has profoundly affected all corners of society, in the UK and globally. Its longer-term impacts are still unfolding and its legacy will be with us for years to come. Our aim with this book has been to curate an enduring collection of the most important and rigorous academic and applied research on the UK voluntary sector's response and adaptation to the pandemic. The contributions gathered in this collection cover the responses of this diverse sector to an unprecedented crisis, the impact of the pandemic on organisations, staff, volunteers and social infrastructure, and the longer-term adaptations made by the sector in response to emerging needs and inequalities.

The voluntary sector, often working in partnership with public agencies and informally with individual or informal groups of citizens, has been central to the response to the COVID-19 pandemic. This edited collection brings together many of the key academics, and voices from practice, carrying out vital and vibrant research into the impact of the pandemic on the sector in the UK, the manifold ways it has responded to new challenges and the longer-term consequences for the sector and its workforce, volunteers and beneficiaries. Collectively, we have sought to document and highlight the ways the sector has responded and adapted, and what can be learnt to maximise its contribution in future crises. The book consists of 18 short and readable chapters, emanating from an open call to UK voluntary sector scholars via the Voluntary Sector Studies Network (VSSN). There has been a tremendous amount of research exploring how the voluntary sector has responded to the pandemic and how the crisis has affected its work, and we aimed to curate and preserve research on a wide range of key topics that might otherwise be lost or hard to access.

We are delighted that the final collection includes contributions from a diverse range of UK-based scholars at different career stages, as well as commentators from within voluntary sector practice and policy, addressing a wide range of topics and covering experiences in all four UK nations. The contents thus reflect an impressive mix of authors from academic and policy-/practice-based research organisations and cover projects funded from a myriad of sources, from large national projects funded by UK Research and Innovation (UKRI) and national charities and foundations, to more focused projects based on researcher and practice collaborations. Each chapter is original, not published elsewhere, but they often build on or connect with wider research projects and agendas.

As well as its diversity of scholarship, the book also encompasses a range of perspectives and aspects of this large and diverse voluntary sector, and includes contributions covering all four UK nations. Part I of the book includes a series of broader contributions that shed light on what happened across the sector and assess both broad impacts and key issues in the recovery of the sector from the pandemic. Part II focuses on a number of significant fields and policy domains within which the sector operates, as well as the position of organisations working with minority groups and addressing inequalities. Finally, Part III contains chapters highlighting a range of essential practice-based concerns and longer-term issues that have emerged during the pandemic, including wellbeing, leadership and social infrastructure. Ultimately, we hope that the collection stimulates further debate about the role of the sector in wider societal responses to COVID-19, and how it might underpin future social resilience and enhanced social justice.

Broad context: the COVID-19 pandemic and the VCS

The UK's pandemic response

COVID-19, a contagious disease caused by Severe Acute Respiratory Syndrome Coronavirus 2 (SARS-CoV-2), first emerged in Wuhan, China in December 2019. Following its rapid spread across the globe, by early 2020 it was causing urgent debate about how governments and wider society should respond to the threat (Farrar and Ahuja, 2021). In the UK, a newly elected Conservative administration led by Prime Minister Boris Johnson, with the priority of 'delivering' Brexit, proved to be ill-prepared to confront the challenge of a global pandemic (Calvert and Arbuthnot, 2021). The Westminster government, distracted and ideologically disinclined to take COVID-19 seriously, was nevertheless forced into a response by mid-March 2020. Johnson appeared in a televised briefing on 23 March 2020 to announce a policy requiring all those who could to remain at home except for essential shopping, basic exercise or for medical treatment; essential key workers – the NHS, frontline transport staff and some charity workers – were exempt. Thus, the whole territory of the UK entered a relatively severe 'lockdown' until the beginning of a gradual easing in May, with the lifting of most restrictions only occurring in early July 2020.

After a slow start, a further raft of policies fell into place in the following weeks, with the stay-at-home order supported by large-scale public spending in the form of a furlough scheme for workers and various grants and loan guarantee schemes for businesses. Despite these unprecedented public health measures, justified in order to 'flatten the curve' of COVID-19 infections, by the end of the first full week of July 2020, as the first wave of the disease was abating, the cumulative death toll in the UK from COVID-19 had reached 41,000. Following the summer reopening, and stimulus policies such as the Treasury's controversial 'Eat Out to Help Out' scheme, a second wave of infections gathered pace throughout autumn 2020, leading to a second stringent national lockdown commencing on 5 January 2021 at the height of the UK's winter. As the second wave in turn abated in early April 2021, some 127,000 people had died within 28 days of a positive COVID-19 test, and the UK had one of the worst death tolls from COVID-19 in Europe (Cuffe, 2021). The broad impact on the UK population was therefore severe, particularly in the first wave, and the unequal impact on different population groups exacerbated existing inequalities, an important theme of this volume (Fancourt et al, 2021).

The huge scale of the initial lockdown and the relative severity, sudden onset and unprecedented nature of the measures put in place caused great uncertainty and dislocation for many citizens, particularly for those considered to be vulnerable and required to 'shield' due to age-related frailty or underlying health conditions. The experience in the UK was a rapid upswell in voluntary and community action to ameliorate the immediate impacts and disruption of lockdown. To some extent, this reflected weak state capacity after years of austerity and neoliberal ideology, perhaps particularly visible in terms of local resilience and support to vulnerable individuals and communities. Interestingly, this appeared to be recognised at a national level within days of the first lockdown being announced: on 24 March 2020, for instance, Health Secretary Matt Hancock called for 250,000 volunteers to 'help the NHS and local services by delivering shopping and medicines to vulnerable people' (*The Guardian*, 2020). An NHS Volunteer Responders scheme was launched, supported by the 'GoodSAM Responders' app, which in the event attracted over 750,000 volunteers. If nothing else, this suggested an extraordinary desire to help fellow citizens in an emergency, and the new-found availability of those who had been furloughed. Unfortunately, there were widespread reports that the system was overwhelmed by the number of volunteers, and some withdrew following delays or a lack of request for their help – there were also concerns that the GoodSAM volunteer force wasn't coordinated with local infrastructure to support effective deployment (Rees et al, 2020).

The voluntary sector response and the impact of COVID-19

Arguably much more significant and broadly based was the explosion of agile, responsive and often innovative voluntary action happening from the bottom up throughout the country (Dayson et al, 2021). Perhaps drawing the most attention was the novel and rapid development of independent local 'mutual aid' groups that emerged across the whole country, encouraged by a central national website but driven by citizens motivated to provide support – primarily food and medicine delivery, and friendly check-ups – to their neighbours and local community members (Wyler, 2020). As Tiratelli and Kaye (2020, p 8) put it, '[t]hese groups were not "nice to have" – they provided essential support to vulnerable people and prevented further negative outcomes emerging from the crisis'. At the level of the more traditional, organised voluntary sector, organisations responded in manifold ways to meet the needs of their local communities or beneficiary groups, often pivoting to deliver services in new ways (especially online and using digital technology), meet new needs and work collaboratively with local government and health agencies, other voluntary organisations (VOs), as well as existing and new community groups, and mutual aid groups (Dayson et al, 2021). It must also be recognised that some shut down completely because they couldn't see how to operate and/or furloughed their workers. Local infrastructure organisations (LIOs) were often centrally involved in coordinating responses with local government and VOs (McMullan and Macmillan, 2021). There is much more to be said about this variety of responses, and this book aims to begin to fill in some of the rich picture of the ways the sector responded in different places, fields of activity and parts of the voluntary sector, based on academic and practice-based research. Numerous contributions to this volume aim to shed light on the different responses in different parts of the country, including within Scotland and Wales.

Another key part of the broader context for the voluntary sector in the early weeks of the pandemic were deep concerns, articulated particularly by the sector's representative bodies, about the impact of the pandemic on its own ability to sustain itself and therefore provide continuing support to beneficiaries and communities. With the government slow to act compared with support for business and individuals, the general view was that proposed government support to the sector was inadequate. As Macmillan (2020, p 130) put it, COVID-19 represented a three-dimensional crisis of 'resourcing, operation and demand'. The sector mounted a behind-the-scenes lobbying of government, and a social media campaign (under the #everydaycounts and #nevermoreneeded hashtags) sought to raise awareness of the work of VOs in responding to the pandemic, and to highlight their financial precarity due to a sudden drop-off in income from fundraising, donations and fees for goods and services. There were also initial concerns that charities would be unable to access the full range of cheap loans made available to businesses due to eligibility restrictions, and that they would be unable to furlough workers due to increasing demand for their services (Chamberlain, 2020). Sector representatives such as the National Council for Voluntary Organisations (NCVO) claimed that civil society would lose £4 billion of income during the first 12 weeks of the pandemic (HoC DCMS Committee, 2020). Ultimately, the sector was provided with a £750 million support package announced by Chancellor Rishi Sunak on 8 April 2020 (see Hargrave, 2020) and from this point on, at least some financial support appeared to be in place for the sector (Craston et al, 2021). Contributions to this volume, particularly in Part I, consider broader perspectives on the impact and response of the sector.

In keeping with Boris Johnson's determination to 'move on', most lockdown restrictions in the UK were lifted on 4 July 2020, though a second wave of infections during autumn and winter 2020 led to the imposition of a new tiered approach to lockdown restrictions based on geographical variations in infection. Throughout the pandemic, the Scottish National Party (SNP)-led government in Scotland and the Labour devolved administration in Wales had tended to push for stronger and more proactive restrictions, with more emphasis on mutual responsibility and care. Meanwhile, at the UK level the opposition Labour Party, while strongly supporting the government's general legislative and policy response to COVID-19, also argued for stronger and earlier action, particularly as time went on and backbench Conservative MPs agitated for lighter public health restrictions. By December 2020 the first vaccines were being delivered (supported by many volunteers), but a second wave – bringing many more deaths and continued pressure on hospitals – was underway and the UK re-entered lockdown on 5 January 2021. Through early 2021 the expanding vaccination programme proved to be highly successful with rapid provision and high uptake in the UK compared with many similar countries. This time, restrictions were removed more gradually, leading to a supposed 'Freedom Day' in England on 29 July 2021. Nevertheless, at the time of writing in early 2022, the country appears to have emerged relatively unscathed from the appearance of the Omicron variant, and all remaining restrictions have been lifted in England from 24 February 2022 as part of the government's 'Living with COVID' strategy (HM Government, 2022). The threat of further waves of disease caused by new variants, and potentially waning vaccine effectiveness and coverage, may continue to cause concern. The voluntary sector sits in this broader context: responding to an initial urgent crisis followed by a continually shifting 'new normal', and the emergence of a growing range of 'downstream' impacts such as mental health and wellbeing concerns (British Academy, 2021).

COVID-19 and the UK voluntary and community sector: experiences, knowledge and implications

Experiences and knowledge

Throughout the two years of the COVID-19 pandemic period, up to March 2022, a sizeable and multifaceted research endeavour has been underway to chart, interpret and understand the significance of the crisis for voluntary and community action in its diverse forms – for the experiences, work and operation of organisations and groups, for informal grassroots and mutual aid activities, and for volunteering and social action. The chapters in this book provide an authoritative guide to some of the leading research-based observations of the impact of COVID-19, from academics and practitioners alike. Voluntary and community sector (VCS) research has been responsive and adaptive, picking up issues as they have emerged. The research response to the pandemic has been iterative, rather like the crisis itself (Bynner, 2021).

As the COVID-19 crisis unfolded, much of the early research effort sought to understand the scale and scope of the immediate impact of lockdown, addressing key questions such as: what kinds of services are needed and possible right now and how can needs be met, and what kinds of resources will be available to make that happen and keep organisations going? Early research took the form of regular snapshot and 'pulse' surveys of organisations to assess what they were facing and how they were coping with the crisis, and what was happening to various income streams, such as contracts, grants, donations and income from trading.

Typically, these surveys identified increased and intensified demand for services, constrained resources for some organisations and apprehension about the short- and medium-term future. The results were often used to present a bigger picture of a sector both stepping into the pandemic response and yet fragile and in need of support and flexibility from funders. This was combined with qualitative reflections from peer-support Zoom calls about how the crisis was being experienced on the ground, and what dilemmas organisational leaders were encountering, such as supporting the wellbeing of isolated staff and volunteers and trying to meet needs online.

Over time, research began to explore in more detail the contribution of different parts of the VCS and how they were faring, for example, in terms of smaller organisations, community business and social enterprise, mutual aid groups and hyper-local community action, groups representing minoritised communities and the sector working in different fields. The early mobilisation of voluntary and community action to support people in need of food deliveries and parcels, meals and medicines began to broaden towards social support, arts and craft activities, and a deepening concern with mental health and wellbeing, debt and enduring poverty.

At the same time, research began to identify a number of cross-cutting themes in the sector's role, contribution and relationships with the state and others. Numerous research reports identified a change in the way voluntary and community organisations engaged with each other and with statutory partners. An 'all-hands-on-deck' emergency response prevailed involving the part and temporary suspension of existing practices, assumptions and hierarchies. Practitioners spoke of positive and proactive relationships and constructive collaboration, coupled with new-found visibility and recognition for the necessary contribution made by the sector. Organisations were able to work beyond existing boundaries and silos, and the coordinating capability of many VCS infrastructure bodies was appreciated. Of course, this was never a universal experience, neither within local areas nor across different localities or the different UK national contexts. Research also began to explore these variations, asking what made for different approaches and experiences. The role of earlier investment in the VCS came to the fore, alongside the importance of pre-existing relationships between the sector and statutory partners.

Finally, as various attempts to envisage life beyond COVID-19 faltered in the face of new variants and waves of infection, so research charted the longer-term impact of the crisis on voluntary and community organisations. This could be seen in terms of staff and volunteer burnout, and in the paradox afforded by the need for ongoing flexibility in the face of changing rules and circumstances, alongside the inertia of strategy in the midst of ongoing and radical uncertainty. In such a context, how could practitioners conceivably think through the intense demands on their organisations and find a pathway beyond COVID-19?

Implications for the VCS moving forward

Although the chapters in this book focus predominantly on the immediate and shorter-term experiences of the COVID-19 pandemic of the voluntary sector in the UK, there will undoubtably also be longer-term implications. At the time of writing, the outlook for the voluntary sector remains incredibly uncertain as the final throes of the pandemic are yet to play out. In the early stages of the pandemic Macmillan (2020) argued that the voluntary sector faced a three-dimensional crisis of resourcing, operation and demand, and these categories remain relevant to the challenges facing the sector two years on.

In terms of *resourcing*, it seems unlikely that significant amounts of extra funding will flow to the voluntary sector in the next few years, particularly in light of increasingly constrained public finances. In parallel, it is also unclear if levels of charitable giving or formal volunteering will return to pre-pandemic levels. In terms of *operation*, while most VOs have been able to recommence pre-pandemic modes of delivery, they are also having to consider whether to retain some of the digital provision which proved so effective during the pandemic. Digital provision, alongside staff needs and wishes for greater flexible, remote or hybrid working, will need to be balanced against benefits of face-to-face interaction with service users and communities. In terms of *demand*, the pandemic has undoubtedly exacerbated inequalities associated with health and social and economic deprivation, meaning need among the people VOs often exist to support is likely to remain high for the foreseeable future. Finding ways to meet these needs while working with constrained resources will be an ongoing challenge for many VOs.

A further area of uncertainty relates to partnership working. As numerous chapters in this book highlight, the pandemic brought renewed and arguably more equal partnership working between the voluntary, public and private sectors. This has meant that small VOs, including those working with the most marginalised and disadvantaged groups, have felt more valued and included than before the pandemic (Thiery et al, 2021, and also Chapter 6 of this volume). Many in the voluntary sector have expressed a wish for these relationships to continue in the same way once the pandemic is over, but there remains concern that they will revert to previous practices which were often characterised by top-down and unequal power relationships and a lack of understanding of the true value of the voluntary sector (Dayson et al, 2021).

It has been argued that the voluntary sector possesses the transformative capacity to play a central role in post-pandemic recovery across the UK but that this potential will be limited without significant policy interventions and resource investment to catalyse this role (Dayson et al, 2021). To date, very few ideas or concrete policy proposals have been forthcoming. An exception is the English 'Levelling-Up White Paper', published in February 2022, which, in acknowledging the vital role of the voluntary sector and wider civil society during the pandemic, includes a recognition that social and community capital is equally critical as boosting economic development and regeneration. Although the White Paper was criticised for not including concrete funding plans and few policy proposals to deliver on its ambition (Pro Bono Economics, 2022), it does at least point towards a rhetorical shift from the adversarial and antagonistic tone that characterised relations between the voluntary sector and the Westminster government at the beginning of the pandemic (Dayson and Damm, 2020; Macmillan and Ellis Paine, 2020). For the voluntary sector, the true test of the White Paper, and other policy developments that may be forthcoming in the next few years, will be the extent to which they help address challenges associated with resourcing, operation and demand, and whether or not they lead to a more equal and equitable partnership with the public and private sectors in years to come.

Overview of the book and chapter contents

The book is organised into three parts with chapters in each reflecting the theme of the part: respectively, broad perspectives (Part I), the view from different parts of the sector (Part II) and practitioner perspectives (Part III).

Part I takes the broadest view, with four empirical and theoretical contributions on the impact on and sustainability of the voluntary sector.

In particular, the chapters in this section contribute enormously to our understanding of the broad impact of COVID-19 on the voluntary sector, and its likely trajectories of recovery.

In Chapter 2 a multidisciplinary research team from across the four UK nations helps set the context for many of the discussions in later chapters, by reporting results from a UKRI-funded study of mobilising voluntary action during the pandemic across the four nations. The authors highlight three key themes from a comprehensive literature review: the importance of mutual aid, informal volunteering and hyperlocal activity; the emergence of new partnerships and demonstrating the value of pre-existing relationships; and volunteer engagement, opportunities and mobilisation. They find clear policy divergences across the UK, based on different assumptions about the role of voluntary action.

Drawing from the long-standing Third Sector Trends study in the north-east of England and Cumbria, in Chapter 3 Tony Chapman addresses the question of whether the sector really faces a cliff edge as a result of COVID-19. Despite stark warnings of collapse through successive crises, third sector organisations (TSOs) seem to endure, and the overall picture over time is one of resilience and continuity rather than upheaval. To explain this paradox, Chapman uses survey findings to argue that the adaptability and robustness of TSOs derives from their independence and flexibility, their ability to alter priorities and change the way they work in view of the resources they can access.

Diarmuid McDonnell, Alasdair Rutherford and John Mohan address a similar question in Chapter 4 but use administrative data from charity and company regulators to explore rates of formation, dissolution and insolvency among charities in the UK. An innovative time series quantitative method is deployed to the data, allowing a comparison of experience before and during the pandemic. Overall, the authors conclude that charity formations were maintained in the early part of the pandemic, but a more dramatic decline has subsequently materialised. However, this has been counterbalanced by a fall in dissolutions and insolvencies. Because of the time lags involved, it remains to be seen how the picture will change beyond the pandemic, though the authors expect to see a noticeable rise in stored-up and delayed dissolutions, as financial support schemes end and reserves diminish.

In Chapter 5, Sarah Smith, Tracey Coule and Daniel King draw on an 18-month UKRI-funded project to explore some of the costs the pandemic has imposed upon VOs and the people who inhabit them. They outline the potential human costs of 'doing good' in crisis contexts, including harm to the wellbeing of both staff and volunteers. While VOs were often in a position to help those in need, the ever-increasing demands upon their services need to be balanced against the need for individuals to maintain boundaries and avoid burnout.

The seven chapters in Part II focus more on particular policy fields, impacts on minority groups (and responses of organisations working with those groups) and the important issue of inequalities exposed by the pandemic.

Chapter 6 addresses two central questions. First, how was the volunteer resource utilised by voluntary organisations, both nationally and locally, during the pandemic? Second, what was the nature of the cross-sectoral collaborations between voluntary organisations and local authorities at the heart of local humanitarian support frameworks? Jon Burchell, Joanne Cook, Harriet Thiery, Erica Ballantyne, Fiona Walkley and Silviya Nikolova argue that voluntary organisations' experiences of the pandemic were not predominantly about the ability of the VCS to recruit new volunteers, but about the skills and resourcefulness of VCS organisations, alongside local authority partners, to coordinate and mobilise existing available resources effectively.

Maureen McBride and colleagues explore, in Chapter 7, the role of voluntary organisations in Glasgow who gave practical and emotional support to refugee and migrant families. Voluntary organisations mobilised quickly and effectively to provide sensitive solutions to a range of challenges including translating public health information, dispelling misinformation and liaising with statutory services to plug gaps in available services. Particularly striking is their description of the work of frontline voluntary organisation workers in supporting families to repatriate the deceased and assisting asylum seekers without accommodation.

In Chapter 8, Abigail Woodward and colleagues highlight the distinctiveness of BAME-led voluntary organisations in their response to the pandemic. They argue that BAME-led voluntary organisations have been successful in proving their distinctiveness from other parts of the sector. Although small amounts of specific funding have been made available to support them, this is mostly short term and has been against a backdrop of funding losses over the last ten years. The challenge is how to ensure BAME-led voluntary organisations continue to be valued through COVID-19 recovery, particularly by the health and care system.

Cookingham Bailey and colleagues discuss, in Chapter 9, how voluntary organisations were seen as a trusted source of support and stability for marginalised communities. New technologies provided opportunities for greater connection but digital technology only worked where there were established relationships of trust. Many staff in advocacy organisations took on multiple roles to support the most vulnerable. This chapter highlights the dilemma for voluntary organisations in policy networks. The pandemic provided an opportunity to influence; however, organisational and financial constraints limit the ability of smaller voluntary organisations to participate.

Community buildings are crucial to the functioning of civil society and community, providing a physical and reliable base for convivial activity, but we would expect them to have been hit hard by COVID-19 and its associated lockdowns and social distancing, and subsequent loss of income. In Chapter 10, Carina Skropke assesses how organisations that own physical assets have responded in practice to the very changed context created by the pandemic, and finds that there is considerable pessimism in this part of the sector and concerns about future resourcing and sustainability.

Few can have failed to notice the disproportionate impact that COVID-19 had on BAME communities, and many expressed unease over the extent to which the pandemic highlighted existing racial (and other) inequalities, while exacerbating existing divides. In Chapter 11, Karl Murray highlights the range of research carried out by both BAME organisations and commentators, and considers the impact on programmes and the sustainability of BAME-led organisations, as well as funders. On a positive note, he highlights the extent of partnership working in the sector during the pandemic, including between infrastructure bodies and a renewed emphasis on Black-led funding and the targeting of funding to address racial disparities.

Chris Dayson and colleagues focus, in Chapter 12, on the role of an interesting form of voluntary action at the forefront of local responses to the pandemic: the 37 neighbourhood networks which cover the city of Leeds, aiming to support older people to live independently and participate in their communities by providing a range of activities and services. As COVID-19 hit, they pivoted quickly to meeting basic needs, demonstrating both *absorptive* capacity, to respond to the immediate impact of the pandemic on the needs of members and to keep operating as voluntary organisations, and then *adaptive* capacity, to adjust their approach as needs and circumstances evolved.

Finally, in Part III we present six chapters providing a broad and diverse range of perspectives from practice and co-produced researcher–practitioner collaboration, but also a focus on the crucial role of community buildings and assets, as well as the wellbeing of workforces, and leadership.

Throughout the pandemic, the Institute for Voluntary Action Research (IVAR) has been hosting peer-support sessions for VCSE leaders to share experiences and receive support from colleagues. The discussions have formed the basis for regular updates and briefings as the crisis has unfolded. In Chapter 13, Vita Terry, Houda Davis and Marilyn Taylor use the material from over 100 peer-support sessions involving leaders from over 200 mainly small and medium-sized voluntary organisations to highlight the emotional impact of the pandemic, and how leaders have responded. The authors conclude that emotions shift and change over time, and therefore providing emotional support needs to be integrated into organisational culture.

In Chapter 14, Sophie Reid, from Power to Change, synthesises findings from five different studies to explore tensions in the response and experiences of community businesses during the pandemic. On the one hand, their 'hybrid' business models, which balance grants with trading income, meant that many community businesses struggled financially during the pandemic. On the other, their local rootedness meant they were well placed to identify and respond to needs in communities meaningfully as the pandemic progressed.

In Chapter 15, Geoff Nichols, Lindsay Findlay-King and Fiona Reid describe how community sports clubs have adapted to the restrictions imposed during the COVID-19 pandemic. They make the case that these clubs are mutual aid organisations, even though their focus is more on the leisure and wellbeing of members rather than food or medicine. They suggest community sports clubs were able to respond quickly to changed circumstances to meet the needs of members, though their focus was generally on continuing to serve their members rather than meeting wider societal needs.

Lucy Smith brings attention to voluntary sector infrastructure organisations, such as Councils for Voluntary Service (CVSs), Voluntary Actions (VAs) and Volunteer Centres (VCs) in Chapter 16. Drawing on two London-based case studies of CVSs in operation during lockdown, she describes how the relationships and embedded positions of these organisations enabled information, resources and aid to flow between otherwise unconnected parties, at a local and regional level. This chapter carefully considers the value and role of infrastructure and shows how infrastructure organisations mobilise social networks in response to a crisis.

The unprecedented nature of the pandemic is nicely captured by Hindley and Wilson's Chapter 17 title, 'How many of us had pandemic in our risk register?', itself a quote from one of their research participants. Community buildings are central to community life and the basic functioning of civil society, but were also heavily impacted by the immediate drop-off in use because of stay-at-home orders and the concomitant loss of income. The value of their study lies in their timely insight into the impact of lockdown on community buildings, and their expectations of the future and financial position. The findings demonstrate the variety of responses, including considerable innovation, but also resilience and survival, although there are question marks over longer-term volunteering.

In Chapter 18, Pat Armstrong discusses the challenges of leading voluntary sector organisations through the pandemic. Based on research and engagement with leaders of voluntary organisations undertaken with Jayne Stuart at the Association of Chief Officers of Scottish Voluntary Organisations (ACOSVO), the chapter highlights the sheer emotional toll on leaders of responding to the crisis. They observe the shifting concerns leaders had as the pandemic developed, noting how they focused on others first – beneficiaries, volunteers and staff – and it took a while before their own wellbeing was considered. The role of peer support becomes a crucial and safe space for leaders to connect with each other and to share experiences and insight.

Finally, as editors we are delighted that Professor Emerita Margaret Harris has provided an Afterword to the volume, in which she succinctly summarises the key themes emerging from the book's diverse chapters. Margaret is in a unique position, following a distinguished research career, to be able to survey and reflect on the agile and collaborative responses emerging from within the sector, and ends the book by looking forward to the near future of recovery from COVID-19 and considering the changes and challenges that are likely to endure.

References

British Academy (2021) *The Covid Decade: Understanding the Long-Term Societal Impacts of COVID-19*, London: British Academy.

Bynner, C. (2021) 'The third sector as key workers and strategic collaborators', [online], Available from: //childrensneighbourhoods.scot/2021/10/21/the-local-third-sector-key-workers-of-the-future/ [Accessed 3 March 2022].

Calvert, J. and Arbuthnot, G. (2021) *Failures of State: The Inside Story of Britain's Battle with Coronavirus*, London: HarperCollins.

Chamberlain, E. (2020) *Government Funding for Charities: An Important Start but More Is Needed*, London: NCVO.

Craston, M., Raynette Bierman, R., Mackay, S., Cameron, D., Writer-Davies, R. and Spielman, D. (2021) *Impact Evaluation of the Coronavirus Community Support Fund: Final Report*, London: Ipsos MORI.

Cuffe, R. (2021) 'Does the UK have highest Covid death toll in Europe?', *BBC News* [online], Available from: www.bbc.co.uk/news/57268471 [Accessed 3 March 2022].

Dayson, C., Baker, L. and Rees, J. (2021) 'The value of small in a big crisis: the distinctive contribution, value and experiences of smaller charities in England and Wales during the first wave of the COVID-19 pandemic', [online], Available from: www.lloydsbankfoundation.org.uk/media/cqhjhftd/lbfew-value-of-small-2021-summary-report.pdf [Accessed 3 March 2022].

Dayson, C. and Damm, C. (2020) 'Re-making state-civil society relationships during the COVID 19 pandemic? An English perspective', *People, Place and Policy*, 14(3): 282–9.

Fancourt, D., Steptoe, A. and Bu, F. (2020) 'Trajectories of anxiety and depressive symptoms during enforced isolation due to COVID-19 in England: a longitudinal observational study', *Lancet Psychiatry*, 8: 141–9.

Farrar, J. and Ahuja, A. (2021) *Spike: The Virus vs the People: The Inside Story*, London: Profile Books.

Hargrave, R. (2020) 'Chancellor unveils £750m coronavirus package for charities', [online], Available from: www.civilsociety.co.uk/news/chancellor-unveils-750m-coronavirus-package-for-charities.html#sthash.yqcUwYnJ.dpuf [Accessed 3 March 2022].

HM Government (2022) *COVID-19 Response: Living with COVID-19*, London: HM Government.

House of Commons DCMS Committee (2020) *The Covid-19 Crisis and Charities: First Report of Session 2019–21*, London: House of Commons.

Macmillan, R. (2020) 'Somewhere over the rainbow - third sector research in and beyond coronavirus,' *Voluntary Sector Review*, 11(2): 129–36.

Macmillan, R. and Ellis Paine, A. (2020) 'Post-war voluntary action helped rebuild Britain – could it happen again after coronavirus?', [online], Available from: //theconversation.com/post-war-voluntary-action-helped-rebuild-britain-could-it-happen-again-after-coronavirus-141234 [Accessed 3 March 2022].

McMullan, J. and Macmillan, R. (2021) *Stepping Up: Coordinating Local Voluntary Sector Responses to the COVID-19 Crisis*, Sheffield: NAVCA/VCS Emergencies Partnership.

Pro Bono Economics (2022) 'Levelling up our social capital, social fabric and wellbeing', [online], Available from: www.probonoeconomics.com/levelling-up-our-social-capital-social-fabric-and-wellbeing [Accessed 3 March 2022].

Rees, J., Caulfield, L., Wilson, S. and Ouillon, S. (2020) *Innovation and Enterprise across the Social Economy in Recovery from Covid-19*, West Midlands Combined Authority, [online], Available from: www.bvsc.org/Handlers/Download.ashx?IDMF=7e9c92b5-976f-439b-9937-66049d9cedec [Accessed 3 March 2022].

The Guardian (2020) 'Matt Hancock calls for 250,000 volunteers to help NHS during coronavirus crisis', [online], Available from: www.theguardian.com/world/video/2020/mar/24/matt-hancock-calls-for-250000-volunteers-to-help-nhs-video [Accessed 3 March 2022].

Thiery, H., Cook, J., Burchell, J., Ballantyne, E., Walkley, F. and McNeill, J. (2021) '"Never more needed" yet never more stretched: reflections on the role of the voluntary sector during the COVID-19 pandemic', *Voluntary Sector Review*, 12(3): 459–65.

Tiratelli, L. and Kaye, S. (2020) *Communities vs Coronavirus – The Rise of Mutual Aid*, London: New Local Government Networks.

Wyler, S. (2020) *Community Responses in Times of Crisis – Glimpses into the Past, Present and Future*, London: Local Trust.

PART I

Experience, impacts and lessons for the voluntary community sector

2

Mobilising the voluntary sector: critical reflections from across the four UK nations

Nick Acheson, Laura Crawford, Jurgen Grotz, Irene Hardill, Denise Hayward, Eddy Hogg, Rhys Dafydd Jones, Matthew Linning, Sally Rees, Alasdair Rutherford, Ewen Speed, Amy McGarvey, Catherine Goodall, Joanna Stuart and Debbie Maltman

Introduction

Individuals, organisations across all sectors and governments seek to mobilise voluntary action in a time of crisis. How and why this is done and the difference it makes can vary greatly. The COVID-19 pandemic, an international public health crisis, has led to significant mobilisation of voluntary action but assumptions, especially about a coherent UK-wide response, need to be critically assessed. The definition of 'voluntary action' we use in this chapter and in the underpinning research was co-produced by the research team and the advisory panel and is broadly based on the definitions of volunteering by Kearney (2001) and in the Northern Ireland Volunteering Strategy (Department for Social Development, 2012):

> Voluntary Action is the commitment of time and energy, for the benefit of society and the community, the environment or individuals outside (or in addition) to one's immediate family. It is undertaken freely and by choice, without concern for financial gain. It comprises the widest spectrum of activity for example, community development, arts, sport, faith based, education, neighbourliness, youth, environmental, health and direct care. This can include activities undertaken through public, private and voluntary organisations as well as community participation and social action in associations and groups which may not be registered or don't have a confirmed structure. (Grotz, 2021)

Since March 2020, the COVID-19 pandemic has had extraordinary effects on the voluntary and community sector across the four nations of the UK. COVID-19 is far more than a medical emergency; it is a social event disrupting not just the economy and everyone's personal lives, but also the practice of voluntary action, as we will explore in this chapter (Teti et al, 2020; British Academy, 2021; Pierson, 2021). For example, during the pandemic, the work of some volunteer-involving organisations had to be paused, the delivery of some projects was reconfigured and new groups and organisations were established to alleviate the economic and social consequences of the crisis (British Academy, 2021). As we move towards recovery in 2022, this chapter focuses on an analysis of the challenges facing the voluntary and community sector across the four UK nations and reflects on the contrasting policy adjustments enacted by them.

In autumn 2020, we began our UK-wide study funded by the Economic and Social Research Council (ESRC) as part of the UK Research and Innovation (UKRI) scheme to develop policy-relevant insights into the economic and social impacts of the pandemic (ESRC, n.d.). The funding scheme focused on the overall UK response to the pandemic, but because of devolution some powers are non-reserved, meaning that they fall within the devolved government's responsibility. This includes volunteering and the voluntary and community sector (Woolvin et al, 2015). The result is that there have been different policy responses across the four UK jurisdictions, which needed to be taken into account.

The advent of the pandemic was preceded by significant shifts in social policy over a protracted period, which has played out differently in the four UK nations. In the decade prior to the pandemic in Wales and Scotland, the spirit of partnership working remained strong (Woolvin et al, 2015). In Northern Ireland, policy making and partnership working have been strengthened by the Good Friday Agreement, where all the main parties in the devolved administration have embraced the sector (Hughes and Ketola, 2021). In England, the pandemic came at the end of a decade of disengagement from the sector (Woolvin et al, 2015), which Macmillan has described as a 'partial decoupling' (Macmillan, 2013). As a result, during the pandemic, an uneven geography has emerged across the four nations. The pre-existing relationships between the state and the sector have significantly shaped differences in policy and the practice of voluntary action (Macmillan, 2020a).

Therefore, our project deliberately involved working across four jurisdictions and policy regimes, involving four national groups of academics and sector experts plus a UK coordinating group, working at a number of spatial scales. We were also supported by a project partner advisory panel, with representatives from key professional networks and organisations, along with related ESRC and British Academy investments.

Study design and approach

Our project sought to review, analyse and evaluate state- and non-state-supported volunteer responses to the pandemic across the four nations of the UK. We examined the different voluntary action policy frameworks adopted by the four nations prior to and in response to COVID-19, mapped changes in the profile of volunteers and assessed plans to sustain their involvement. We also aimed to offer examples of what worked well and what was less successful, and whether learning was transferable and under what circumstances.

The study was explicitly co-designed and co-delivered, practising the principles of the co-production of knowledge (Hodgkinson et al, 2002; Bannister and Hardill, 2014). The study employed a mixed methods approach across five work packages undertaken in iterative stages:

1. Emerging findings from research undertaken during the pandemic
2. Policy documents
3. Voluntary action surveys
4. User data from digital volunteer-matching tools
5. Government and stakeholder interviews

The work packages were guided by a co-produced analytical framework to identify core components for analysis (Grotz, 2021). This chapter reports on our findings from work packages 1 and 2.

Emerging findings from published research

In 2020, the voluntary sector and the social science research community quickly mobilised, supported by a number of research funders, sometimes working together to understand, address and mitigate the adverse impacts of the pandemic on everyday life, including voluntary action. We identified and thematically reviewed more than 70 research reports on the impact of the pandemic on voluntary action, researched and written by a range of organisations across the UK including voluntary sector umbrella organisations, volunteer-involving organisations (VIOs) and local authorities, some involving social science researchers. Many of these reports focused on the impact of the first UK lockdown from March 2020, perhaps, with the benefit of hindsight, prematurely reflecting on what recovery would look like (Crawford, 2021). This thematic review surveyed the strength of the existing research and identified knowledge gaps which were addressed in our four national surveys.

Policy documents

In each of the nations, partners identified and assembled relevant policy documents. For each jurisdiction, a 'within-case' analysis of these documents was undertaken in context, such that only policies relating to that particular jurisdiction were considered, wherever this was possible. Subsequently, for the UK an 'across-case' analysis was then completed, using selected key documents, identifying a number of points of concurrence and departure across the four jurisdictions (Speed, 2021). Most notably, there were clear differences on the social value afforded to voluntary action across the jurisdictions. For example, in the English context, voluntary action tended to be characterised as a transactional activity that occurred in civil society, beyond the remit of the state, evident in the Civil Society Strategy (Cabinet Office, 2018). In Scotland and Wales, the value afforded to voluntary action was much more collaborative and it was given a more central role in policy and practice, as seen in Volunteering for All: Our National Framework (Scottish Government, 2019). Northern Ireland seemed to operate within a compatibilist space where voluntary action was somewhere in between a transactional and a collaborative undertaking, where voluntary action policy was somewhat hamstrung by the lack of an effective policy-making context due to the period of suspension of the Northern Irish Assembly.

Emerging findings from existing research publications

Three key themes emerged from the review of existing evidence about the impact of the pandemic on voluntary action (Crawford, 2021).

The first key theme was the importance of mutual aid, informal volunteering and hyperlocal activity as a pandemic response. It is widely acknowledged that these groups responded at speed, providing emergency support to those shielding or isolating across the UK. As Tiratelli and Kaye (2020, p 28) note, 'these groups are not a "nice-to-have" – they are of decisive importance to the health and welfare of thousands of people'. The informal nature of this activity enabled agile responses which were not constrained by bureaucracy or 'red tape' (Welsh Parliament Equality, Local Government and Communities Committee, 2021; Curtin et al, 2021). The notion of place was central here; activity was driven by a response to a local need and delivered at the local scale. This also characterised the spirit with which community members provided support; as Alakeson and Brett (2020, p 19) note, 'it is their home too and they are trusted because they are not providing a service so much as supporting the place where they live'.

The second theme was the significance of collaboration, with the pandemic leading to the emergence of new partnerships and demonstrating the value of pre-existing relationships. As a council member in one study succinctly asserts, 'you need to build these relationships before you need them' (Cretu, 2020, p 34). Coutts (2020, p 20) noted that the pandemic 'pushed aside more competitive relationships' and involved 'dropping your own personal/ organisational ego'. Collaborative working was identified within and between organisations, involving a range of formal and informal actors operating at different spatial scales. Collaboration not only required a willingness to work in partnership but a recognition that different actors were perhaps better suited to certain roles (Cretu, 2020). Tiratelli and Kaye (2020) emphasised the importance of local government adopting a 'facilitative approach' to enable community activity to thrive. However, such a position was often difficult to achieve in practice, with formal organisations concerned about risk management and safeguarding (Macmillan, 2020b). Across the existing research, the degree and quality of collaborative working varied considerably, and in areas where there was a history of investment and community engagement the response was generally more joined up (Wilson et al, 2020; 2021; Tiratelli and Kaye, 2020). Conversely, failure to work collaboratively resulted in duplication causing confusion for staff, volunteers and those who required support (Macmillan, 2020b; Tiratelli and Kaye, 2020). Some reports already expressed concern about sustaining collaborative working models in the face of the societal challenges that recovery from the pandemic would inevitably entail.

A third key theme broadly encompassed volunteer engagement, opportunities and mobilisation. In March 2020, UK Prime Minister Boris Johnson celebrated the 750,000 people who stepped forward to volunteer in England as part of the NHS Volunteer Responder scheme, suggesting this demonstrated that "there really is such thing as society" (Johnson, 2020). Meanwhile, organisations were grappling with matching volunteer supply with demand. National recruitment platforms were criticised for contributing to the oversupply of volunteers by attempting to create 'top-down centralised solutions to local issues' (Thiery et al, 2020, p 30). This pattern was reported across the UK, with organisations commenting on the difficulties of finding roles for all those who stepped forward, generating concerns about the impact on future enthusiasm to volunteer (Ellis Paine, 2020; Welsh Parliament Equality, Local Government and Communities Committee, 2021). Ellis Paine (2020) highlighted the complexity of pandemic volunteering patterns, acknowledging that alongside a surge in new volunteers, many others were forced to step back and shield or isolate, take on new roles or carry out pre-existing roles in different ways. Moreover, government restrictions in all four nations affected what organisations were able to deliver and impacted the health and wellbeing of volunteers who stepped down or were stood down (Grotz et al, 2020). The large-scale move to digital delivery was one of the most significant operational shifts during the pandemic, yet 'going digital' was not a seamless or universally applicable approach (Boelman, 2021). A lack of digital skills, technology, reliable internet access or desire to interact virtually all acted as barriers to digital engagement. The suitability of digital provision was heavily influenced by the demographic profile of both volunteers and service users as well as the nature of the proposed activity. While face-to-face befriending could be reimagined as a virtual or telephone service, activities like lunch clubs, which typically support older adults in community settings, were harder, and in many cases impossible, to move online. As a result, some volunteer-involving organisations were more acutely affected by the pandemic restrictions, unable to use digital technology as an adaptation strategy.

There were recurrent themes in the research undertaken in 2020 of both hope and concern for the future. On the whole, there was a sense that the pandemic had evidenced the viability of working in innovative and collaborative ways. New relationships built on trust and appreciation were formed, council staff redeployed to frontline roles developed closer relationships with the communities they served (Coutts, 2020) and a 'newfound respect' for the voluntary and community sector developed through collaborative cross-sector interactions (Cook et al, 2020, p 13). Nevertheless, there was widespread uncertainty about the future, with concerns this precariousness could prompt the return of siloed working. As Cook et al, (2020, p 2) stress, one of 'the key challenges facing us all now is how to embed these gains to resist the bureaucratic creep and retain these great leaps forward'. Furthermore, the pandemic has 'exacerbated and brought into sharper focus pre-existing inequalities, as well as leading to the emergence of new pockets of need' (Crawford, 2021, p 4). These societal needs are likely to play a pivotal role in where and how volunteers are deployed.

Our thematic analysis revealed that the strength of the evidence across the four nations was unequal, and it was clear that organisations within the four nations were at very different stages in reflecting on what happened during the pandemic. As the Bevan Foundation (2020, p 13) observed, some organisations remained 'entirely focused on day-to-day outputs while others were looking to the long term'. Moreover, to speak of the response to COVID-19 as a singular event did not reflect the realities of volunteer mobilisation across the sector, and the length of the ongoing emergency brought with it additional problems, such as staff burnout (Ecclesiastical, 2020).

The thematic review demonstrated a significant degree of convergence around the key issues the voluntary sector and statutory services were facing. However, given the diversity of the UK's constitutional system, there was a need to consider how the policy context of each jurisdiction impacted volunteer mobilisation and to what extent voluntary action was embedded within the broader pandemic response. These themes will be explored in the next section.

Policy divergence and policy adjustments

As we noted earlier in this chapter, the voluntary action policy frameworks differ between the four nations of the UK and this has had significant implications for the ability of volunteers and voluntary and community sector organisations to play a part in alleviating unmet need in the pandemic. Due to policy differences in what the best public health response might be, for example different policies in terms of mandated mask wearing, working from home, social distancing and so on, the COVID-19 pandemic functioned to make much more explicit the ways in which unreserved policy making occurs within the devolved jurisdictions. The need for an ongoing and developing public health response to the pandemic, and divergence across jurisdictions as to the best ways of responding, made the devolved nature of UK politics a central feature of the pandemic response at a level never seen before. There was clear and consistent divergence across all four jurisdictions; and these differences have persisted throughout.

Our research sought to establish points of similarity and difference across the four jurisdictions with regards to the impact this divergence made for the role of voluntary action in pandemic responses.

We found clear policy differences between the four jurisdictions. There is more demonstrable congruence between Northern Ireland, Wales and Scotland in terms of how the social value of voluntary action is both defined and operationalised in the implementation of voluntary action policy. There is also more congruence across these three jurisdictions in terms of a commitment to ensuring a diverse range of volunteering opportunities and how they can be accessed in relation to participating in voluntary action.

England's volunteering policy framework tends to focus more on pressing new agents into voluntary action roles. It is couched within a transactional mode of exchange between the state and individual citizens, where citizens are encouraged to be engaged in activities that were previously offered or coordinated by the state. There is little attempt to engage existing voluntary action organisations in this activity; the appeal for action tends to be made directly to citizens. In this sense, it is a policy that facilitates a retraction of the state from the field of voluntary action.

Our analysis specifically considered the ways in which voluntary action played out across the four jurisdictions in the 12 months from 23 March 2020 when the first UK lockdown began. Sector experts across the four UK jurisdictions identified a sample of 21 COVID-19 voluntary action policy documents for analysis (Speed, 2021). The analysis of these documents demonstrates the ways in which the prevailing policy contexts in the four jurisdictions are simultaneously similar and different. There were clear differences in the overall policy context, which determined both the available policy options and the subsequent policy responses, particularly in relation to voluntary action and COVID-19. For example, the English context was structured by a transactional model of voluntary action where governance of voluntary action has been ceded by the state. This resulted in the English policy response being much more about pragmatic guidelines for sustaining voluntary activities, compared with the Welsh context, for example, where the emphasis was on collaborative working to address public health concerns. In this context, it was much more difficult for English policy to identify a national-level response that aligned with existing policy commitments to voluntary action, largely because this prior commitment did not exist. The responses were predicated more on the need for reactive novel activity and policy rather than a proactive adaptation of existing activity. This more proactive approach is what tended to happen in Scotland and Wales.

The lack of a legislative assembly in Northern Ireland in the three-year period to January 2020 meant that a number of policy instruments which could have impacted on the pandemic response were not in place or had not been refreshed, for example the Civil Contingencies Framework or the Volunteering Strategy. The Emergencies Leadership Group established by the Minister for Communities at the start of the pandemic sought to fill the gap in linking the voluntary and community response, including volunteering, into the government-led emergency response. The sector has worked effectively with government, for example, to deliver the vaccination programme involving volunteers.

Scotland and Wales have both mobilised more of a national-level strategic policy response, and it is one that has explicitly identified and collaborated with an identified range of relevant voluntary action organisations and actors. With regard to Scotland, a national-level strategic approach has been operationalised, which has been integrated with the broader multi-agency approach to resilience – see, for example, the Communities and Volunteering Circle recommendations to the Social Renewal Advisory Board (2021). In effect, the response built upon existing arrangements as well as introducing some bespoke new ones. For example, the Scottish government's pre-pandemic core funding direct to third sector interfaces (TSIs) and other trusted partners; the Scottish government's third sector unit's role in the development and delivery of bespoke COVID-19 funding for the voluntary sector; the contribution of the Scottish government Resilient Communities Team and the formation of the Voluntary and Community Sector Resilience Advisory Group; the establishment of the 'Scotland Cares' campaign to handle spontaneous volunteering; and, later, the establishment of the 'National Vaccination Centre hub' to assist the vaccination, testing and other COVID-19 response arrangements. The interface between Wales Council for Voluntary Action (WCVA), as the voluntary sector infrastructure body, and Third Sector Support Wales, working collaboratively with the Welsh government's third sector unit, was maximised during COVID-19 and crucial to how voluntary action was and is being delivered to communities of need.

In Wales, the WCVA has directly disbursed government funds for COVID-19 relief, while the Scottish government provided COVID-19 funding directly to the voluntary and community sector through trusted partners such as the Scottish Council for Voluntary Organisations (SCVO) and the Corra Foundation. Donated funding for voluntary and community sector organisations was coordinated by the National Emergencies Trust (NET) and distributed by Foundation Scotland, assisted by SCVO and partners on the newly established Scottish Emergency Funding Advisory Board.

Discussion and conclusion

In this chapter, we have reported on a UK-wide study exploring the impact of the pandemic on mobilising voluntary action, reviewing, analysing and evaluating state- and non-state-supported volunteer responses. We have analysed evidence of the way in which the landscapes of voluntary action have been transformed in different and in similar ways across the four nations of the UK. The findings of the study add to some of the recurring themes we identified in evidence from a range of sources collected during the pandemic: namely, the importance of mutual aid and hyperlocal activity, especially in the first lockdown of 2020, to address unmet need largely at the local level; and collaboration and partnership working at various spatial scales between and within the four nations.

We set the context by explaining that public policies towards mobilising voluntary action are devolved, and that the pandemic was preceded by a period during which social policy had been renegotiated, 'a restructuring of Beveridgean proportions', especially in England (Taylor-Gooby, 2012, p 62). Combined, the workstrands of this study highlight the ways in which the uneven geography of devolution has been compounded by policy making in the pandemic impacting on the mobilisation of voluntary action. The workstrands illustrate that the pandemic has resulted in significant upheaval in assumptions, expectations and positions about the role of voluntary action in the four nations of the UK, and that the debate is ongoing and unresolved both within and across the nations. While there are similar concerns in the four nations, such as retention of new volunteers, the ways the nations seek to frame these questions and identify solutions, and how stakeholders collaborate, vary greatly.

This study started with what turned out to be the flawed assumption that by the time we write up its findings, the pandemic would be behind us. This is not the case, so our findings must be seen within the context of this ongoing crisis. The protracted nature of the pandemic has seen the volunteer response ebb and flow and a shift in the ways in which services are delivered.

Individuals have been moved to help non-kin, giving their time in diverse ways (Woolvin and Harper, 2015; Eden Communities, 2021). The practice of voluntary action during the pandemic has highlighted the need for a more fluid understanding of voluntary action as the pandemic has changed how voluntary action is mobilised, as an embodied practice. It is much more clearly seen as a spectrum of participation, formally and informally constituted. We have long recognised that individual involvement in voluntary action changes over one's lifetime (Brodie et al, 2011). We have also demonstrated that the way voluntary action is mobilised varies across the four UK nations with potentially significant consequences for the ability to respond to crises and to rebuild after. The sheer scale of unmet need appears daunting, and Pierson (2021) questions the ability of the under-resourced UK-wide welfare state to cope. Some of the pressures organisations are facing include fragile finances, staff being under severe strain, juggling the delivery of blended services and forging new partnerships. Voluntary action has changed but it remains very much 'who we are' and 'what we do' (Brewis et al, 2021). What we can say with some certainty, though, is that the approaches to mobilising voluntary action in the four nations of the UK will be different and that any future research needs to recognise this.

References

Alakeson, V. and Brett, W. (2020) *Local Heroes: How to Sustain Community Spirit beyond Covid-19*, [online], Available from: www.powertochange.org.uk/blog/local-heroes-sustain-community-spirit-beyond-covid-19/ [Accessed 25 February 2022].

Bannister, J. and Hardill, I. (2014) *Knowledge Mobilisation and the Social Sciences: Research Impact and Engagement*, London: Routledge.

Bevan Foundation (2020) *Coronavirus: Community Responses in Merthyr Tydfil*, [online], Available from: www.bevanfoundation.org/resources/coronavirus-community-responses-in-merthyr-tydfil/ [Accessed 25 February 2022].

Boelman, V. (2021) *Volunteering and Wellbeing in the Pandemic. Part II: Rapid Evidence Review*, [online], Available from: www.youngfoundation.org/wp-content/uploads/2021/06/Volunteering-and-wellbeing-in-the-pandemic.-Part-2-Rapid-evidence-review.pdf [Accessed 25 February 2022].

Brewis, G., Ellis Paine, A., Hardill, I., Macmillan, R. and Lindsey, R. (2021) *Transformational Moments in Social Welfare: What Role for Voluntary Action?*, Bristol: Policy Press.

British Academy (2021) *Shaping the COVID Decade: Addressing the Long-Term Societal Impacts of COVID-19*, [online], Available from: www.thebritishacademy.ac.uk/publications/shaping-the-covid-decade-addressing-the-long-term-societal-impacts-of-covid-19/ [Accessed 25 February 2022].

Brodie, E., Hughes, T., Jochum, V., Miller, S., Ockenden, N. and Warburton, D. (2011) *Pathways through Participation: What Creates and Sustains Active Citizenship?*, London: NCVO, IVR, Involve.

Cabinet Office (2018) *Civil Society Strategy: Building a Future that Works for Everyone*, London: Cabinet Office.

Cook, J., Thiery, H., Burchell, J., Walkley, F., Ballantyne, E. and McNeill, J. (2020) *Report #1 Lessons from Lockdown*, [online], Available from: www.cvsce.org.uk/sites/cvsce.org.uk/files/MoVE_WP1_Report_1.pdf [Accessed 25 February 2022].

Coutts, P. (2020) *COVID-19 and Communities Listening Project: A Shared Response*, [online], Available from: www.carnegieuktrust.org.uk/publications/covid-19-and-communities-listening-project-a-shared-response/ [Accessed 25 February 2022].

Crawford, L. (2021) 'Working paper 2: what the existing research tells us, mobilising UK voluntary action during COVID-19 (MVAin4)', [online], Available from: www.mvain4.uk/resource-details/working-paper-2-what-the-existing-research-tells-us/ [Accessed 25 February 2022].

Cretu, C. (2020) *A Catalyst for Change. What COVID-19 Has Taught Us about the Future of Local Government*, [online], Available from: www.nesta.org.uk/report/catalyst-change/ [Accessed 25 February 2022].

Curtin, M., Rendall, J., Roy, M., and Teasdale, S. (2021) *Solidarity in a Time of Crisis: The Role of Mutual Aid to the Covid-19 Pandemic*, [online], Available from: www.gcu.ac.uk/media/gcalwebv2/ycsbh/yunuscentre/newycwebsite/The-role-of-mutual-aid-COVID-19_YunusCentreReport.pdf [Accessed 25 February 2022].

Department for Social Development (2012) *Join In, Get Involved: Build a Better Future: A Volunteering Strategy and Action Plan for Northern Ireland*, Belfast: Department for Social Development.

Ecclesiastical (2020) *Ecclesiastical Charity Risk Barometer 2020*, [online], Available from: www.ecclesiastical.com/documents/charity-risk-barometer-2020.pdf [Accessed 25 February 2022].

Eden Communities (2021) *The Spectrum of Volunteer Participation*, [online], Available from: www.edenprojectcommunities.com/sites/default/files/volunteer_report.pdf [Accessed 25 February 2022].

Ellis Paine, A. (2020) *Briefing 5 Rapid Research COVID-19. Volunteering through Crisis and Beyond: Starting, Stopping and Shifting*, [online], Available from: //localtrust.org.uk/wp-content/uploads/2020/09/COVID-19-briefing-5-3.pdf [Accessed 25 February 2022].

ESRC (n.d.) 'Covid call', [online], Available from: //esrc.ukri.org/files/news-events-and-publications/news/esrc-covid-19-activity/ [Accessed 25 February 2022].

Grotz, J., Dyson, S. and Birt, L. (2020) 'Pandemic policy making: the health and wellbeing effects of the cessation of volunteering on older adults during the COVID-19 pandemic', *Quality in Ageing and Older Adults*, 21(4): 261–9.

Grotz, J. (2021) 'Working paper 1: a picture is worth a thousand words', [online], Available from: www.mvain4.uk/resource-details/apictureisworthathousandwords/ [Accessed 25 February 2022].

Hodgkinson, G.P., Herriot, P. and Anderson, N. (2002) 'Re-aligning the stakeholders in management research: lessons from industrial, work and organizational psychology', *British Journal of Management*, 12: S41–8.

Hughes, C. and Ketola, M. (2021) *Neoliberalism and the Voluntary and Community Sector in Northern Ireland*, Bristol: Policy Press.

Johnson, B. (2020) Twitter video, [online], Available from: https://twitter.com/borisjohnson/status/1244339182690066433 [Accessed 25 February 2022].

Kearney, J. (2001) 'The values and basic principles of volunteering: complacency or caution?', *Voluntary Action*, 3(3): 63–86.

Macmillan, R. (2013) 'De-coupling the state and the third sector? The 'Big Society' as a spontaneous order', *Voluntary Sector Review*, 4(2): 185–203.

Macmillan, R. (2020a) 'Somewhere over the rainbow – third sector research in and beyond coronavirus', *Voluntary Sector Review*, 11(2): 129–36.

Macmillan, R. (2020b) *Briefing 3 Rapid Research. Grassroots Action: The Role of Informal Community Activity in Responding to Crises*, [online], Available from: //localtrust.org.uk/wp-content/uploads/2020/07/COVID-19.-Briefing-3.pdf [Accessed 25 February 2022].

Pierson, C. (2021) *The Next Welfare State? UK Welfare after COVID-19*, Bristol: Policy Press.

Scottish Government (2019) *Volunteering for All: Our National Framework*, [online], Available from: www.gov.scot/publications/volunteering-national-framework/documents/ [Accessed 25 February 2022].

Social Renewal Advisory Board (2021) *Social Renewal Advisory Board Communities & Volunteering Circle*, [online], Available from: www.gov.scot/binaries/content/documents/govscot/publications/independent-report/2021/01/not-now-social-renewal-advisory-board-report-january-2021/documents/final-draft-communities-volunteering-circle-recommendations/final-draft-communities-volunteering-circle-recommendations/govscot%3Adocument/final-draft-communities-volunteering-circle-recommendations.docx [Accessed 25 February 2022].

Speed, E. (2021) 'Working paper 3: preliminary analysis of policy differences across the four UK jurisdictions', [online], Available from: www.mvain4.uk/resource-details/working-paper-3/ [Accessed 25 February 2022].

Taylor-Gooby, P. (2012) 'Root and branch restructuring to achieve major cuts: the social policy programme', *Social Policy and Administration*, 46(1): 61–82.

Teti, M., Schartz, E. and Linbenberg, L. (2020) 'Methods in the time of COVID-19: the vital role of qualitative inquiries', *International Journal of Qualitative Methods*, 19(1): 1–5.

Thiery, H., Ballantyne, E., Cook, J., Burchell, J., Walkley, F. and McNeill, J. (2020) *Report #3: Building Local Responses to Identify and Meet Community Needs During COVID-19*, [online], Available from: //doit.life/channels/11997/move-findings/file/md/142043/report-3-building-local-responses-to-ide [Accessed 25 February 2022].

Tiratelli, L. and Kaye, S. (2020) *Communities vs Coronavirus: The Rise of Mutual Aid*, [online], Available from: www.newlocal.org.uk/publications/communities-vs-coronavirus-the-rise-of-mutual-aid/ [Accessed 25 February 2022].

Welsh Parliament Equality, Local Government and Communities Committee (2021) *Impact of Covid-19 on the Voluntary Sector*, [online], Available from: //senedd.wales/media/d4jh52zz/cr-ld14075-e.pdf [Accessed 25 February 2022].

Wilson, M., McCabe, A. and Macmillan, R. (2020) *Briefing 4 Rapid research COVID-19. Blending formal and informal community responses*, London: Local Trust. Available from: localtrust.org.uk/wp-content/uploads/2020/08/COVID-19-BRIEFING-4.pdf [Accessed 25 February 2022].

Wilson, M., McCabe, M. and Macmillan, R. (2021) *Briefing 10 Rapid Research COVID-19. Community Responses to COVID-19: Striking a Balance between Communities and Local Authorities*, [online], Available from: localtrust.org.uk/wp-content/uploads/2021/03/COVID-19-Briefing-10.pdf [Accessed 25 February 2022].

Woolvin, M. and Harper, H. (2015) 'Volunteering from 'below the radar'. Informal volunteering in deprived urban Scotland: research summary', [online], Available from: www.volunteerscotland.net/media/624210/mw_phd_summary_30_07_15.pdf [Accessed 25 February 2022].

Woolvin, M., Mills, S., Hardill, I. and Rutherford, A. (2015) 'Devolved responses to national challenges? Voluntarism and devolution in England, Wales and Scotland', *Geographical Journal*, 181(1): 38–46.

3

Bouncing back: the employment of sector attributes to recover from crises

Tony Chapman

Judging from media stories in the national and third sector press, charities, social enterprises and community organisations seem to have been in a more or less permanent state of turmoil over the last 20 years. Sector 'crises' have been predicted in response to significant shifts in government policy affecting the third sector together with unforeseen global events including the global economic crash of 2008 and the COVID-19 pandemic which began in 2019. This begs the question: if the third sector has had to endure so many 'perfect storms' or so-called 'existential crises', then why does it still exist?

The situation of the third sector, in reality, is better described in terms of 'general improvement' or 'continuity' rather than tumultuous change. NCVO's long-established and annually renewed *UK Civil Society Almanac* demonstrates (see NVCO, 2021 and Figure 3.1) that over the last 20 years, sector income and expenditure has risen relatively smoothly and substantially from £34 billion to £54 billion.

Furthermore, there is much more evidence of continuity than there is of change in the size, shape and structure of the sector over the last two decades. And as Figure 3.1 also shows, the number of organisations has increased, but only marginally so, from 146,000 charities in 2000/01 to 167,000 by 2017/18. Similarly, the percentage of the population which regularly volunteers has remained relatively stable in the range of 22 to 29 per cent (more recently, lower percentages reflect a change in the way data are collected). None of these indicators suggest recurrent deep crises.

The third sector is more robust than it is given credit for. Certainly, third sector organisations (TSOs) have faced significant challenges over the last two decades, but as this chapter will show, most have shown themselves to be sufficiently adaptable and robust to keep going – sometimes against the odds. The purpose of this chapter, therefore, is to identify key attributes of TSOs which help them to tackle problems that come their way.

Figure 3.1: Continuity and change in the third sector

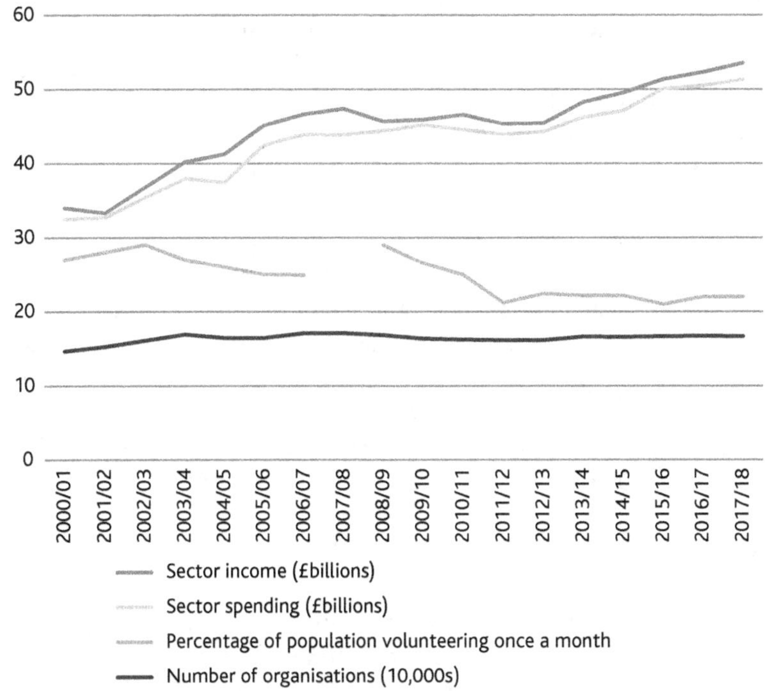

- Sector income (£billions)
- Sector spending (£billions)
- Percentage of population volunteering once a month
- Number of organisations (10,000s)

Source: NCVO Civil Almanac 2021

Sector adaptability and robustness in the face of crises

This chapter takes a step back from the immediate impact of the current COVID-19 pandemic and takes a broader view on sector adaptability and robustness in the face of significant challenges. It does so by looking at the ups and downs of the sector as a whole and the situation of individual TSOs over the last 15 years using evidence from a large-scale, long-term study of the sector in the north of England – the Third Sector Trends Study (TSTS).

Some aspects of change in the situation of the third sector derive from government policy. For example, under the New Labour governments from 1997 to 2010, there was a shift towards New Public Management techniques (Pestoff et al, 2013). Government invested in capacity-building programmes to 'professionalise' the sector and facilitate greater financial sustainability by tackling 'grant dependency'. By encouraging TSOs to set up profit-making trading ventures and/or to deliver public sector services under contract, it was hoped that a strong socially enterprising culture would emerge. A second policy shift came from the coalition and Conservative governments between 2010 and 2019, which promoted the idea of a 'Big Society' where civil society was expected to fill the space created by austerity policies which sought 'smaller government' (Macmillan, 2013).

Two other key challenges to the sector over the last two decades were driven by global factors. The first was the global financial crash of 2008 which led to a substantive economic downturn. In response, governments sought to contain public expenditure and drew back from investment in social programmes which had supported the activities of many TSOs. The second, and still current, crisis is the COVID-19 pandemic which has produced significant economic and social impact (see Chapter 1 of this volume).

This chapter will show that adaptability and robustness of TSOs derives, firstly, from their different relationship with key resources supporting their work when compared with the private sector or public sector institutions. Secondly, it is argued that TSO leaders are more able to sustain organisations than their counterparts in private businesses or vulnerable public sector bodies because they have both the independence and flexibility in their access and use of resources to allow them to reshape and/or repurpose to meet current circumstances.

Sources of evidence

Research reports from think tanks and third sector umbrella organisations over the last 20 years have continually portrayed the third sector as being on the edge of a precipice.[1] Too often, findings are presented which are based on research which was generated to prove a point (rather than to 'find out' what is actually going on), to position the sector favourably in political or resource terms (that is, to direct more funding in its direction) or that has delivered partial or misleading messages selectively culled from analysis to produce stories that 'cut through' in the media.

With the exception of crucial long-term analysis of national data primarily from the Charity Commission in the annual *NCVO UK Civil Society Almanac* (NVCO 2021), research often involves small unrepresentative samples of TSOs which cannot persuasively substantiate claims. And because they are 'one-off' or 'snapshot' studies, there is little or no scope to make comparative assessments to test reliability and assess the extent to which change has actually occurred, why that happened or what its consequences were.

In recognition of these shortcomings, Northern Rock Foundation commissioned the TSTS study in north-east England and Cumbria to explore the structure and dynamics of the third sector in the context of change.[2] The original plan was for the study to run for seven years to 2015. However, the Community Foundation serving Tyne and Wear and Northumberland, with support from a number of other funding bodies (including Power to Change, Garfield Weston Foundation, Joseph Rowntree Foundation and Charity Bank, among others), extended the study across the north of England. The study will begin its sixth wave of surveys in June 2022.

What makes the third sector different?

The third sector is a contested terrain. There is little agreement about how the sector is defined and which types of organisations should be included, what objectives it should pursue and who or what it serves, how it should work in practice and how to value or measure what it achieves. Furthermore, there is disagreement on where the sector sits in relation to other sectors. Some argue that the sector constitutes a 'third pillar' alongside the state and private sector (Rajan, 2019), while others see it as an 'in between' place sitting within a triangle of the state, the private sector and private life (Evers and Laville, 2004).

Following the lead of Evers and Laville, TSTS has adopted the position that it is easier to say what the third sector is not, rather than what it is (see also Alcock and Kendall, 2011). In the context of this chapter, this can help to demonstrate why TSOs work in different ways from public organisations or private businesses – and why they occupy a distinctive position which helps them navigate through difficult times.

How are TSOs different from private sector organisations?

Private businesses exist, primarily, to make a profit. They achieve this by selling goods and services at a higher price in the marketplace than it costs for them to produce. To get started or to grow, businesses need capital to buy or rent property, pay for equipment and raw materials, and take on employees to get work done. Like TSOs, businesses sometimes get grants to help them get going, but most new or growing businesses rely primarily upon loans, usually from financial institutions such as banks, to meet these costs.

Businesses are inherently economically vulnerable because they borrow money, but also because they are in competition with other companies, which can limit or destroy their profitability. Business vulnerability is aptly demonstrated by the private sector's high levels of closure and is reflected in the short duration of most businesses when compared with charities. The average age of TSOs in the TSTS survey database is 31.4 years. While data sets are not directly comparable, the indication from government statistics is that the average age of UK companies is 8.5 years (Chapman et al, 2020, p 7).

Most people who run businesses care about what they do and who they serve, but no matter how strong their emotional attachment may be to their work, they must recognise when it is time to stop (otherwise they risk losing their livelihood, assets and status) or are forced to do so by their creditors or shareholders. The people who govern TSOs are not immune from personal risk or liability, but that risk is comparably lower and this allows them to keep organisations going by, for example, reducing the scale and scope of activities, or by changing practices or the purpose of their work.

How are TSOs different from public sector organisations?

Public sector organisations are different from TSOs (and private businesses) in two main ways. First, they are primarily reliant on fiscal resource rather than profitability. As such, they must work within budgets which are framed or set by government. Second, while public bodies may hold significant powers, they are less autonomous than TSOs and private businesses because they cannot direct and exercise their power freely. In strategic and practice terms, public bodies clearly have some room for manoeuvre, but are nevertheless held accountable to meet statutory obligations to deliver services.

Furthermore, shifts in political priorities at central government level can undermine the powers of public sector organisations. For example, local authorities once controlled local educational institutions and delivered public housing and transport, among other things. These powers have progressively been whittled away by national government (Dollery and Robotti, 2008). Similarly, the resource base of public authorities can alter significantly in response to government policy, such as the deep cuts produced by government 'austerity' policies from 2010 to 2019 (Gray and Barford, 2018). Public bodies, such as state-funded, semi-autonomous, non-departmental public bodies (NDPBs or 'quangos')[3] can be repurposed or abolished, such as, for example, the demise of regional development agencies and government offices for the regions which were closed by the 2010–15 coalition government led by Prime Minister David Cameron.

What is distinctive about TSOs?

TSOs differ from each other in many ways, depending upon factors such as their size, purpose and practice. What they share in common is that they occupy a different territory from private businesses and public sector bodies. In a similar way to private businesses, TSOs are autonomous bodies which are able to make their own decisions on what their purpose should be. They are substantively different from private firms, however, because they rely on a much wider range of resources to get their work done, including earned income, grants and gifts, in-kind support (from other TSOs and the public and private sectors) and freely given work time provided by trustees and volunteers.

Within the realm of civil society, TSOs have the autonomy to make decisions on issues they want to tackle, where they want to work, who they wish to serve and how they go about doing so in practical terms. Unlike the public sector, they are not constrained to provide universal services or those targeted to prescribed constituencies of the population. Nor, crucially, are they burdened by statutory obligation to deliver their services uniformly and continuously. TSOs are, therefore, able to be flexible because, within the constraints of their current resources, they can choose when to start, continue or stop delivering services.

TSOs are legally autonomous bodies that must decide how to respond to current circumstances, but they may not feel as if they are in control. This is because they can face real and often immanent threats to their organisational wellbeing, such as failure to win grants and contracts, or to engage successfully in trading activities. The exhaustion of reserves, the inability to harness support from volunteers or a loss of demand for their services can also undermine TSOs.

Nevertheless, the risk of sudden closure, when compared with private businesses, is likely to be much lower. The probable reason for this is TSOs' relative lack of financial vulnerability. Unlike businesses which rely heavily upon borrowed money, TSOs tend to live within their means. Indeed, as NCVO has shown (see Figure 3.1), on no occasion in the last 20 years has the third sector's expenditure exceeded its income.

Flexibility as a way of life

As autonomous entities, TSOs can alter their priorities and change the way they work in accordance with the resources they have to hand. Running organisations can be difficult, however, as it may be necessary to manage continually fluctuating resources within a fluid policy and funding context and a competitive practice environment. To understand this process more fully, the TSTS research programme involved a qualitative longitudinal study of 50 TSOs, initiated in 2008, to complement the recurrent rounds of survey work (Chapman, 2017a).

By 2021, this qualitative research work had reached its fourth iteration (Chapman, 2022). Of the original 50 TSOs selected in 2008, 44 were still in operation by September 2021, among which near-complete financial records were available for 32 organisations. Data on income and expenditure from the Charity Commission has been retained on an annual basis running back to 2004. Analysis reveals that TSOs typically experience significant income fluctuations irrespective of their size (with the exception of the sub-sample of ten large national charities operating in north-east England and Cumbria, which tended to exhibit smoother income profiles).[4]

For illustrative purposes, Figure 3.2 presents data on 11 of the medium-sized TSOs in the sample (with income between £100,000 and £1 million) to illustrate patterns of financial turbulence. The overall picture of ups and downs in TSOs' finances is quite 'chaotic' and, certainly, there is no clear indication that they coincide neatly with major events such as the 2008 financial crash or the austerity programme from 2010 to 2019.

Figure 3.2: Fluctuations in the income of medium-sized TSOs in north-east England and Cumbria, 2004–20

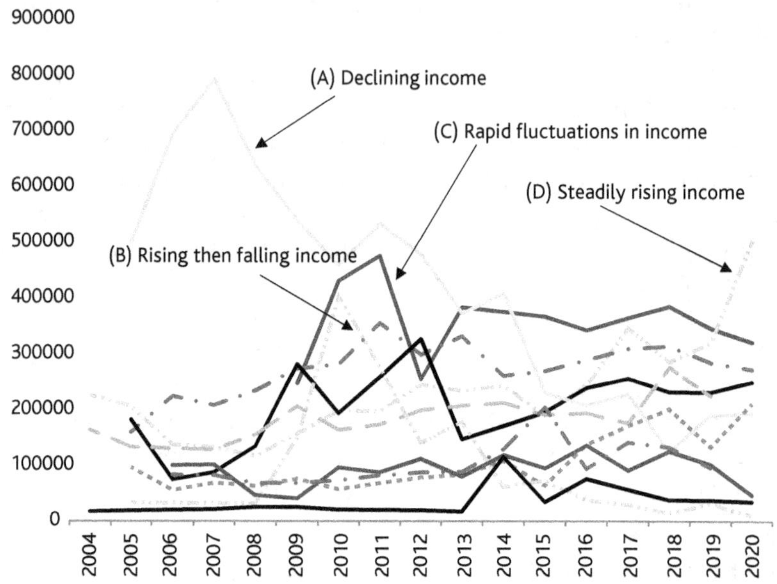

[Line chart showing income fluctuations from 2004 to 2020, with y-axis from 0 to 900000. Four categories labelled: (A) Declining income, (B) Rising then falling income, (C) Rapid fluctuations in income, (D) Steadily rising income.]

Source: Data from Charity Commission Register 2022

Of the sample of 32 regional or locally based TSOs, four distinct categories can be delineated: those which experienced a trend of long-term continual growth (three TSOs), those tackling the consequences of continuous long-term decline (two TSOs), those which experienced significant growth and concomitant decline in income (two TSOs) and, finally, those which had to manage recurrent fluctuation (25 TSOs). Among these 25 TSOs, ten experienced 'dramatic' shifts in income levels (that is, more than a 50 per cent change in either direction from the baseline income point); among the remainder, income shifts were 'moderate' (less than a 50 per cent change in either direction). No organisations enjoyed anything approaching 'level' funding throughout the period of study.

As the analysis presented above indicates, all locally or regionally based organisations in the TSO50 study have experienced turbulent financial fortunes. While at the individual organisational level this could undoubtedly sap their energy and test their resilience, a strong sense has also been gained from the qualitative research that organisational leaders are accustomed to this situation – it is part and parcel of life in the third sector (Chapman, 2022).

Financial pressure was felt keenly by CEOs or chairs of medium- and larger-sized organisations which needed more money to keep their organisation going. Throughout the period of study, CEOs reported worries about sustaining the jobs of their employees and keeping services running for beneficiaries. In smaller TSOs, which employed no or few staff, such financial worries were less pronounced, but instead shifted into other arenas such as maintaining voluntary and in-kind support.

Financial uncertainties led organisational leaders to minimise the risk of sudden and precipitous financial ruin by drawing upon a 'basket of mixed resources'. TSTS longitudinal survey data can be used to show how perceptions of reliance on different types of resources has changed between 2008 and 2019. Figure 3.3 illustrates the changing levels of perceived reliance on resources in 'relative terms' over the last ten years.[5]

As these data demonstrate, *grants* from trusts and foundations, and government and private sector businesses, were regarded as the most important type of income (relative to other types of income) in the third sector since 2010 (and the perceived level of importance of grants has risen slightly over time). Even among larger, more formal TSOs (with income above £250,000), the perceived importance of grants grew substantially over the decade, while the perceived importance of contracts declined between 2010 and 2019.

The reality is that *public service delivery contracts* have never represented a significant source of income for the majority of TSOs (Clark et al, 2009). Larger TSOs are more likely to be in a position to take on contracts, though some medium-sized and smaller TSOs may be sub-contracted to do elements of the work. Attitudes about contracts have changed little over the last decade. Over two thirds of respondents are either unaware of such opportunities or are not interested in this option. A similar proportion of the sector (15–20 per cent) have not tendered for contracts on the basis that they need more support, more information or because they perceive other barriers to winning contracts. The percentage of TSOs which do bid for or win contracts has grown from 14 per cent to 17 per cent in a decade, but this is still a very small proportion of the sector. Among the largest organisations (with income above £1 million), a third still do not engage in public service contract delivery and focus instead on self-defined objectives.

From the turn of this century, a belief that socially enterprising activity can contribute towards organisational sustainability and growth has often been voiced. As Figure 3.3 demonstrates, there was a jump in the perceived importance of *self-generated trading* activity between 2010 and 2012, possibly in response to the global financial crash and to offset the impact of government austerity policies. Since 2012, however, the perceived importance of trading activity has remained level at about 17 per cent.

Figure 3.3 indicates that *borrowing* money is rarely regarded as an essential element of organisational finances. There was a major policy drive to encourage social investment in the last decade, but this has yet to catch the imagination of the sector as a whole: fewer than two per cent of TSOs perceive borrowing money to be an important part of their mix of resources. Even among the biggest TSOs, borrowing is the least important

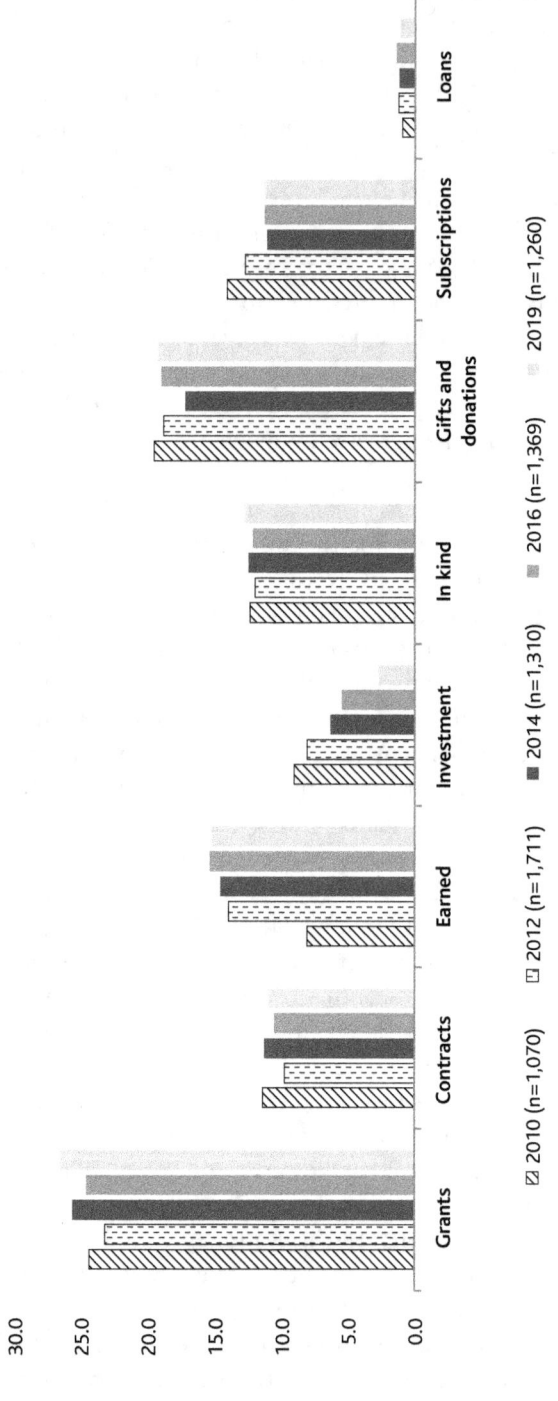

Figure 3.3: Relative importance of income sources to TSOs (Third Sector Trends, north-east England and Cumbria, 2010–19)

Source: Third Sector Trends surveys 2010–19

element of income in the mix. This is likely to reflect TSOs' financial 'prudence' rather than 'risk aversion', as is sometimes asserted by critics (Chapman, 2017b).

The perceived value of *investment income* to TSOs, in relative terms, has plummeted over the last decade. This suggests that TSOs are less inclined to perceive investments as a reliable source of income in comparison. That said, NCVO analysis demonstrates that while the financial yield of investment is low, the scale of sector investments has held up well over the last decade. Indeed, in 2017/18 the net assets of the sector in the UK grew to £142 billion. NCVO concluded that 'investments were the main driver in the overall growth of assets and grew by £4.1bn'.[6]

As also shown in Figure 3.1, *public giving and donations* and *subscriptions* are perceived as crucial sources of income by TSOs. NCVO have demonstrated that public giving is the single most important source of income for the third sector: 47 per cent of sector income is derived from public giving.[7] But this income is not distributed evenly across the sector. According to a reanalysis of NCVO Charity Commission data, just 4.4 per cent of gift and legacy income is received by micro organisations (those with annual incomes below £10,000), while 14.2 per cent is received by TSOs with annual incomes between £10,000 and £1 million. By contrast, 81.4 per cent of the money donated by the public is given to TSOs with annual incomes of £1 million or more.[8]

Money is a crucial element in the resource mix, but TSOs also rely heavily on non-financial resources. TSTS data show that in-kind support (such as free training, use of space and facilities, pro bono consultancy or professional services, help from employee supported volunteers and so on) is also regarded as an important element – especially among smaller TSOs (Chapman, 2021).

But another vital resource is the contribution of time by volunteers. In the north of England, 80 per cent of TSOs indicate that they rely mainly on volunteers who commit time on a regular basis and 70 per cent say they rely mainly on volunteers who can work unsupervised. Smaller organisations, and especially those without employees, are the most reliant on regular volunteers: 94 per cent of TSOs with income below £10,000 state that they could not survive without volunteers compared with 52 per cent of TSOs with income over £1 million.

There is little evidence from TSTS to suggest that the extent of sector reliance on volunteers has changed significantly since 2008. But there is a strong likelihood that there has been substantive change since the onset of COVID-19. As NCVO have shown, there has been a marked decline in the population who volunteer once a month from 23 per cent in 2019–20 to 17 per cent in 2020–21 (NCVO, 2021). It is also likely that the composition of the volunteer workforce may change (Ellis Paine, 2020). For example, previous reliance on older retired volunteers (McGarvey et al, 2019) may shift to other constituencies of the population.

Swings and roundabouts

The third sector has faced many challenges over the last two decades. This has led commentators to issue dire warnings about financial vulnerability. This chapter has presented longitudinal evidence to show that the third sector is, in fact, much more resilient than might be expected. And against some criteria, such as overall income of the sector, there has been modest but steady growth.

The security of individual TSOs, like private businesses, is affected by resource issues, but the difference from an analytical point of view is that businesses are less able to spread their risk and are much more vulnerable to seismic shifts in market conditions due to their need to maintain turnover and sustain profitability. This helps to explain why around 10 per cent of businesses close on average per year compared with about 2 per cent of charities.[9]

Perceptions of sector vulnerability are, nevertheless, explicable. As shown from the TSTS study of 50 TSOs over the last 15 years, fluctuation in the financial fortunes of individual organisations is the norm, not the exception. So it is not surprising that feelings of insecurity are strong among people who lead individual organisations who must constantly manage high levels of uncertainty about their resource base.

To help them manage uncertainty, TSOs garner financial and non-financial resources in such a way as to avoid having all their eggs in one basket. They are accustomed to juggling a wide range of resources to help them do their work. Financial resources include grants, contracts, self-generated earned income, subscriptions, gifts, donations and investments – but unlike private businesses, only rarely do TSOs rely upon borrowed money. Non-financial resources include in-kind support (such as the receipt of pro bono expertise, employee-supported volunteers or the provision of free use of space, facility or consumables) and freely given time by trustees and volunteers.

At any point in time, parts of this resource base may be under threat due to circumstances within or beyond control of the organisation. So organisational leaders have to learn how to manage this precarious balance – arguably to the extent that it has become part of the sector's 'way of life'.

This helps to explain a conundrum that emerges from the TSTS research evidence. While TSO leaders undoubtedly and continually voice worries about the vulnerability of the wider sector's resource base, they are much more positive when making predictions about their own organisation's future prospects.

As TSTS research has consistently demonstrated, within the private confines of individual TSOs, an 'optimistic' point of view tends to prevail, of at least maintaining financial resource levels or increasing them substantially.

Figure 3.4: Mismatch between expectations and reality on rising income, 2009–21

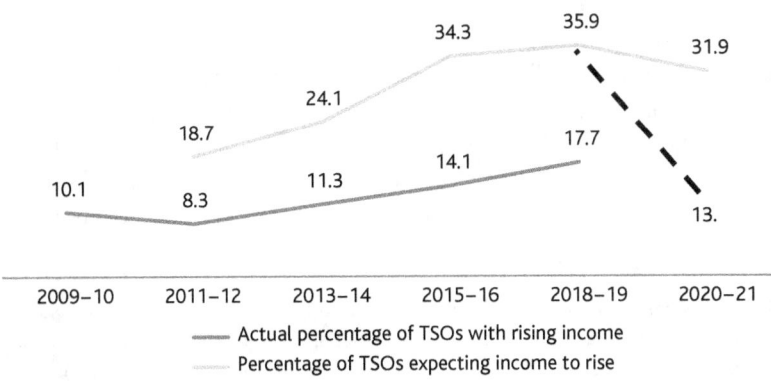

Note: Dashed line represents predictions from the June 2020 survey
Source: Third Sector Trends surveys 2010–19

The problem, however, is that expectations about increasing income are rarely realised, as indicated in Figure 3.4.

Somewhat paradoxically, concerns about sector wellbeing may be exacerbated by this general tendency of organisational leaders to be over-optimistic about future levels of financial resources – perhaps leading to a continual sense of disappointment when things do not work out as expected. For example, even following the global economic crash, 19 per cent of TSOs expected that income would rise significantly in the next two years. But when the reality was checked in the 2012 survey, only 8 per cent of TSOs actually had significantly rising income.

Over the years, optimism about rising income rose steadily from 19 per cent in 2010 to 36 per cent in 2019. In reality, the percentage of TSOs with significantly rising income rose too, but to a lesser extent than expected, rising from 10 per cent in 2009–10 to 18 per cent by 2018–19.

After the COVID-19 pandemic had become established in the UK, a sub-sample of respondents were asked how they felt about the future. Optimism about significantly rising income over the next two years fell from 32 per cent in December 2019 to 13 per cent in June 2020. But it remains to be seen whether these expectations were well founded.

Organisational and sector leaders may perceive a positional advantage by being downbeat about financial prospects, in the hope that they might pull on the heartstrings of those organisations and individuals who give them money to do good work. Continual references to 'perfect storms' or being 'on the edge of a precipice' have become so common that there is a risk that those who volunteer, or offer in-kind or financial support, may feel less inclined to invest resources. In response to the COVID-19 pandemic, that does not seem to have been the case, however. In fact, there has been a surge in voluntary action and funding bodies have been flexible and generous in their response to the sector's needs.

As a long-term strategy, however, projecting a 'care-worn' image of the third sector by continually making headline-grabbing claims of its imminent demise may undermine confidence. The evidence presented in this chapter indicates that sector resilience and robustness is plain to see – perhaps it would be best to build on this and recognise that investment in a strong sector is a more attractive option than rescuing one which is close to collapse.

Notes

1. In my first research project in this field, I fell into the same trap because I had no access to longitudinal data. Indeed, the project brief specifically demanded that 'threats' to sector sustainability were demonstrated and led to the adoption of what turned out to be a misleading title to the report (see Chapman, T., Crow, R., Brown, J. and Ward, J. (2006) *Facing the Future: A Study of the Impact of the Changing Funding Environment on the Voluntary and Community Sector in the North East of England*, Middlesbrough: Social Futures Institute). The inherent limitations of this kind of snapshot study analysis led, ultimately, to the establishment of Third Sector Trends.
2. All publications from the Third Sector Trends study are available at this web address: www.communityfoundation.org.uk/knowledge-and-leadership/third-sector-trends-research/.
3. The Cabinet Office defines a non-departmental public body (NDPB) as a 'body which has a role in the processes of national government, but is not a government department or part of one, and which accordingly operates to a greater or lesser extent at arm's length from ministers'. See: www.gov.uk/guidance/public-bodies-reform#:~:text=A%20non%2Ddepartmental%20public%20body,at%20arm%27s%20length%20from%20ministers%E2%80%9D.
4. The TSO50 study included ten organisations from each of the five sub-regions of northeast England plus Cumbria. Each area included the same range of organisational sizes, but focused on different thematic areas (for example, youth organisations in Tees Valley). Full details can be found in Chapman (2017a).
5. In this study, TSOs were asked "How important are the following sources of income for your work?" A separate response is given for each income source in the following range: 'Most important', 'important', 'of some importance', 'least important' and 'not important'. Data do not therefore refer to the sum of income, but perceptions of reliance upon a range of resources which can be compared over time. The bar graphs show relative importance of income sources to each other in each year of study (hence, the percentages add up to 100 each year to ensure that the data are intelligible and comparable). Reliance upon and the value gained from volunteer resources are addressed separately in the survey. Given the limited space available in this short chapter, Figure 3.3 reports only sector-wide perceptions; interpretation is bolstered by background analysis for organisations of different sizes. More complete analysis by organisational size is available in regional Third Sector Trends reports published in 2020, which are available online at: www.communityfoundation.org.uk/knowledge-and-leadership/third-sector-trends-research/.
6. *NCVO Civil Society Almanac 2020*: //data.ncvo.org.uk/financials/. TSTS analysis shows pronounced variations in the extent of TSOs' assets according to their age. 86 per cent of TSOs established since 2010 have no investment assets, compared with only 41 per cent of organisations established before 1945. It is worth noting that older 'asset-rich' TSOs are among the least likely to consider social investment options or indeed to take loans of any kind.

7   *NCVO UK Civil Society Almanac 2020*: //data.ncvo.org.uk/financials/.
8   *NCVO UK Civil Society Almanac 2020*: Re-analysis of background Table C2: //data.ncvo.org.uk/financials/.
9   Business closure data – ONS: www.ons.gov.uk/businessindustryandtrade/business/activitysizeandlocation/bulletins/businessdemography/2019. Charity deregistration data – Charity Financials: www.charityfinancials.com/insights/insider/press-release-number-of-uk-charities-closing-quadrupled-after-the-last-recession-a-warning-for-covid-19.

References

Alcock, P. and Kendall, J. (2011) 'Constituting the third sector: processes of decontestation and contention under the UK Labour governments in England', *Voluntas*, 22: 450–69.

Chapman, T. (2017a) 'Journeys and destinations: how third sector organisations navigate their future in turbulent times', *Voluntary Sector Review*, 8(1): 3–24.

Chapman, T. (2017b) 'The propensity of third sector organisations to borrow money in the UK', *Policy Studies*, 38(2): 185–204.

Chapman, T. (2021) *Going the Extra Mile: How Businesses Support the Third Sector in England and Wales*, London: Pro Bono Economics.

Chapman, T. (2022) *Navigating Third Sector Organisations through Turbulent Times: Reflections on Leadership Challenges 2008–2022*, Newcastle: Community Foundation Serving Tyne & Wear and Northumberland.

Chapman, T., Longlands, S. and Hunter, J. (2020) *Third Sector Trends Survey 2020: Covid-19 and its Potential Impact on the Third Sector in the North*, London: IPPR.

Clark, J., Dobbs, J., Kane, D. and Wilding, K. (2009) *The State and the Voluntary Sector: Recent Trends in Government Funding and Public Service Delivery*, London: NCVO.

Dollery, B. and Robotti, L. (2008) *The Theory and Practice of Local Government Reform*, Cheltenham: Edward Elgar.

Ellis Paine, A. (2020) 'Volunteering through crisis and beyond: starting, stopping and shifting', [online], Available from: //localtrust.org.uk/wp-content/uploads/2020/09/COVID-19-briefing-5-3.pdf [Accessed 22 December 2021].

Evers, A. and Laville, J.L. (eds.) (2004) *The Third Sector in Europe*, Cheltenham: Edward Elgar.

Gray, M. and Barford, A. (2018) 'The depths of the cuts: the uneven geography of local government austerity', *Cambridge Journal of Regions, Economy and Society*, 11(3): 541–63.

Macmillan, R. (2013) 'Decoupling the state and the third sector? The "big society" as a spontaneous order', *Voluntary Sector Review*, 4(2): 185–203.

McGarvey, A., Jochum, V., Davies, J., Dobbs, J. and Hornung, L. (2019) *Time Well Spent: A National Survey on the Volunteer Experience*, London: NCVO.

NCVO (2021) *The UK Civil Society Almanac 2021*, [online], Available from: //beta.ncvo.org.uk/ncvo-publications/uk-civil-society-almanac-2021/ [Accessed 7 October 2021].

Pestoff, V., Brandsen, T. and Verschuere, B. (eds.) (2013) *New Public Governance, the Third Sector and Co-Production*, Abingdon, Oxon: Routledge.

Rajan, R. (2019) *The Third Pillar: The Revival of Community in a Polarised World*, London: William Collins.

4

The impact of COVID-19 on the formation and dissolution of charitable organisations

Diarmuid McDonnell, Alasdair Rutherford and John Mohan

Introduction

The onset of the COVID-19 pandemic in early 2020, and the associated lockdown of economy and society, prompted the vociferous expression of concerns about an existential threat to many charitable organisations.[1] Some of the headline figures focused on the enormous losses of income likely to be visited upon major charities, some of which were fixtures in the public's perception of the charitable landscape. Several of these depended on sales of goods and services, as is evident from their strong presence in retail, but this visibility was also a source of vulnerability, since activities such as trading through charity shops were not going to be feasible under lockdown restrictions.

Aside from the risks faced by prominent individual organisations, there was a sense from initial surveys of a potential threat to very large numbers of organisations. At times, the evidence verged on the apocalyptic. Media coverage and evidence given to public enquiries highlighted dramatic examples of individual organisations either facing closure within a matter of weeks or contemplating the almost total loss of key income streams and therefore operating on a substantially reduced basis at a time when demand for their services was increasing significantly (Wilding, 2020). The position of small- and medium-sized organisations, often exemplified as the beating heart of the voluntary sector and on the frontline of immediate responses to emerging needs, featured strongly in the conversation.

With these worrying predictions from early survey evidence, there is a pressing need to understand the implications of the pandemic on the sustainability of the voluntary sector, especially given the role these organisations play in the UK's 'mixed economy of welfare' (Rees and Mullins, 2016). This chapter analyses trends in the formation and dissolution of charitable organisations during the COVID-19 pandemic, and places these in the context of longer-term patterns. The chapter's empirical focus is on charitable organisations in Scotland, England and Wales, with some international comparison.

What we know about the formation and dissolution of charities

There is a long-running and rich scholarly tradition of studying the formation and demise of charitable organisations. Such studies matter, as new charitable organisations offer many benefits to the communities and individuals they serve; while their disappearance can result in the loss of community assets and public goods/services, outlets for creative and compassionate pursuits, and employment and volunteering opportunities. Analyses of formation are commonly found in literature focusing on 'nonprofit density', and seek to relate the number of organisations per capita for a given geographic area to a range of organisational, individual and community-level factors. For example, Kim (2015) finds a negative association between the number of nonprofits founded in US counties and levels of social need; that is, as social need increases, fewer nonprofits are founded. Sharkey et al (2017) identified a causal link between the number of crime- or community-focused nonprofits and the levels of violent crime in a city.[2]

Research on the demise or 'failure' of charitable organisations often falls under the 'nonprofit dissolution' literature. Dissolution is a contested phenomenon, subject to various conceptualisations including resource reduction, market exit and organisational mortality (Mellahi and Wilkinson, 2004; Helmig et al, 2014). Empirical studies have focused on explaining dissolution as a function of deterministic and voluntaristic factors (Mellahi and Wilkinson, 2004): the former include factors such as organisational size, age and density, the latter strategic and governance behaviours (Callen et al, 2010).

Clifford (2018) offers a rare examination of both the formation and dissolution of charitable organisations. He finds that in England, between 1996 and 2011 fewer charities were formed in more deprived areas, compared with less deprived, and that once founded, charities in more deprived areas have a higher hazard (chance) of dissolution.

The empirical studies that constitute the broad field of nonprofit density and dissolution typically select organisations as their units of analysis; for example, what is the probability of dissolution for a given charitable organisation, conditional on relevant factors? There is a lack of empirical work that adopts a macro perspective on the phenomena of charity formation and dissolution; that is, what are the trends in formations and dissolutions at the level of whole charity sectors or jurisdictions? In this chapter, we demonstrate the value of employing a macro perspective to evaluate the impact of the pandemic on these phenomena.

Impact of COVID-19 on charitable activity

A number of rapid response research projects were initiated in 2020 and 2021 to try to capture the real-time impact of the pandemic on the UK charity sector. Many have taken the form of repeated surveys of small samples of voluntary organisations at a given point in time during the pandemic. Headline figures from these various surveys present a broadly consistent picture: that the financial position of these organisations has deteriorated within a given reference period, that they anticipate COVID-19 to have a clear negative impact on delivering their objectives and that they believe there to be an enhanced likelihood that their organisation would cease to operate at some point in the near future. To give one example, the 'Respond, recover, reset: the voluntary sector and COVID-19' project (Nottingham Trent University, 2020) uses surveys to produce regular snapshots of the UK voluntary sector (charities, social enterprises, mutual aid associations and so on). With between 380 and 700 respondents, the survey has been monitoring the position of voluntary organisations since September 2020. It contains several indicators which are repeated monthly, though individual surveys tend to focus on particular topics. For example, when asked whether they believe their organisation is unlikely or very unlikely to be operating next year, between 8 per cent and 14 per cent have agreed (Nottingham Trent University, 2020; 2021). This compares with a typical dissolution rate for registered charities of no more than 2–3 per cent per annum.

The Scottish Third Sector Tracker surveyed 585 TSOs based or operating in Scotland, and sought to describe the impact of COVID-19 on the operations of these organisations since March 2020. Conducted in the summer of 2021, the research revealed considerable disruption to planned services, an increase in demand for services and a substantial proportion of organisations (48 per cent) experiencing a decrease in income (Scottish Council for Voluntary Organisations, 2021). In addition, 22 per cent of organisations had to temporarily stop operating altogether at some point during the pandemic (Scottish Council for Voluntary Organisations, 2021). A 2021 survey by the Charity Commission for England and Wales found that 60 per cent of charities experienced a drop in income from charitable activities during the pandemic, and 40 per cent had to draw upon their reserves (Charity Commission, 2021). When asked about their future financial viability, 62 per cent of charities expected this to be at risk over the next 12 months, though only 1 per cent expect that threat to jeopardise the organisation's survival.

The advantage of these surveys is timeliness, and it has always been a criticism of reliance on data from regulators that there is a substantial time delay (Kennedy, 2021). However, the trade-off is that by using surveys, we capture sentiment about financial vulnerability: real concerns expressed by organisations, but which may or may not play out as organisational dissolution.

Given the aforementioned time delay, there are a limited number of studies that used administrative data from UK regulators to study the impact of the pandemic on the charitable organisations. Such regulatory data can provide a more representative sample of charitable organisations and more valid indicators of financial resources and vulnerability. Clifford et al (2021) constructed a panel of c.50,000 charities that filed an annual return for a financial year ending between mid-June and December 2020 inclusive. Using this panel, they examined long-run trends in annual income growth/decline between 2000 and 2020, and found that the typical charity experienced a 15 per cent real-terms decline in their income in 2020, a much more distinctive drop than during the recession and period of public spending austerity which followed the 2008 financial crash (2009–14).

Combined, these extant studies provide a rich account of the lived experience of voluntary organisations during the pandemic, and suggest what might happen to these organisations in the future as a result of rising demand, and financial and operational disruption. By definition, however, these studies only reflect the experience of organisations that survived long enough to be surveyed or have their financial returns analysed. Nor, in many cases, will these studies have captured responses from organisations newly formed during the pandemic, as they may not yet appear on email or membership lists that served as sampling frames, or been required to file annual returns with a regulator. Thus, there is a gap in our understanding of the impact of COVID-19 on the UK charity sector: to what degree have the rates of new organisations being formed and existing organisations dissolving been altered since March 2020?

Regulatory data on charities

Data for this study come primarily from the publicly available charity registers[3] of two regulatory agencies: the Charity Commission for England and Wales, and the Office of the Scottish Charity Regulator. In addition, we show international comparisons drawing on data from Northern Ireland (Charity Commission for Northern Ireland), Australia (Australian Charities and Not-for-profits Commission), New Zealand (Charities Services), Canada (Canada Revenue Agency) and the United States of America (Internal Revenue Services). The charity register data were collected in January 2022 using a Python web-scraping script that has been running on the 28th of each month since August 2020.

For charities in Scotland, England and Wales, data on insolvency reports made to Companies House by charitable companies are also collected. Charitable companies represent an economically significant subset of the charitable sector, and tend to comprise larger charities because company status is more likely to be taken out by organisations which are engaging in trading and delivering contracts, and/or managing significant property assets and employing staff. While much rarer than dissolution, this duty to notify when a company is insolvent means that reports are made in a more timely fashion and so this sub-sample provides us with a measure of charities in financial distress prior to their completing the deregistration process with the relevant charity regulator. Data from Companies House is extracted through the Companies House online database using the company number attached to the charity's record.

We restrict analysis to the period 2015–21: this is in line with similar analyses of excess events/deaths (see Office for National Statistics, 2021), as it places contemporaneous observations in the context of recent trends. We feel this is justified on the grounds that charity regulation in the UK (and regulators) has evolved considerably over the longer period (for example, Charities Act 2011), and thus such historical patterns may not provide a relevant baseline to compare current trends.

Modelling the impact of COVID-19 on charity formations and dissolutions

The main phenomenon of interest is the impact the COVID-19 pandemic has had upon formation and dissolution rates of charitable organisations. Here, we define 'formation' as the registration of a charity with its respective regulator, and 'dissolution' as the deregistration of a charity with its respective regulator. Thus, formations are a subset of all new charitable organisations established in a given year (as some do not need to register with the Charity Commission for England and Wales if they are below a certain income threshold). A dissolution is a general term for the wide variety of ways in which a charity can cease to exist (for example, it can merge with another organisation, revoke its charity status but continue operating, change legal form, become insolvent and wind up).

The pandemic is an exceptional event and thus posited to alter the expected or 'normal' levels of formations and dissolutions. To measure this impact, we draw upon two analytical approaches: one descriptive ('excess events') and one causal (Interrupted Time Series Analysis). The 'excess events' approach measures the impact of the pandemic in terms of deviations from expected annual levels of formation and dissolution (and is analogous to analyses of 'excess deaths' that have come to the fore during the pandemic). We do this by comparing the numbers of formations and dissolutions in 2020 and 2021 to the averages observed over the period 2015–19. We do this for five other jurisdictions also to provide comparisons for what occurred in Scotland, England and Wales.

We then use Interrupted Time Series Analysis (ITSA) to model the shift in the level and trend of charity formations and dissolutions during the pandemic (Penfold and Zhang, 2013). For example, a decline in charity formations in 2020 may have been expected regardless of the pandemic; thus, we need a robust method for isolating the potential impact of the pandemic from longer-term trends. ITSA is particularly suitable for analyses of macro-level interventions/changes occurring at a discrete point in time (Briesacher et al, 2013). ITSA divides a time series – repeated observations of a single outcome over time – into two segments: before and after an intervention/change. The ITSA model is estimated using data relating to periods before the pandemic (pre-April 2020), and the predictions from the model used to forecast what would have happened in 2020/21 if the pandemic hadn't occurred. We then compare the prediction to what we observed for 2020/21 to see if the pandemic has shifted the level and/or trend in formations and dissolutions.

How exceptional were 2020 and 2021 for charity formations and dissolutions?

Were 2020 and 2021 typical or atypical years in terms of the level of charity formations and dissolutions observed? How does the UK experience compare with charity jurisdictions internationally? Figure 4.1 plots the difference between actual and expected numbers of formations for seven charity jurisdictions: circles represent years between 2015 and 2019; triangles represent 2020; and diamonds represent 2021. As the absolute number of formations varies by jurisdiction (for example, USA: 72,760 in 2020; Scotland: 812 in 2020), we standardise these differences by calculating how far above or below the 2015–19 average a year was for each jurisdiction: observations to the left of the vertical line capture years where formations were below average; observations to the right of the vertical line represent years where formations were above average. There is considerable variation across UK jurisdictions: in 2020, formations are slightly above average in England and Wales, slightly below average for Northern Ireland and much less than average for Scotland. In fact, only Canada has recorded a larger deviation from average levels of formations than Scotland in 2020. It appears that for all jurisdictions, formations in 2021 are below the 2015–19 average, with the exception of the USA (data were not available for 2021 for Canada).

Figure 4.2 replicates Figure 4.1 but this time focusing on differences between actual and expected numbers of dissolutions. Dissolutions in 2020 and 2021 are below average levels for most jurisdictions (data were not available for 2021 for Canada), with the exception of the US and Northern Ireland – in the case of the latter, this is almost certainly a function of regulatory issues around the registration and deregistration of charities in

The impact of COVID-19 on charities

Figure 4.1: Deviation from average level of formations for seven charity jurisdictions, 2015–21

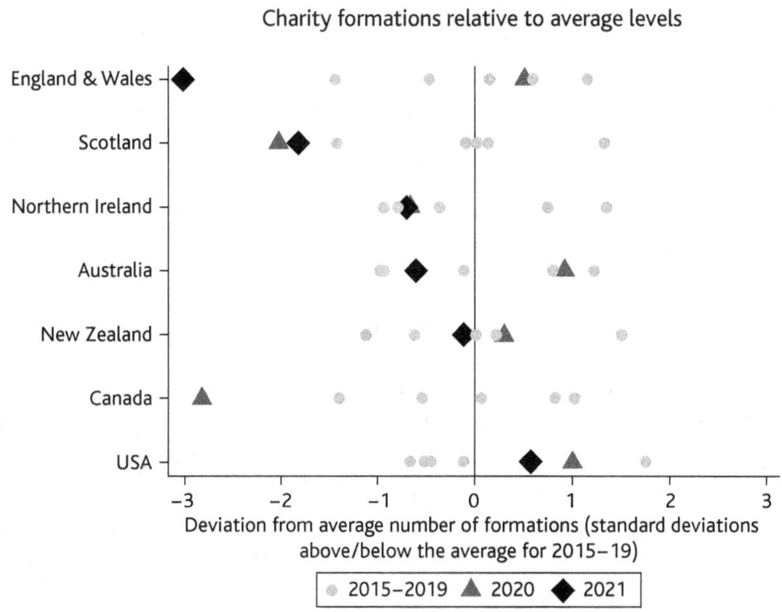

Charity formations relative to average levels

[Chart showing deviation from average number of formations (standard deviations above/below the average for 2015–19) for England & Wales, Scotland, Northern Ireland, Australia, New Zealand, Canada, USA, with markers for 2015–2019, 2020, and 2021]

Source: Data from multiple sources; see pp. 49–50

Figure 4.2: Deviation from average level of dissolutions for seven charity jurisdictions, 2015–21

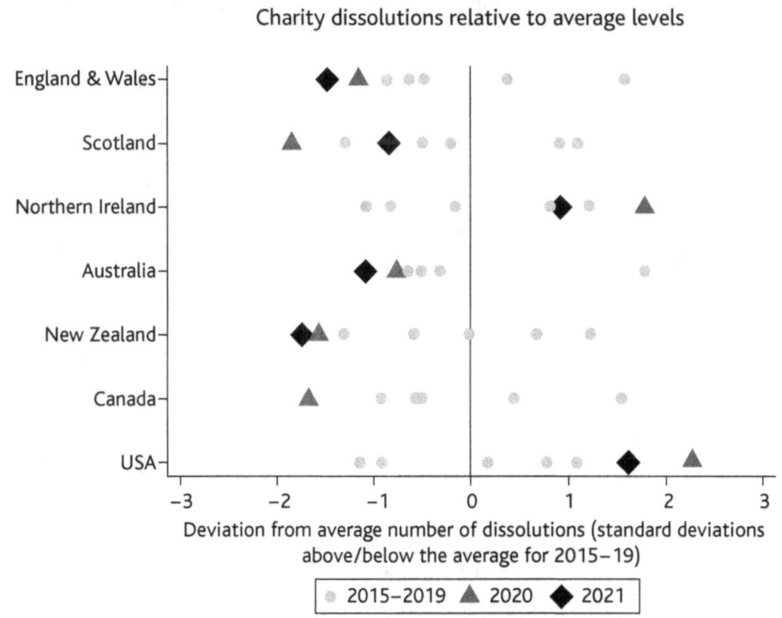

Charity dissolutions relative to average levels

[Chart showing deviation from average number of dissolutions (standard deviations above/below the average for 2015–19) for England & Wales, Scotland, Northern Ireland, Australia, New Zealand, Canada, USA, with markers for 2015–2019, 2020, and 2021]

Source: Data from multiple sources; see pp. 49–50

this jurisdiction.[4] The decrease in dissolutions compared with the historic (2015–19) average is noticeable but not beyond conventional statistical significance thresholds (that is, two standard deviations).

The above analyses are helpful for identifying years where formations or dissolutions were considerably different than expected. However, this is not evidence of the specific impact of the pandemic on these outcomes: perhaps formations and dissolutions were declining year on year in the run-up to the pandemic, and thus a decrease was to be expected? To help us address this alternative explanation, we turn our attention to the temporal trends in charity formations and dissolutions across Scotland, England and Wales in more depth.

Trends in the formation of charities

The formation rate – the number of new charities registered in a given year divided by the number of charities that continue to operate (shown by filing a non-zero annual return in the previous year) – has remained steady at c.4 per cent per annum, including for 2020. In a given year, 5,463, and 901, new charities would be expected to be formed in England and Wales, and Scotland, respectively (based on the 2015–19 averages). However, in England and Wales in particular, there appears to have been a significant drop-off in the number of formations in 2021.

There is a clear seasonal pattern in the number of formations, with these highest during October and November, and lowest in February,

Figure 4.3a: Trends in the formation of charities in England and Wales

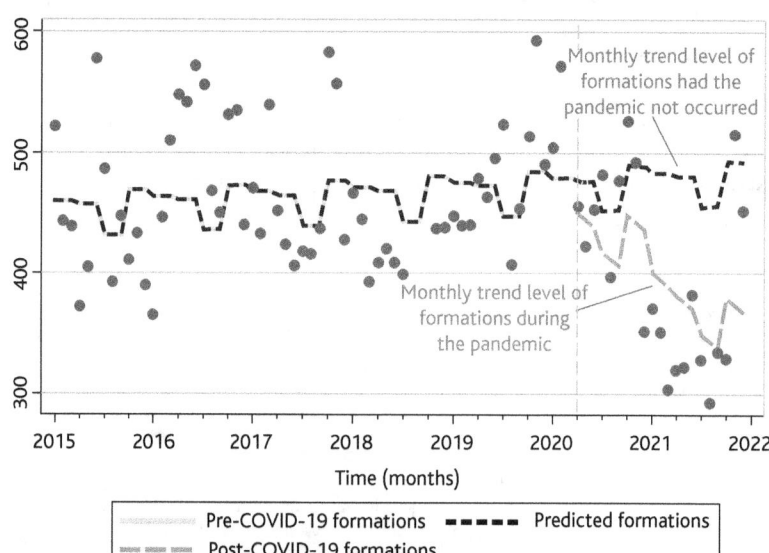

Source: Data from the Charity Commission for England & Wales, January 2022

Figure 4.3b: Trends in the formation of charities in Scotland

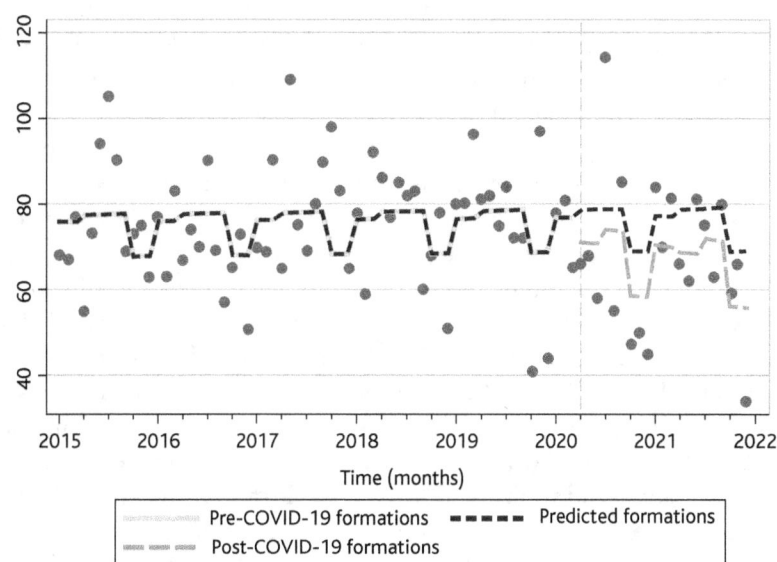

Source: Data from the Scottish Charity Regulator, January 2022

March and August. There does not appear to be an immediate post-March 2020 decrease in formations, though there may be a sustained decline in new charities.

The scatter plots in Figures 4.3a and 4.3b show the monthly number of charities formed in (a) England and Wales, and (b) Scotland (represented by the circles). The solid dark line shows the level of formations predicted by our model of the longer-term trend before COVID-19, including seasonal variation. The dashed line shows the forecast of this prediction beyond March 2020, assuming that the pre-pandemic patterns had continued. The grey dashed line shows the ITSA model, which estimates changes in the level of and trend in formations as a result of the pandemic. England and Wales have seen a sharp decline in the formation of new charities, with typical numbers registered in the months immediately following lockdown, but far fewer than expected in late 2020 and early 2021. Scotland, in contrast, shows a much less pronounced drop in new charities, with registrations historically low but without a continuing decline through the COVID lockdown.

Trends in the dissolution of charities

The dissolution rate – the number of charities deregistered in a given year divided by the number of charities that continue to operate (shown by filing a non-zero annual return in the previous year) – shows some minor fluctuations around the average of c.3 per cent in both jurisdictions, in particular for 2019 and 2021. In a given year, 4,691, and 690, charities would be expected to dissolve in England and Wales, and Scotland, respectively (based on 2015–19 averages). Again, there is a clear seasonal pattern in the number of dissolutions, with these highest during January and February, and lowest in May, August and September. Therefore, the post-March 2020 decrease in the level of dissolutions may simply be a function of an expected seasonal decrease heading into summer months.

The scatter plot in Figures 4.4a and 4.4b shows the number of charities removed from the charity registers in each month for (a) England and Wales, and (b) Scotland. The solid dark line shows the trend level of dissolutions before COVID-19. The dashed line shows the forecast of this prediction beyond March 2020, assuming that the pre-pandemic patterns had continued. The grey dashed line shows the ITSA model, which estimates changes in the level of and trend in dissolutions as a result of the pandemic. England and Wales experienced a sharp drop in the level of dissolutions since the pandemic, though there is less evidence of a shift in the long-run trend (slight growth before the pandemic; flat trajectory after the pandemic). Scotland shows a similar decline in the level of dissolutions in the immediate post-pandemic period but it appears that dissolutions are returning to typical levels (though perhaps without months where dissolutions are particularly high).

Figure 4.4a: Trends in the dissolution of charities in England and Wales

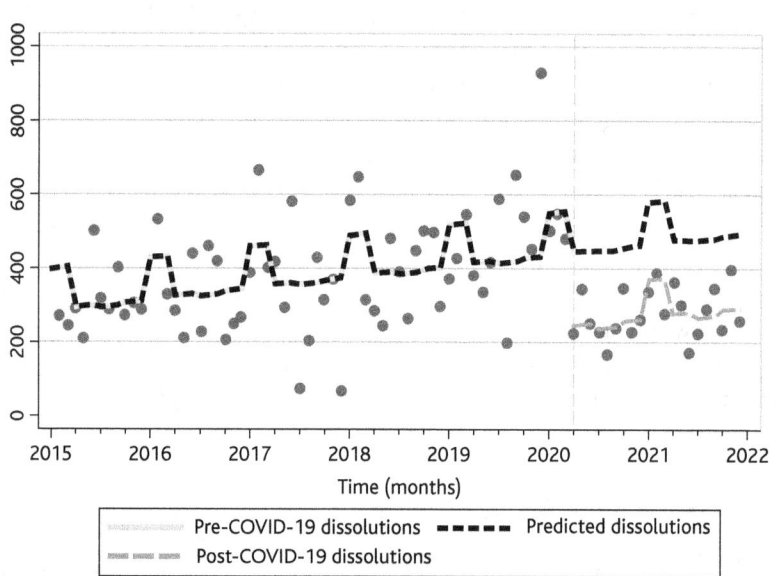

Source: Data from the Charity Commission for England & Wales, January 2022

Figure 4.4b: Trends in the dissolution of charities in Scotland

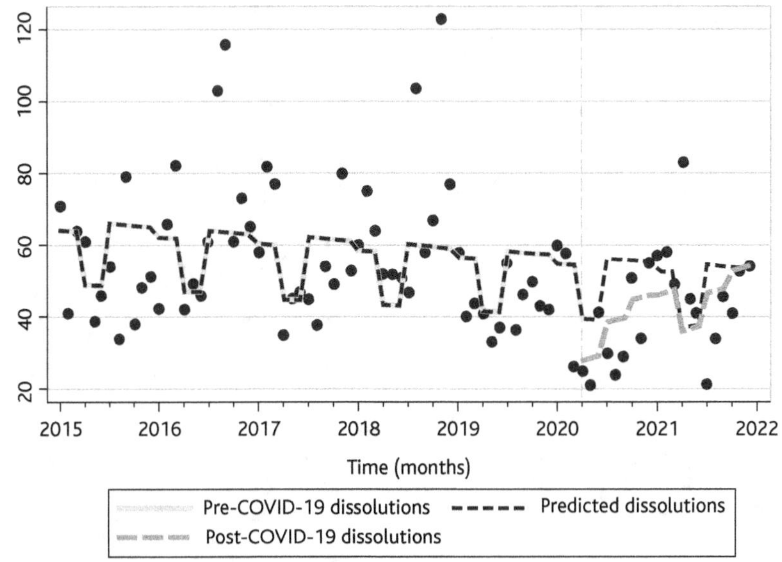

Legend: Pre-COVID-19 dissolutions; Post-COVID-19 dissolutions; Predicted dissolutions

Source: Data from the Scottish Charity Regulator, January 2022

Insolvency

Finally, we focus in on charities experiencing insolvency. This restricts our sample to charities with the legal form of company, and also to the more extreme outcome of being insolvent when the charity ceases to operate. There are advantages and disadvantages in examining this data. On the positive side, it is much more immediate as companies which are insolvent must inform Companies House while they are still operating, whereas charities being removed from the register is the last step in the dissolution process. This allows us to detect financial vulnerability earlier than with charity dissolutions. However, the data covers a sub-sample of the sector because not all charities are companies, and only records the rarer event of insolvency. Limited company is also a legal form which is more likely to be used by larger and more established charities, so it primarily gives an insight into their financial experience during the pandemic.

The scatter plot in Figure 4.5 shows that there were typically about six to eight charitable company insolvencies every month in the pre-pandemic period. These numbers were maintained at the very start of the pandemic but then declined to three or four insolvencies per month in late 2020 and 2021. This suggests that, at least for charitable companies, the risk of insolvency has actually been lower during most of the pandemic period, with no sign yet of the risk increasing again. This may reflect the uneven experience of pandemic disruption, which fell more heavily on smaller charities

Figure 4.5: Trends over time in the insolvencies of charitable companies in England and Wales

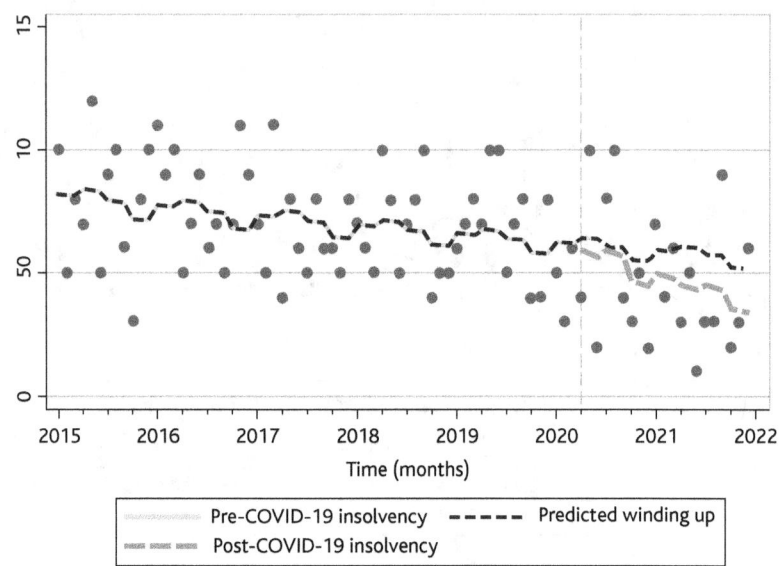

Source: Data from Companies House API, January 2022

with lower reserves, as well as the (temporary) protective effect of the support such as the UK government's Job Retention Scheme (furlough) and emergency grants. Monitoring insolvencies could provide an early warning of emerging issues, but at the end of 2021 it is an alarm that has not yet sounded.

What does the pattern of charity formations and dissolutions tell us about the sector during and after the pandemic?

In order to be effective, voluntary organisations require a degree of permanence and predictability, as well as the availability of favourable conditions ('enabling resources') for establishing new forms of voluntary activity (Musick and Wilson, 2008). As observed in North American scholarship, 'birth' and 'death' notices are rarely published in the voluntary sector and the causes of the demise of individual organisations are difficult to trace. But an essential preliminary to an understanding of the effects of the COVID-19 pandemic is to obtain a sense of aggregate trends. This chapter responds to Macmillan's (2020, pp 133–4) call for a 'longitudinal examination of large-scale third sector datasets' in order to 'ascertain what kinds of organisations ... appear to hold up or struggle through the crisis'.

In considering this data, we are faced with two questions. What does it tell us about the state of the UK charitable sector during COVID-19? And what does it lead us to expect to happen to the sector as we come out of the pandemic? We argue that charity regulator data suggests that the doom-laden messages of early surveys have not yet been substantiated by a fall in the number of charities. However, this crisis has been exceptional in both how it has played out (disrupting both income and service provision) and in the support available (with policies such as furlough schemes and emergency grants providing a temporary lifeline). In addressing these questions, our analysis highlights two findings.

Charity formations were maintained in the early part of lockdown, but have since seen a more dramatic decline, particularly in England and Wales. This may represent the lead time involved in setting up a charity, with those registered in mid-2020 based on groundwork conducted before the pandemic, and it is only in late 2020 and early 2021 that we start to see the consequences of disruption to charity formation. Declining levels of charity formation are not inherently problematic, as there is a regular turnover of charities in normal times with limits on the density of voluntary organisations that can operate in a given field or geographic area (Paarlberg et al, 2018). However, this decrease may not be equally or equitably distributed across fields or geographic areas, potentially leaving under-resourced areas in even greater need of voluntary activity (Lecy and Van Slyke, 2013). This is particularly salient given the association between social and economic inequality, and the unequal impact of the pandemic on households and individuals (Blundell et al, 2020). Given the apparent effect of the pandemic on charity formations, it seems likely that we will see continued lower rates of new charities until we are well on our way out of the pandemic. Even with just a return to normal levels of new charities, there will therefore be a longer-term persistent effect of the smaller number of charities founded in 2020 and 2021.

On the other hand, perhaps the reduction in charity formation is counterbalanced by a decrease in the level of dissolutions? There is some evidence this is the case: there was a significant drop in the number of dissolutions recorded on the registers of UK charity regulators, even allowing for disruptions to regulatory operations. Pandemic restrictions introduced in the UK in March 2020 (the 'lockdown') led to large numbers of people working from home or being furloughed, as well as the suspension of many non-essential businesses and services. The fall in the number of charity insolvencies through 2021, after a small rise early in the UK's first lockdown in spring 2020, is some comfort as it suggests that there has not been a persistent effect on the solvency of larger charities following the initial lockdown shock. But the historically low levels of insolvency in 2021 is somewhat surprising, and we will also need to monitor how this evolves.

This result seems counter-intuitive given the observable implications of the pandemic response (for example, the shutting of charity shops, the cessation of much volunteering activity) and the apocalyptic reports and prognostications founded on survey snapshots throughout 2020. But it is possible that policies such as the UK government's furlough Coronavirus Job Retention Scheme and some emergency COVID-19 grants have allowed charities to continue who might otherwise have ceased, even in normal times. It might hint at a situation where significant numbers of voluntary organisations are in stasis: currently not operating and perhaps no longer intending to, but yet to notify the charity regulator. If true, it would imply a coming surge in charity dissolutions.

Predicting the future is hard, and the key unknown here is whether there will be a surge of charities failing on the horizon. While we would expect charity formations to begin to return to normal as pandemic restrictions are eased, we do not anticipate a large increase in formations that would make up for lost ground, given that formations have so far continued to fall even as restrictions eased during 2021. This will mean that the effect of the lower number of charity formations will have a longer-term impact on the total number of charities, particularly in England and Wales. In contrast, however, the broader evidence base on financial vulnerability combined with the survey results of charities' experiences of financial disruption means that we would expect that there will be a discernible rise in stored-up dissolutions whose administration has simply been delayed by the pandemic, particularly as financial supports end and reserves are run down. A significant number of these will simply be organisations that we might have expected to cease even in normal times. The open question is: how many charities ceased to exist because of the pandemic, with this effect yet to be seen in the data?

Notes

[1] We would like to acknowledge the financial support of ESRC under the UKRI Covid-19 Rapid Response scheme for research on 'Assessing financial risk and vulnerability in the UK's charities during and beyond the Covid-19 crisis', grant reference ES/V004859/1.
[2] See McDonnell et al (2020) for a detailed summary of the nonprofit density literature.
[3] The charity registers are lists of organisations that a) possess charity status, and b) are registered with the relevant regulator. In Scotland, the register contains all organisations granted charity status, while in England and Wales there are charitable organisations that operate outside the oversight of the charity regulator. In most jurisdictions, the regulator has a legal mandate to create, maintain and publish a charity register, instilling confidence that these records are of sufficient quality for use in scholarly research (McDonnell and Rutherford, 2022).
[4] www.charitycommissionni.org.uk/news/legal-update/

References

Blundell, R., Costa Dias, M., Joyce, R. and Xu, X. (2020) *COVID-19 and Inequalities*, London: Institute for Fiscal Studies.

Briesacher, B.A., Soumerai, S.B., Zhang, F., Toh, S., Andrade, S.E., Wagner, J.L., Shoaibi, A. and Gurwitz, J.H. (2013) 'A critical review of methods to evaluate the impact of FDA regulatory actions', *Pharmacoepidemiology and Drug Safety*, 22(9): 986–94.

Callen, J.L., Klein, A., Tinkelman, D. (2010) 'The contextual impact of nonprofit board composition and structure on organizational performance: agency and resource dependence perspectives', *Voluntas: International Journal of Voluntary and Nonprofit Organizations*, 21: 101–25.

Charities Act 2011 (c.25) (2011), London: The Stationary Office Limited, www.legislation.gov.uk/ukpga/2011/25/contents [Accessed 19 May 2022].

Charity Commission for England and Wales (2021) *COVID-19 Survey 2021*, London: Charity Commission for England and Wales.

Clifford, D. (2018) 'Neighborhood context and enduring differences in the density of charitable organizations: reinforcing dynamics of foundation and dissolution', *American Journal of Sociology*, 123(6): 1535–600.

Clifford, D., Mohan, J. and Rutherford, A.C. (2021) *Patterns of Financial Vulnerability in English and Welsh Charities after the Onset of Covid*, Birmingham: Third Sector Research Centre.

Helmig, B., Ingerfurth, S. and Pinz, A. (2014) 'Success and failure of nonprofit organizations: theoretical foundations, empirical evidence, and future research', *Voluntas: International Journal of Voluntary and Nonprofit Organizations*, 25: 1509–38.

Kennedy, J. (2021) 'Elaborating on collaborating', [online], Available from: www.dsc.org.uk/content/elaborating-on-collaborating/ [Accessed 6 February 2021].

Kim, M. (2015) 'Socioeconomic diversity, political engagement, and the density of nonprofit organizations in U.S. counties', *The American Review of Public Administration*, 45(4): 402–16.

Lecy, J. and Van Slyke, D. (2013) 'Nonprofit Sector Growth and Density: Testing Theories of Government Support', *Journal of Public Administration Research and Theory*, 23(1): 189–214.

Macmillan, R. (2020) 'Somewhere over the rainbow – third sector research in and beyond coronavirus', *Voluntary Sector Review*, 11(2): 129–36.

McDonnell, D. and Rutherford, A.C. (2022) 'Researching risk in the voluntary sector: the challenges and opportunities of regulatory data', in J. Dean and E. Hogg (eds.) *Researching Voluntary Action: Innovations and Challenges*, Bristol: Policy Press, pp. 122–134.

McDonnell, D., Mohan, J. and Norman, P. (2020) 'Charity density and social need: a longitudinal perspective', *Nonprofit and Voluntary Sector Quarterly*, 49(5): 1082–104.

Mellahi, K. and Wilkinson, A. (2004) 'Organizational failure: a critique of recent research and a proposed integrative framework', *International Journal of Management Reviews*, 5: 21–41.

Musick, M.A. and Wilson, J. (2008) *Volunteers: A Social Profile*, Indianapolis, IN: Indiana University Press.

Nottingham Trent University (2020; 2021) *Respond, Recover, Reset: The Voluntary Sector and COVID-19*, [online], Available from: //cpwop.org.uk/what-we-do/projects-and-publications/covid-19-vcse-organisation-responses/ [Accessed 25 February 2022].

Office for National Statistics (2021) *Excess Deaths in your Neighbourhood during the Coronavirus (COVID-19) Pandemic*, [online], Available from: www.ons.gov.uk/peoplepopulationandcommunity/birthsdeathsandmarriages/deaths/articles/excessdeathsinyourneighbourhoodduringthecoronaviruscovid19pandemic/2021-08-03 [Accessed 13 December 2021].

Paarlberg, L.E., An, S.-H., Nesbit, R., Christensen, R.K. and Bullock, J. (2018) 'A field too crowded? How measures of market structure shape nonprofit fiscal health', *Nonprofit and Voluntary Sector Quarterly*, 47: 453–73.

Penfold, R.B. and Zhang, F. (2013) 'Use of interrupted time series analysis in evaluating health care quality improvements', *Academic Pediatrics*, 13(6): S38–44.

Rees, J. and Mullins, D. (2016) *The Third Sector Delivering Public Services: Developments, Innovations and Challenges*, Bristol: Policy Press.

Scottish Council for Voluntary Organisations (2021) *Scottish Third Sector Tracker: Wave One Findings*, Edinburgh: Scottish Council for Voluntary Organisations.

Sharkey, P., Torrats-Espinosa, G. and Takyar, D. (2017) 'Community and the crime decline: the causal effect of local nonprofits on violent crime', *American Sociological Review*, 82(6): 1214–40.

Wilding, K. (2020) '"Every day counts" as charities still wait for government support', [online], Available from: www.ncvo.org.uk/about-us/media-centre/press-releases/2748-every-day-counts-as-charities-still-wait-for-government-support [Accessed 10 February 2021].

5

Paying the price of 'doing good' in the face of crisis

Sarah Smith, Tracey M. Coule and Daniel King

Introduction

The COVID-19 pandemic is 'double-trouble' for many voluntary organisations (VOs) that are simultaneously subject to higher demand for services in response to the unfolding crisis, alongside a decrease in the money available to fund their work. This has prompted a good deal of scholarship examining the immediate adverse, and often economic, impact of the crisis on such entities and/or the positive benefits achieved for external constituents through their 'good' work. Early findings from an 18-month UKRI-funded project into COVID-19 and VOs, however, show some of the human costs of 'doing good' in crisis contexts, to those who inhabit the organisation. This chapter will explore the propensity for the wellbeing of staff and volunteers to be sacrificed in the name of 'doing good' and delineate the various features of nonprofit work that may lead to this condition. We call for scholars and practitioners to resist framing VOs only in terms of what (financial) impact COVID-19 has had on them and what (good) is being done by them at the expense of seeing what is going on in organisations to achieve such social goods:

> 'A lot of charities expect huge amounts of time and emotional energy from their staff. And ... I feel like I'm watching [them] crumbling in front of me from the pressure ... I think the culture in a lot of charities almost rewards that by saying oh, they're so busy.' (Senior manager, national infrastructure organisation, England)

While there are multiple motivating factors in choosing to work in the voluntary, community and social enterprise (VCSE) sector, throughout our interviews participants frequently talked about their desire to support and help beneficiaries and to make a difference: "You want to help everybody, that's why we have a passion for working in this sector" (CEO, national infrastructure organisation, England). The cost of doing good can often be a human one; 18 months into the pandemic, many organisations, projects and services are stretched to breaking point, and staff are increasingly feeling the strain from the sheer amount of work it has taken to keep services running during the crisis. This chapter examines the nature of voluntary organisations, their work and those who do it to explore what drives them to go 'over and above' in a time of crisis, and beyond. In doing so, it explores the human impacts on staff and leaders in the sector. The chapter concludes with some questions this raises for the sector more broadly as we move through different phases of the pandemic.

Methodology

The results of this study are part of a wider project looking at the impact of COVID-19 on the VCSE sector funded by the Economic and Social Research Council (ESRC). This project had three parts: a monthly repeated cross-sectional barometer survey, which was a temperature check on the impact of the pandemic on the sector; a panel survey occurring quarterly in 2021, looking at crisis leadership and resilience; and 300 in-depth, semi-structured interviews, exploring how individuals and organisations have responded to the pandemic. The interviews typically lasted 50–60 minutes and were conducted via teams. Our sample strategy sought to be inclusive and capture a wide range of organisations. Our interviewees came from across the whole of the UK, organisations of different sizes, sub-sectors and organisational types including community interest companies, funders and foundations, and national and local infrastructure bodies. Predominately, our interviewees were from middle or senior levels within the organisation, although some were more frontline workers. These initial findings were presented as a series of reports (see CPWOP, n.d.). The interviews were all recorded, fully transcribed and are available via the UK Data Service (for more details please contact the research team).

The research team met regularly to discuss emerging themes from across the interviews, using a series of tools such as padlets and team meetings, to surface interesting and reoccurring themes. The data was then divided into 'buckets' around these key themes which could then be drilled down into within these more manageable chunks.

The tension between the feeling of doing 'good' and the human costs of this quickly emerged as a reoccurring theme for interviewees, particularly where they described their experiences in what is widely described as the first wave of the pandemic (the original lockdown in the UK from late March 2020 to July 2020). Interviewees described, sometimes in graphic terms, the emotions and struggles that they were facing. While these tensions between work and home life were challenges that many people experienced during that phase of the pandemic, our interviewees were describing a particular and distinct experience which arose due to their role *within* the VCSE sector.

The emotional challenge of working for a cause or serving a community which was meaningful and seemed urgent and important, while at the same time personally struggling, seemed to us an experience pertinent to the sector. We identified ten interviews where this theme came up. Primarily, they were from the early interviews which occurred soon after the first lockdown in 2020, where these experiences were often still raw and present for interviewees, but as we analysed other interviews we added to this pool.

We analysed the data by reading the transcripts that we had identified several times, before thematically coding the data in NVivo. Analysis was iterative, first-order coding of recurrent terms used by interviewees (Gioia et al, 2013), focusing on the specific experiences. We looked for themes of what constituted doing good and the impacts that it had on individuals as well. These codes were developed into themes, of doing good as organisational identity, doing good work through first response and being a good employee, and then the costs – focusing on individual experiences.

We present these personal accounts as quotes and as vignettes. A vignette is 'a short, carefully constructed description of a person, object, or situation, representing a systematic combination of characteristics' (Atzmüller and Steiner, 2010, p 128), used to illustrate aspects of a phenomenon (Reay et al, 2019). Vignettes are particularly useful to provide insights into a person's experience, capturing the emotion and feel of a situation. In line with our research ethics, our interviewees were given pseudonyms. We have sought to protect their identity while still maintaining enough context to make their accounts meaningful.

In the following section we turn to our findings, starting with accounts of what constitutes 'doing good' before looking at the human costs this can entail.

Constituting 'good' in a crisis

In this section, we focus on three interrelated themes that, for our interviewees, were central to the idea of 'doing good' during the COVID-19 pandemic, namely, doing good as organisational identity; doing good work through first response; and being a good employee. We then move on to explore some of the human costs of 'doing good' in crisis contexts in the section that follows.

Doing good as organisational identity

At a basic level, organisational identity is a collection of statements that organisation members or inhabitants believe to be core, distinctive and enduring to their organisation (Albert and Whetten, 1985). Organisational identities can act as a guide for (management) decision making and action, particularly in contexts of change (Fox-Wolfgramm, Boal and Hunt, 1998), as an interpretive lens through which members make sense of events and issues (Gioia and Thomas, 1996) and as a reference point for comparison between current and envisioned identity, or between identity and decision/action, in order to assess legitimacy of the latter (Dutton and Dukerich, 1991).

In our research, members of VOs regularly talked about their work as "more than a job", about feeling a sense of purpose or meaning. For many, their sense of self is bound up with the work they deliver to achieve the organisation's social purpose. In other words, VO staff often weave individual and organisational purpose into a symbiotic relationship within their narratives:

> 'When you really care about what you do and you see a little bit of this in the health service, if you can no longer deliver the service that you want to deliver and you see people suffering because of that, there's a much bigger emotional impact than ... I'm struggling not to say just losing your job ... Quite often it's losing your purpose and the fact that you can do good ... and a replacement job might not give you that.' (CEO, National infrastructure organisation, Scotland)

Psychologists use the term 'moral injury' to refer to the recognition of not being able to effectively do a job and seeing people suffer as a result (Litz et al, 2009). Williamson et al (2020) define this as 'the profound psychological distress which results from actions, or the lack of them, which violate one's moral or ethical code'. This can be experienced in a range of different sectors and settings; Litz et al (2009) use the example of the armed forces and Williamson et al (2020) point to the UK health service, and through our research we have seen examples of this in the voluntary sector.

> 'I think the incentive of what makes me work harder is knowing we're supporting others. We all didn't want to just sit around and ... just hold our services or stop our services ... We've got a great incentive to try and support people, that was my incentive to work hard and keep working, because I know we're going to make a difference and we'll help people.' (Line manager, national voluntary organisation, sport, England)

In this sense, the enduring core identity of 'who we are' (that is, the intangible abstract sense of 'doing good') remained stable during the pandemic, but there was significantly more plasticity and instability in the outer layers of organisational identity (Gustafson and Reger, 1995) which refer to the more tangible, substantive matters of 'what is done' at a given time or in response to particular external events. With the onset of the COVID-19 pandemic and associated local and national 'lockdowns', VOs were faced with the question of how to provide existing services in a meaningful way. While some organisations focused on expanding services due to higher demand, others found they were simply unable to provide their services in the same ways. The latter often faced a choice between pausing services, continuing through alternative, remote delivery models and/or moving into new delivery niches in order to support their communities. For some, this raised concerns about a crisis of legitimacy linked to comparisons between their current identity, familiar to all constituents (users, members, partners, funders and so on) in 'normal times', and their envisioned identity and role in the crisis:

> 'One of the big reasons that our members tell us they join … is for the networking opportunities and the opportunity to engage peer to peer. So we had to be sure that we're still offering that, otherwise there's a real risk that people don't see the value in us as an online entity as much.' (Senior manager, national infrastructure organisation, England)

As the pandemic endures over the long term, this tension between quickly expanding scope and focus, in a turbulent environment, in order to meet immediate needs, and effectively refocusing when the environment stabilises into a 'new normal', can become more acute for organisations.

Doing good work through first response

The pandemic has intensified the notion of voluntary organisations as innovators or first responders, meeting immediate needs and filling the gaps left by other provision (Wyler, 2020; Dayson et al, 2021; Langdale et al, 2021). Indeed, this is an enduring, normative assumption about such organisations (Coule and Patmore, 2013; Coule and Bennett, 2016). This identity marker seemed to intensify at the onset of the crisis for interviewees, particularly those from smaller, grassroots, community-based organisations identifying and responding to gaps in provision within their immediate and wider communities, when it seemed that nobody else could: "For us, personally there was no time … to take a step back and look strategically at the entire city. And also, who's role is that? It's probably not our role. But it didn't really feel like anybody was doing that" (Line manager, voluntary organisation, art and creativity, northern England). One such organisation completely changed their remit at the start of the pandemic. Initially an arts organisation which relied on in-person services, it became apparent that they were unable to continue working in this way. The majority of the staff were furloughed and services were paused. However, a small team of three, managing the volunteer programme, were approached by their local council to mobilise volunteers into the community to do daily tasks such as shopping and dog walking for those who were vulnerable and shielding.

This plasticity in the outer layers of organisational identity (that is, substantive matters of *what* is done) was common in interview accounts, with VOs breaking entirely with 'business as usual'. Certainly, in the early stages of the pandemic, workers (whether paid or unpaid) engaging with some of the most vulnerable communities and groups experienced little tension in this shift because it fit with their core identity of 'doing good', despite new activities being different from their normal activities: "I look now and I think no matter what happens in the future we did that. There was a time in history that everyone will always remember and I think we had such a big part to play in that and I feel really, really proud" (Line manager, voluntary organisation, art and creativity, northern England).

There was genuine worry and fear about how to continue new methods of support and engagement through the crisis and what would happen to people if this stopped. It seems to us that the enduring core identity of 'doing good', coupled with the 'moment of crisis' presented by the pandemic, motivated many VOs, and their staff, to 'do whatever it took' to meet immediate need.

Feelings of guilt and luck were also frequently discussed among interviewees, and seemed, at least to some degree, to motivate or drive individual behaviour. For some, there was a sense of feeling lucky to have a job or keeping their organisation running when colleagues were furloughed, other organisations were pausing services, and beneficiaries and service users were struggling: "There were times when I felt quite guilty that we were doing okay because we have been quite lucky" (CEO, national infrastructure organisation, Scotland). "Overwhelmingly, I feel incredibly grateful that I still have a job because I know that not just colleagues but friends and family that I have, have not been so lucky" (Senior manager, voluntary organisation, support for armed forces, England). Guilt at their perceived privileged position often led to working long hours to deliver projects. Furloughed staff also experienced guilt at not being able to work alongside their colleagues at a time of crisis, and in some instances, staff chose to take on a different role rather than being furloughed. These roles were often ones they were not trained for and created different stresses either because staff felt that they were out of their depth or because they were greatly removed from the job they regularly did. For furloughed staff, this connection between what the organisation represents and who they themselves are created different stresses; they were unable to do what they perceived they do best at a time when it was most needed.

Being a good employee

A key challenge of binding organisational and personal identity together is that it creates a collision of personal and professional life, and this was thrown into stark relief as a result of working from home. Those working remotely were facing all the demands of home life that many of us navigated but on top of this were taking into their homes emotionally draining work, at a time when their previous support networks and ways of dealing with this work had changed. Consequently, it was common during interviews to hear leaders of VOs talking about the challenges of supporting volunteers, staff and colleagues while setting work–life boundaries.

While Terry et al (2019) problematise the notion of 'leadership' in the sector questioning what constitutes a leader, many of the interviewees in our research described themselves as 'leading' their organisations. With the acknowledgement that 'leaders' or CEOs, directors and managers are also members of staff and are therefore subject to the same pressures felt across the organisation, there were also specific pressures on those who managed other members of staff. For these people, expressions of concern over difficulties in checking in on staff wellbeing was common. Conversations around mental health and wellbeing can be challenging and the process of remote working, for some, created further barriers. Managers and leaders were concerned about how to have these conversations with their staff and worried that they were missing the signs that members of their organisation were facing difficulties with their mental health and wellbeing:

'I think as a director I have probably become more involved with staff in terms of being more upfront about asking personal questions. Just because of needing to check because I presume you don't necessarily pick up the same body language … so you have to be far more explicit and say – are you okay?' (Senior manager, voluntary organisation, disability, Wales)

"In terms of emotionally, I have really struggled, mental health-wise. Knowing that your staff are struggling, yes it's been hard … there have been times where I have struggled, where I haven't done previously. It's a different type of work altogether" (CEO, voluntary organisation, families and children, east of England).

Conversely, some interviewees found that they were unable to talk to their managers about their health and wellbeing. For some working in the sector, there was a perception that the focus of the organisation was solely on beneficiaries at the expense of staff. This is not a new problem for the sector, for example Wrixon (2021) revisits her work on bullying in the sector, but the pandemic has created added challenges and tensions. While many in our study described their work environment in positive terms pre-pandemic, the pressure of the pandemic made some of these environments a very different place. Additionally, while most participants did not explicitly state that they felt they were being bullied, there was a clear feeling among some that their needs were not taken into account by those managing them: "I think it's difficult to stomach when you know that your manager is very concerned about young people losing out on opportunities but doesn't seem to care about the staff who are supposed to be providing the support" (Frontline staff, voluntary organisation, young people, East Midlands, England).

The organisational and personal drive to do good, alongside feelings of luck and guilt, meant that many staff did not seek support from others when they were facing increasing workloads or emotionally challenging work. There was a recognition that their colleagues were also facing the same levels of work and were 'Zoomed out' or tired of video calls. For some in VOs, it was only when they were able to take a break that these work levels caught up with them:

> 'That's been hard … we're trying to brake, turn left, turn right and accelerate all at the same time … and that takes its toll. A lot of us got COVID, myself included, in December, only obviously when we'd closed. So that adrenalin, that thing that happens when you're working in an emergency and you work and work and work until the emergency ends and then you all fall over sick. That happened to us.' (CEO, voluntary organisation, civil and advocacy, London, England)

This particular organisation had worked from March until December at crisis levels; while initial emergency responses may require extra work, time and energy, sustaining this over longer periods, in this instance nine months, often results in burnout. In the wider examples throughout this section, being a good employee came at the expense of personal relationships. Increased workloads created tensions over where priorities lay. Those with children often faced feelings of guilt over where they concentrated their energies and this in turn caused tensions with partners over conflicting work priorities. Others found little time to commit to personal and family relationships and these relationships suffered as a result.

The impact of doing good

To explore the impacts of doing good in a time of crisis we present three vignettes which provide snapshots of the challenges faced by three of our interviewees.

Laura's story

Laura works for an art and creativity voluntary organisation providing local support in the north of England. In March 2020, it became clear that their services could no longer continue on an in-person basis so most of her colleagues were furloughed. However,

> Laura and two other members of staff were approached by their local council to mobilise the volunteers they managed into the local community to do everyday tasks. This resulted in an intense period of work for her and her colleagues: "It was really, really hard. Probably the hardest thing I've had to do in my working life".
>
> This small team worked round the clock managing the increasing demand for help from their local community and supporting volunteers. The workload took its toll on Laura; working from home meant that she was unable to step away from her work which was emotionally demanding and ultimately her relationships with her partner broke down as a result.
>
> Laura also felt that blanket organisational policies around taking leave by a specific date could have been made more flexible throughout the pandemic, particularly given that she was working intensively and others had been furloughed. This created tensions:
>
>> 'It made me really bitter. And it was like I know it's not their fault at all. So if you're head curator of a gallery that's shut, how are you supposed to work? I couldn't be mad at that individual or whatever but it was just the whole situation, it just made me feel really bitter.'

Laura's story raises questions about how organisations heal the rifts created by staff workloads. While this example is not indicative of all organisations, significant numbers furloughed part of their workforce and as a result staff had different experiences of the pandemic depending on whether they were furloughed, changed jobs or had increased workloads. As we saw in the first section of this chapter, furloughed staff often felt guilty or disconnected from the organisation. Others, however, who were dealing with high workloads felt resentful towards colleagues who were furloughed or towards their managers for not furloughing them. Given the nature of working in a VO, the need to work towards a common good, these tensions, if unresolved, could be problematic to organisations in the future.

Andrew's story

> Andrew is the CEO of an LGBT+ and empowerment national infrastructure organisation. He and his small team of nine staff have worked remotely for a number of years and are spread across the country. He recognised that they were in a unique position to offer support to their members on remote working and so developed webinars which they began to deliver in March 2020.

Their members experienced a huge demand for their services and as a result demand for Andrew's organisation "was going through the roof". Andrew said:

'When you're working in identity politics it is a real challenge because you're dealing with issues you have lived experience of and so there are those additional stresses all the time ... field. And then adding those additional stresses of COVID and working with groups who are again working with individuals, and many of the people running those groups are the volunteers themselves facing those issues of suddenly not being able to access food, trans people not being able to access medication. That adds to that emotional pressure as a professional team.'

Like Laura in the example above, Andrew experienced challenges around establishing a work–life balance, and this was further complicated by the death of his dog, care for which had provided much needed structure to the home-working day. He admitted to experiencing sleepless nights and having to recognise that he simply couldn't help everyone. He felt that advice from the government and large organisations to furlough staff was not helpful to his organisation simply because they were seeing such an increased need for their services which they as a team had to meet.

Andrew's story demonstrates the levels of anxiety those in the sector felt for and towards their service users and as a result their needs often came before the needs of those working in VOs. Significantly, for organisations like his, which were experiencing an increase in demand, much of the support and advice for dealing with the pandemic was not relevant because it focused on those who needed to pause or pare back their service. Andrew's story also shines a light on the emotionally challenging nature of the work those in the sector are doing. In this instance, the nature of the work also intersected with the 'lived experience' of the staff doing it, which creates additional challenges of mental health and wellbeing. For Andrew, the needs of both his staff and his service users came before those of his own and this raises questions of who ensures the wellbeing of senior leaders.

Claire's story

Claire is a senior manager in a national infrastructure organisation. In March 2020, she and her immediate family were ill with what she now thinks was COVID-19. But seeing a rise in demand for her organisation's services, she continued to work. Claire felt that a key reason members joined their organisation was for the opportunity to meet and network with other organisations, so faced challenges of ensuring the legitimacy of the organisation to meet the needs of their members. She also felt the stress of her role

> more specifically due to the ever-changing nature of guidance and information from the government:
>
> > 'When you work in policy and there's announcements being made, it can feel like somebody is pushing you along to a timeline that is not of your making and it's very out of your control – that was happening a lot in the early days when ... government are announcing this policy ... and then you think, well, what if I'm not representing members, there's an opportunity here to get their voice in and I'm letting them down if I'm not doing it.'
>
> In addition to work pressures, Claire had the pressures of home life; her husband was also working so childcare and home schooling fell to her: "So his job, in very basic terms, trumped mine. His job was keeping children alive and safeguarded and mine was arguing with the government about some money which is very important but you know, conversely." For Claire, who had always worked with her partner to ensure that home life was a shared responsibility, this represented a huge shift in who she was. Ultimately, she felt that she was unable to keep on top of everything she was responsible for and asked her manager to furlough her. Her manager encouraged her to take time off to recover from her initial illness and from the levels of stress work and the pandemic had created in her life.

Claire's story, like Andrew and Laura's, raises questions for how VO staff begin to redraw work–life balance boundaries that have been undone as a result of the pandemic. A number of our interviewees discussed the increased difficulties they had found in stepping away from their work at the end of the working day. This, coupled with a clear increase in need for their services and the desire to support those in need, has made it even harder to step away, to recognise that good is good enough.

Conclusion

The health and wellbeing of many members of VOs has suffered greatly because of the workload and emotional challenges placed on them to support service users and beneficiaries through the pandemic. Through this chapter, we have examined what has driven people in the sector and explored the costs to health and wellbeing as a result. The desire to 'do good' is a key driver of behaviour. Underlying this is a deep understanding of the issues faced by people in their geographical local communities or in the communities created through specific issues or identities. At the start of the pandemic, there was a recognition from organisations that they were in a position to provide help and support, even when this was outside of their usual remit, simply because other organisations were not. With an ever-growing need for their services, the pressure to support their communities has, in many cases, remained with these organisations.

One of the key challenges VOs face as we move into new phases of the pandemic is how to avoid making these crisis levels of work the 'new normal'. It is likely that organisations within the sector will face future crises whether on a macro or micro level and there is key learning that can be taken from their experiences of the pandemic that can help them to navigate some of the challenges to staff health and wellbeing, brought to the fore through the pandemic. Firstly, honest questions and reflections which enable staff to voice what has worked and what has not worked during the pandemic. Conversations like these can be challenging but are an opportunity to give some insight into not only what has been difficult but what has been successful and ultimately create a starting position for longer-term change. Secondly, the pandemic has opened up conversations about mental health and wellbeing; organisations in our research often talked about barriers around these conversations having been broken down. The key question now is whether these lines of conversation stay open by continuing some of the organisational working practices developed through the pandemic which allowed individuals to talk more freely about their mental health and wellbeing in the workplace. Finally, many organisations have learnt throughout the pandemic that there are choices that can be made in the different ways everyday things can be done. While there are often limits to how big these changes can be, even small changes can have big impacts.

References

Albert, S. and Whetten, D.A. (1985) 'Organizational identity', *Research in Organizational Behavior*, 7: 263–95.

Atzmüller, C. and Steiner, P.M. (2010) 'Experimental vignette studies in survey research', *Methodology*, 6(3): 128–38.

Coule, T. and Bennett, E. (2016) 'Rhetoric, organizational category dynamics and institutional change: a study of the UK welfare state', *Public Administration*, 94(4): 1059–76.

Coule, T. and Patmore, B. (2013) 'Institutional logics, institutional work and service innovation in non-profit organizations', *Public Administration*, 94(4): 980–97.

CPWOP (n.d.) *Respond, Recover, Reset: Report Archive*, [online], Available from: //cpwop.org.uk/respond-recover-reset-report-archive/ [Accessed 3 March 2022].

Dayson, C., Bimpson, E., Ellis Paine, A., Gilbertson, J. and Kara, H. (2021) 'The "resilience" of community organisations during the COVID-19 pandemic: absorptive, adaptive and transformational capacity during a crisis response', *Voluntary Sector Review*, 12(2): 295–304.

Dutton, J.E. and Dukerich, J.M. (1991) 'Keeping an eye on the mirror: image and identity in organizational adaptation', *Academy of Management Journal*, 34(3): 517–54.

Fox-Wolfgramm, S.J., Boal, K.B. and Hunt, J.G. (1998) 'Organizational adaptation to institutional change: a comparative study of first-order change in prospector and defender bands', *Administrative Science Quarterly*, 43(1): 87–126.

Gioia, D.A. and Thomas, J.B. (1996) 'Institutional identity, image, and issue interpretation: sensemaking during strategic change in academia', *Administrative Science Quarterly*, 41(3): 370–403.

Gioia, D.A., Corely, K.G. and Hamilton, A.L. (2013) 'Seeking qualitative rigor in inductive research: notes on the Gioia methodology', *Organizational Research Methods*, 16(1): 15–31.

Gustafson, L.T. and Reger, R.K. (1995) 'Using organisational identity to achieve stability and change in high velocity environments', *Academy of Management Best Papers Proceedings*, 1: 464–8.

Langdale, E., Macmillan, R., O'Flynn, L., Oxborrow, L. and Wilson, M. (2021) 'Community responses to COVID-19: Community hubs as social infrastructure', [online], Available from: //localtrust.org.uk/wp-content/uploads/2021/08/COVID-19-Briefing-13-FINAL-1.pdf [Accessed 3 March 2022].

Litz, B.T., Stein, N., Delaney, E., Lebowitz, L., Nash, W.P., Silva, C. and Maguen, S. (2009) 'Moral injury and moral repair in war veterans: a preliminary model and intervention strategy', *Clinical Psychology Review*, 29(8): 695–706.

Reay, T., Zafar, A. and Monteiro, P. (2019) 'Presenting findings from qualitative research: one size does not fit all!', in T.B. Zilber, J.M. Amis and J. Mair (eds.) *The Production of Managerial Knowledge and Organizational Theory: New Approaches to Writing, Producing, and Consuming Theory*, Bingley: Emerald Publishing Limited, pp 201–16.

Terry, V., Rees, J. and Jacklin-Jarvis, C. (2019) 'The difference leadership makes? Debating and conceptualising leadership in the UK voluntary sector', *Voluntary Sector Review*, 11(1): 99–111.

Williamson, V., Murphy, D. and Greenberg, N. (2020) 'COVID-19 and experiences of moral injury in front-line key workers', *Occupational Medicine*, 70(5): 317–19.

Wrixon, K. (2021) 'In plain sight: has anything changed almost 2 years on', [online], Available from: www.acevo.org.uk/2021/04/in-plain-sight-has-anything-changed-almost-2-years-on/ [Accessed 3 March 2022].

Wyler, S. (2020) *Community Responses in Times of Crisis*, [online], Available from: //localtrust.org.uk/wp-content/uploads/2020/05/22040_Community-responses-in-times-of-crisis_online_lr.pdf [Accessed 3 March 2022].

PART II

Key policy fields and inequalities

6

Shifting sands: challenges and opportunities for the voluntary sector during the COVID-19 pandemic

Jon Burchell, Joanne Cook, Harriet Thiery, Erica Ballantyne, Fiona Walkley and Silviya Nikolova

Introduction

The COVID-19 pandemic and subsequent national lockdowns placed unprecedented strains on communities across the UK.[1] The access to local services (public, private and community) became severely limited, as most people were ordered to stay at home (Brown and Kirk-Wade, 2021). Restrictions on social movement and the resulting partial economic shutdown both intensified existing social challenges and unearthed new ones. The immediacy of the situation and the unique challenges it presented placed intense pressure on both voluntary and community sector (VCS) organisations and local authorities (LAs) as they sought to rapidly identify and meet the needs of their communities (Burchell et al, 2020).

The pandemic caused considerable upheaval within the VCS. On one hand, it threw the sector into crisis, raising critical sustainability challenges as demand for services soared and primary revenue streams were cut off (Nottingham Trent University, 2021). Although emergency grants were quickly made available, this funding was short term and was not evenly distributed across the sector (Walkley et al, 2021). Other organisations faced the challenge of mothballing their operations during lockdown as venues closed, staff were furloughed and many existing volunteers were forced to isolate. At the same time, the pandemic has created opportunities for more innovative, collaborative ways of working, both within and outside of the sector. The VCS has partnered with the public sector to play an integral role in delivering fast-acting emergency support. This increase in cross-sectoral collaboration has led scholars to suggest that we have arrived at an important juncture in local state–civil society organisation relations (Dayson and Damm, 2020; Macmillan, 2020; Harris, 2021).

This chapter focuses upon VCS organisations' experiences of the COVID-19 pandemic and the challenges facing the sector looking forward. Two central questions emerge: first, how was volunteer resource utilised, both nationally (through centralised volunteering platforms) and locally, through informal community groups, during the pandemic? And second, what was the nature of the cross-sectoral collaborations between VCS organisations and LAs at the heart of local humanitarian support frameworks. Focusing upon evidence across these two areas, the chapter argues that the experience of the pandemic was not about the ability of the VCS to recruit *new* volunteers but about the skills and resourcefulness of VCS organisations, alongside LA partners, to strengthen the capacity to coordinate and mobilise *existing* available resources effectively.

Methods

Data for this chapter are drawn from the Mobilising Volunteers Effectively (MoVE) research project. The research examines LA, VCS and community responses to the pandemic, particularly how volunteers were mobilised to meet community needs in England, Scotland and Wales. Findings discussed here draw primarily from data gathered in phase one of the project: 49 semi-structured interviews conducted from June to September 2020 with LAs, VCS organisations and mutual aid organisers. It also draws on data from later phases of the project, involving more extensive research with mutual aid groups. This includes 31 interviews and eight focus groups with a total of 59 mutual aid participants from 12 different LA areas in England and Wales, carried out from January to September 2021.

The research methodology draws from participatory action research (PAR) (Bradbury, 2015), which views participants as partners in the research process, prioritising 'working with' rather than 'doing research on' (Barnes, 2004). The research created a space for participants to share their experiences of coordinating community responses and to reflect on the challenges and opportunities, utilising a common set of themes but encouraging participants to raise issues that were important to them. The themes discussed in this chapter were drawn from established thematic coding methods (Mason, 2002; Spencer et al, 2013). An initial framework was developed based upon emerging themes and the data was then synthesised and analysed to model general trends. This chapter includes participant quotes to evidence common experiences or perspectives shared by multiple participants, unless otherwise stated.

Findings

Building a national army for a localised response: challenges and limitations of national volunteer schemes

During the early stages of the pandemic, calls were made to increase the numbers of people volunteering. In England and Scotland, national volunteer campaigns were launched centrally via NHS England and the GoodSAM platform (recruiting 750,000 volunteers), and Scotland Cares and Ready Scotland (recruiting 76,000 volunteers). These campaigns were driven by the scale of the pandemic alongside the identification that many traditional volunteers and volunteer organisations had had to step back (Buchan, 2020). While the large-scale response showed an exceptional willingness on the part of the British public to offer support, translating registrations into tasks was slow, raising questions about whether an 'army' of volunteers was truly needed, particularly in the context of communities mobilising effectively and quickly themselves (Butler, 2020).

Within the MoVE research, most interviewees who discussed the role and impact of the national volunteering platforms expressed frustration with both the concept and the implementation of these schemes, summarised by the below quotes:

'The national volunteer scheme ... a) it was late, and b) it didn't add anything to the party really, and actually, even though we never actually officially had the data shared with us in terms of the number of contacts that were made in our patch ... we've had very low take-up of the national scheme, ... and I think that's in part due to the fact that we had our volunteers up and running quite quickly.' (LA #13)

'I would have to be just absolutely straight and say that Ready Scotland really made our lives more difficult. It was a classic example of centralised political thinking and over-controlling on how to respond to something like this – there was really no need for a national recruitment campaign.' (VCS infrastructure organisation #10)

'It felt like a bit of a red herring to us or, a bit of a PR thing, you know, where they wanted to get the story out ... so they could report on the good news that three quarters of a million people volunteered and that was really good, and we just can't ignore that, it's amazing. But there was no local knowledge.' (VCS infrastructure organisation #7)

Broadly, critiques of these platforms centred upon three key problems. Firstly, respondents noted that the national campaigns were driven by the false perception of a volunteer shortage, when most areas already had a large pool of both formal and informal volunteers in operation. There was therefore little need for the new volunteers, leaving many to be under-utilised or never called upon through the NHS Responders system. "They did a call for volunteers, and we were all saying 'Don't, please don't' because we've got lots of volunteers who can't be used just now" (National

VCS organisation #1). "[Community groups] very much said 'we are overwhelmed with volunteers', and the government were pushing to say 'use the NHS volunteers' and we were saying 'well actually, we haven't got a use for them at the moment'" (LA #20).

The second issue raised was by participants whose organisations *had* sought to utilise the national platforms but were unable to access the information that they needed. By the time volunteer data was made available to LAs and their partners, it was too late as localised systems of support had already become well established.

> 'They didn't talk to anybody about how it would work ... obviously when people signed up, they didn't include sharing their data with the people ... and RVS are nothing in [region]. They don't exist in [region]. Had they been able to give us a database of who all the NHS Responders registered in [region] were ... at the beginning, we could really easily have used them, and instead we've been using redeployed members of staff.' (LA #4)

> 'I think the council were thinking "when are we going to get our list then?", of all the people in our areas who are our volunteers, but of course it doesn't work that way and they never did. So it didn't really feature in the volunteering in [region].' (VCS infrastructure organisation #7)

Reflecting on the issues highlighted above, the third challenge focused upon the limitations of imposing a centralised solution on to a problem that required localised knowledge and understanding. There was a perception that the national platforms were out of sync and out of place, as a result of trying to respond to the pandemic with a top-down framework. Participants suggested that the national platforms struggled to align with the activities of local VCS organisations and groups. Many felt that local approaches had proved to be swifter and more effective, arguing "we could be more proactive because structures were already in place" (VCS infrastructure organisation #9). There was frustration at the challenges associated with accessing and utilising these volunteers, and a sense that, ultimately, this was a wasted resource.

Interestingly, in comparison, the Welsh approach avoided many of these criticisms. Following dialogue with the Welsh Voluntary and Community Association, the Welsh government decided against an equivalent NHS Responders scheme, opting instead to link up existing local infrastructure:

> 'We concluded that [a new national platform] wouldn't be helpful, because it would cut across, it didn't plug into the local infrastructures

that we had, that was the fear, with hindsight that was absolutely right, ... I think it could have been disastrous – it could have really got people's backs up, it could have undermined the infrastructure that we had.' (MVCS6)

Volunteers were directed to their local County Voluntary Council, who created a new opportunity on their website (usually geared towards formal volunteering), where they were labelled as a 'COVID response volunteer'. These volunteers could then either be matched with individuals who had called for support, or passed on to the LA or to other voluntary organisations or informal groups, depending on need. While this ultimately was seen as a more effective response to the national platforms, there was still criticism regarding the amount of time taken for these decisions to be made and thus a lack of clarity during the first national lockdown. It should also be noted that Wales also experienced oversupply of volunteers with many being under-utilised or not called upon at all.

Local responses for local needs: flexing capacity to meet demand

While the picture of an oversupply of willing volunteers, ready to act but under-utilised, might in many ways appear surprising or disappointing, a closer look at the nature of the community responses across the UK offers an interesting explanation. At its heart was the ability of local communities to draw upon and utilise a range of resources, skills and support, which enabled them to meet demand quickly and effectively. This included the effective redeployment of staff across both LA and VCS organisations, the creation of local humanitarian response frameworks which collated and coordinated volunteer resources, and the critical role of informal community groups, like mutual aid.

Redeploying staff to meet community needs

Most LAs and VCS organisations redeployed their staff to work together in a coordinated effort. As LAs were forced to suspend some services, such as libraries and leisure services, entire teams became available for alternative roles. This resulted in many of the newly created pandemic roles being filled by redeployed LA employees, rather than new volunteers. Staff from both LAs and VCS organisations took on new and diverse roles during the pandemic, dependent upon evolving needs and required skills. Staff were often redeployed for delivery, food distribution, communications (calling shielding groups), manning the volunteer helpline and matching volunteers with needs. "Our workforce became really fluid and it just moved into the space where people needed us" (LA17). "We've been working really well with the local authority staff. For instance, they've seconded to us, we have five library staff working with us, they do lots of the triage calls with us" (LIO11). Some participants commented on the positive impact that this fluidity had on their organisational culture, establishing cross-sectoral and inter-organisational working, as different teams worked together to support a common objective. The redeployment of staff who might otherwise have been furloughed thus reduced the need for new volunteers to support the response.

The influx of local volunteers

A primary reason for the utilisation of redeployed staff rather than volunteers related to capacity constraints of managing new volunteers. While many established volunteers were forced to self-isolate, new volunteers came forward in large numbers as the national messaging filtered down to the local level. In most locations, participants spoke of how the numbers of volunteers far exceeded their requirements or capacity to support.

In these areas, messaging was focused on directing volunteers to one place, such as the local infrastructure organisation, or the council's website, for a coordinated approach. Once registered, they might then be matched directly with a volunteering opportunity, such as shopping for someone shielding who had phoned up the helpline. Although a welcome display of civic action and kindness, these new volunteers presented a further challenge for LAs and the VCS, as they faced the daunting task of safely and effectively matching volunteers with community needs. Participants also talked about the challenge of how to engage with those volunteers who were never utilised. Many organisations looked to pass on volunteers to other organisations (for example, food banks or pharmacies in need of drivers), while others sought to signpost them to more informal, mutual aid groups or to check in on neighbours. "You get a crisis and suddenly everybody wants to help, but the problem is that they don't know ... they think by just saying 'we're here to help' that's something that's really useful to people, but the problem is managing that help" (LA16). "I should say, the end of this story is there's loads of volunteers that weren't used, it isn't a 100 per cent success story, because far more people offered than could be involved" (MVCS6). "Because you've got this massive movement, you can just see this wave coming towards us, of volunteers and they're all saying, 'I haven't been mobilised yet, what do you want me to do?'" (LA3).

Communities doing it for themselves: the role of mutual aid groups

Quickest to respond to local needs, well in advance of national platforms and LA systems, were mutual aid groups. Before the announcement of the first lockdown, proactive neighbours began mobilising in preparation for restrictions and were active throughout the crisis. Their initial primary focus was to supply food, medicine and other essentials to their neighbours and to connect with people suffering from loneliness and social isolation, although mutual aid activities evolved to include much more over the course of the pandemic.

Where national platforms were slow and bureaucratic, mutual aid groups were swift and agile. In our discussions with groups, they cited several factors that enabled them to move so quickly. Participants frequently reflected on the importance of keeping it small and confining their geographic location: "and we had to mobilise really, really quickly. And the closer you are to the ground, the quicker you're going to be able to mobilise" (S5MAFG1, admin). Their informal and flexible structures of organising allowed them to make decisions and coordinate activity at speed, using digital communication platforms like WhatsApp to share requests for help, which garnered responses from available, local volunteers in a matter of seconds:

> 'It wasn't a case of having to wait for a phone call for somebody to volunteer, the fact it was done … normally within five milliseconds of a post going out, somebody had responded, you know, there's somebody with their phone in their hand, five milliseconds, "oh, missed again", but that was the nature of it at the very beginning.' (S3MAFG2, volunteer)

Some mutual aid participants had registered with the GoodSAM platform but were unable to access opportunities local to them and joined their mutual aid group instead. The ease of getting involved (without the usual forms, checks and training[2]) was a key draw for volunteer participants:

> 'the lack of red tape, and it just set up, we filled in a form just to make sure that we were, you know, okay, and that was it, we got started … it was just simple, it was straightforward … with the NHS Responders, I mean, I'm sure they do similar things but it's just so much more complicated, and that's modern life. And I think it was just lovely to be able to jump straight in and get on with it, with minimal fuss, and I think that made it special as well.' (S3MAFG2, volunteer)

Mutual aid groups were rich in skills and experiences, well embedded within their localities and connected to community groups, organisations and infrastructure. Where the national volunteer platforms had not been able to link in with local capacity, mutual aid groups collaborated with existing community initiatives and contributed to a rich landscape of activity.

The role of cross-sectoral collaborations in coordinating community responses

In many areas, the pandemic sparked a major overhaul in LA–VCS relationships. This was driven by the recognition of the need to pull together resources to meet unprecedented levels of need across the country (Harris, 2021). The rise of these cross-sectoral collaborations, although representing a rapid escalation, was not entirely out of the blue. In recent years, debates have centred on the ability of LAs to work in partnership with communities, to facilitate and support new models of engagement to enhance social action and to increase community voice in decision making (Burchell et al, forthcoming). The COVID-19 pandemic brought these challenges into stark focus, requiring a level of community coordination and collaboration that has not been seen in the post-war era.

Across the country, the breadth and scale of community need required a pooling of capacity and resources that enabled innovative models of cross-sectoral partnership. Therefore, models of working emerged that had previously only been utilised on a small scale; the pandemic provided the impetus to drive forward this agenda more quickly and extensively than previously imagined. While the specific nature and format of these newly emerging relationships varied across the UK, some key features appeared to predominate.

The value of pre-existing relationships and investment in community infrastructure

Most emergency community response frameworks were built upon pre-existing partnerships between LAs and VCS organisations. Time spent investing in these relationships prior to the pandemic was cited in many interviews as allowing LAs to draw upon the support of a broad network of organisations and enabling quick identification of what resources were available across communities. Community engagement programmes were identified as being invaluable frameworks for creating these channels of engagement and building stronger connections between LA staff and communities. In many cases, the volunteering coordination sat alongside the activities of programmes like Local Area Coordination and social prescribing, allowing such programmes to offer support where need was more complex.

By building upon pre-existing relationships, groups were able to share and distribute roles and responsibilities to make the most of existing capacity and resources. Key to unlocking this potential was the ability of both LAs and VCS organisations to work flexibly and innovatively, enabling partnerships to circumvent some of the lengthy pre-existing processes that surrounded issues such as risk, procurement and safeguarding, and which had often previously created major barriers to collaborative working. Previous experiences of responding to crises such as flooding and swine flu were also identified as providing an important foundation for developing the trusting relationships and procedures that were applied during the pandemic. Research participants summarised the importance of these relationships as follows:

> 'We were fortunate in that we had a lot of the building blocks, or the things in place, that enabled us to be able to just plug into our normal engagement routes, and to say "Okay, what does this mean for us, how are we going to manage this?" ... because we'd spent a lot of time building what I think is the right environment, or the sort of environment that enables us to have open conversations and a good dialogue with our sector, it didn't feel like it was our problem, it was a collective problem.' (LA #13)

> 'I think it does come down to the fact that we are really well known and I think there are key members of each partner that works really closely together, I think that meant that we could push this forward really quickly. I think that if we'd have had to have learnt any of that, and get to know, because you have to get to know how each organisation works as well. I think we are all similar, like-minded and just wanting to do best for the community and that was a massive reason why we could be so quick and proactive ... and I think it's taken time to get these relationship ... as soon as this happened, you couldn't have just gone "right, let's go to all organisations in the community, let's go forward" – that was because we know each other and we have done for a long time.' (VCS infrastructure organisation #6)

The level of pre-existing collaboration and investment in LA–VCS relationships also affected the extent to which VCS infrastructure organisations in many cases were willing or able to play a major coordinating role. Where successful, VCS infrastructure organisations enabled a fast and coordinated response, often providing a vital bridge between LA staff and services and community organisations and volunteers. However, in some locations, it was noted that infrastructure organisations were either not strong enough or not in a position to be able to undertake such a coordinating role. Interviewees cited significant periods of disinvestment in community infrastructure in their locations as an important factor in shaping this outcome. These findings support Macmillan (2021)'s assertion that the pandemic has brought about a renewed recognition of the value of VCS infrastructure.

Coordinating responses through cross-sectoral response cells

Cross-sectoral cells were the most common LA response systems in our sample. These command structures were often multi-agency collaborations with members coming from a broad range of organisations and departments, across the public and voluntary sectors. In many areas, this represented a significant transition from traditional silo working towards a place-based response.

This process of bringing together organisations and LA departments was highlighted as a key factor behind a quick and effective response to the scale and diversity of community needs. Equally central was the extent to which VCS representatives were brought directly into these decision-making processes and given equal voice alongside their LA counterparts. VCS organisations spoke about the increased levels of engagement and access available to them across both NHS and LA structures and recognised the increased value of being able to discuss and engage across organisations as part of the community response. Building stronger cross-sectoral understanding and respect was seen as an important outcome of the community response.

> 'I think after two or three weeks ... there were more than enough meetings that involved our sector and statutory organisations, and in fact, in many ways ... we'd gone from one extreme to the other, we'd gone from not speaking, to literally, I'm pretty sure between our chief exec, my executive manager, and me ... I'm pretty sure, from Monday to Friday, and indeed Saturdays as well during the early part, we could have sat ... in meetings from nine til five every day, at various levels ... so we were invited into the big tent.' (VCS infrastructure organisation #4)

> 'I've had a lot of positive feedback from [council colleagues within the volunteering hubs], and from further up the hierarchies in both the council and the Health and Social Care Partnership and the NHS, from people saying it's been great working with us, but it's also been great working with community groups, we think of the third sector quite differently, it's been so refreshing.' (VCS infrastructure organisation #10)

Enhanced collaborative working and information sharing

One foundation to making the collaborative response cells effective was the flattening of power structures amid a genuine commitment to collaborative working, and the sharing resources. Many participants felt that this form of partnership working was the only way in which it was possible to generate the knowledge, expertise and capacity to deliver the required support. Strengthening established communication frameworks facilitated shared decision making at pace and optimised the deployment of VCS capacity and LA staff resources. Greater sharing of resources offered an up-to-date understanding of support networks available, the resource requirements and needs mapping, all of which are key factors in enabling the coordination of a massive community response. Likewise, the removal of barriers in LA systems meant the focus was on who was best placed to take the lead where skills and expertise existed.

In many cases, LAs recognised that they were not always best placed to provide support and were prepared to cede control and devolve responsibilities to VCS organisations. Authorities often undertook an enabling role, acting as the 'safety net', providing back-up resources to enable other organisations to provide the 'hands-on' support. "In other areas you can just see the council is kind of retrenching and saying, 'well, we need to deal with all these people ourselves'. Up here, they didn't, they said 'we can't deal with this ourselves, but these guys can'" (VCS infrastructure organisation #88). In a few areas, LAs developed partnerships with mutual aid groups, whereby requests coming into their central helpline could be signposted on to a local group, facilitating community solutions, where possible. The collaboration was reciprocal, with groups signposting more complex needs back to the LA, as well as receiving support in the way of guidance, training and funds from the council. These relationships were built upon trust, recognition, support and transparent two-way communication.

While this collaborative, place-based form of engagement was championed and praised in many locations across the country, it was not universal; some locations struggled to transition away from established frameworks. In these areas, interviewees shared challenges regarding information being withheld from partners, or of traditional 'silo mentality' blocking the potential to develop new ways of working. In examples where collaborative working proved more difficult to instigate, participants cited a reluctance from organisations (both LA and VCS) to be flexible and described how relationships got bogged down in bureaucracy and procedure.

As Gilchrist (2016) argues, bureaucratic processes often create major barriers to collaborative working with communities. Some councils were criticised for trying to be too controlling and intervening with grassroots community action, expecting them to conform to established procedural rules. Similarly, some VCS groups were seen to have been slow to respond due to an inability to 'pivot' and adapt processes and allow groups to be involved when not formally constituted. This was a source of frustration for some mutual aid groups, who reached out to their LAs and VCS organisations, but were rebuffed.

Flattened structures and greater decentralisation

The focus within the collaborative models on flatter, decentralised organisational structures enabled a transformation in cross-sectoral engagement processes, with an emphasis on sharing decision making, greater collaboration and more subsidiarity, and an objective to devolve action to the most appropriate localised levels. A strong emphasis was placed upon demarcating between activities that could be delivered by communities and VCS organisations with support from LAs, and those that necessitated support through statutory service provision. For example, requests for the delivery of shopping could most effectively be handled by a mutual aid group. More high-level needs, such as support for complex mental health, could be triaged to the appropriate public or VCS service.

This process required a clear understanding, and in some cases mapping, of the skills and resources available within the community and a willingness to hand over control where appropriate. Consequently, LA roles displayed a stronger emphasis towards enabling and facilitating rather than assuming the predominant delivery position. LAs facilitated the creation of the COVID-19 helplines and websites, utilising redeployed staff, and provided key information and support to community organisations and volunteers regarding risk, and health and safety issues, where appropriate.

Conclusion

When restrictions on social movement were imposed in March 2020, LAs faced the dual challenge of identifying needs and coordinating responses quickly and effectively. This demanded identifying who in the community might need support, determining what kinds of needs they had and understanding where resourceful communities had already mobilised. The findings discussed here highlight the centrality of linking in with local knowledge, as well as the importance of flexibility and adaptability to different community contexts.

In light of the complex and shifting patterns of need, it is unsurprising that what we found across locations was not a one-size-fits-all response, but a variety of local approaches. Support was adapted to individual contexts, not just across our interview sample, but within their own geographical contexts, from village to village and from one part of a city to another. A combination of redeployed staff, VCS organisations, and formal and informal volunteers were mobilised to respond.

Large numbers of volunteers came forward, to the extent that mobilising all, or indeed most, of those willing to help was a key challenge. We found a variety of approaches to recruiting and deploying volunteers, drawing on the local infrastructure organisation, hubs of community organisations or multiple community networks – including mutual aid groups – to allocate the new volunteers. Across these approaches, building relationships was key to effectively and safely matching volunteers with need.

Linking in with local knowledge, resources and infrastructure has been crucial. From additional community intelligence to supplement government shielding lists, to localised volunteer recruitment, the value of localised approaches rather than centralised ones was a consistent theme. To access this knowledge, working in partnership with public sector partners, local infrastructure organisations, the broader VCS and informal groups of volunteers has been central. Understanding who would need support, and where that support was already being organised, necessitated a relationship and open dialogue with the actors and organisations that held that knowledge.

Notes

[1] National lockdown was imposed through public health legislation, with separate regulations made in the UK, Scottish and Welsh parliaments. Although the first national lockdowns in March 2020 were almost identical, approaches taken by the devolved parliaments towards social distancing rules and restrictions have varied at different stages of the pandemic (Brown and Kirk-Wade, 2021).

[2] Some organisations expressed concerns about the lack of formal safeguarding processes within mutual aid groups and the potential risks of fraud, abuse and data mismanagement. We do not suggest that all mutual aid groups always took appropriate measures to safeguard volunteers and communities. However, the groups in our sample took their responsibility to keep their communities safe extremely seriously, and as far as our participants were aware, there had been no negative outcomes because of their informal approach.

References

Barnes, M. (2004) 'User participatory research', in S. Becker and A. Bryman (eds.) *Understanding Research for Social Policy and Social Work: Themes, Methods and Approaches*, Bristol: Policy Press, pp 108–14.

Bradbury, H. (ed.) (2015) *The SAGE Handbook of Action Research* (3rd edn), London: SAGE.

Brown, J. and Kirk-Wade, E. (2021) 'Coronavirus: a history of 'lockdown laws' in England', *House of Commons Library Research Briefing*, [online], Available from: researchbriefings.files.parliament.uk/documents/CBP-9068/CBP-9068.pdf [Accessed 19 May 2022].

Buchan, L. (2020) 'Coronavirus: government launches urgent appeal for 250,000 NHS volunteers', *The Independent* [online], Available from: www.independent.co.uk/news/uk/politics/coronavirus-nhs-volunteers-hospitals-cases-deaths-matt-hancock-a9422251.html [Accessed 19 May 2022].

Burchell, J., Cook, J., McNeill, J. and Walkley, F. (forthcoming) *The Enabling Social Action Programme 2018–2020, End of Programme Report*.

Burchell, J., Walkley, F., Cook, J., Thiery, H., Ballantyne, E. and McNeill, J. (2020) *Report #2 Models and Frameworks for Coordinating Community Responses During COVID-19*, [online], Available from: //doit.life/channels/11997/move-findings/file/md/141257/report-2-models-and-frameworks-for-coord [Accessed 25 February 2022].

Butler, P. (2020) 'NHS coronavirus crisis volunteers frustrated at lack of tasks', *The Guardian*, [online], Available from: *www.theguardian.com/world/2020/may/03/nhs-coronavirus-crisis-volunteers-frustrated-at-lack-of-tasks* [Accessed 19 May 2022].

Dayson, C. and Damm, C. (2020) 'Re-making state-civil society relationships during the COVID-19 pandemic? An English perspective', *People, Place and Policy*, 14(3): 282–9.

Gilchrist, A. (2016) *Blending, Braiding, Balancing: Strategies for Managing the Interplay between Formal and Informal Ways of Working with Communities. Third Sector Research Centre Working Paper 136*, Birmingham: University of Birmingham.

Harris, M. (2021) 'Familiar patterns and new initiatives: UK civil society and government initial responses to the Covid-19 crisis', *Nonprofit Policy Forum*, 12(1): 25–44.

Macmillan, R. (2020) 'Somewhere over the rainbow – third sector research in and beyond coronavirus', *Voluntary Sector Review*, 11(2): 129–36.

Macmillan, R. (2021) 'A surprising turn of events – episodes towards a renaissance of civil society infrastructure in England', *People, Place and Policy*, 15(2): 57–71.

Mason, J. (2002) 'Qualitative interviewing: asking, listening and interpreting', in T. May (ed.) *Qualitative Research in Action*, London: SAGE, pp 225–41.

Nottingham Trent University (2021) *Respond, Recover, Reset: The Voluntary Sector and COVID-19*, Nottingham: Nottingham Trent University.

Spencer, L., Ritchie, J., Ormston, R., O'Connor, W. and Barnard, M. (2013) 'Analysis: principles and processes', in R. Lewis, J. Lewis, C.M. Nicholls and R. Ormston (eds.), *Qualitative Research Practice: A Guide for Social Science Students and Researchers*, London: SAGE, pp 269–90.

Walkley, F., Bojke, C., Howdon, D., Burchell, J., Thiery, H., Cook, J., Ballantyne, E. and McNeill, J. (2021) *Report #4 Resilience of the Voluntary and Community Sector across Yorkshire and the Humber*, [online], Available from: //doit.life/channels/11997/move-findings/file/md/181765/report-4-resilience-of-the-voluntary-and [Accessed 20 December 2021].

7

At the COVID-19 frontlines: voluntary sector support for refugee and migrant families in Glasgow

Maureen McBride, Elaine Feeney, Clara Pirie and Jane Cullingworth

Introduction

High levels of pre-existing social and economic inequalities, insecure legal status and the structuring forces of racism left refugee and migrant families particularly vulnerable to the impact of the pandemic. These families relied heavily on voluntary sector workers who have the relational skills and trusted relationships required to provide crisis support to vulnerable people and families. In this chapter, we explore voluntary sector organisations' (VSOs) practical and emotional support for refugee and migrant families in Glasgow, based on research undertaken by a place-based research project working to improve outcomes for children, young people and their communities. VSOs were able to mobilise quickly and effectively to provide sensitive solutions to the range of issues experienced by refugee and migrant families – including translating public health information, dispelling misinformation and communicating/liaising with statutory services given the absence of translation services. Particularly emotionally draining work included having to find solutions to repatriating bodies and supporting asylum seekers who had been forced from their homes.

The chapter is structured as follows. Firstly, we outline the relevant literature on pre-existing inequalities experienced by refugee and migrant families, the voluntary sector's response to these in the context of austerity and gaps in provision, and what is known about the COVID-19 pandemic in terms of how the voluntary sector mobilised to support refugee and migrant families. Following a brief overview of the methodology underpinning our research, we present our findings via four key themes: the flexibility and adaptability of VSOs, the importance of the trusted relationships that workers have developed with refugee and migrant communities, the 'bridging' role between communities and statutory services, and the important VSO work of navigating and challenging policy during the pandemic. Our study highlights the essential role of VSOs, and, in particular, the diverse skill set and emotional labour carried out by voluntary sector workers in their support of, and advocacy for, vulnerable migrant families experiencing a range of intersecting inequalities. Further, the evidence underlines the importance of providing fair and sustainable funding to the sector.

In this chapter, we use 'refugee and migrant families' to encompass a number of groups, including refugees, people seeking asylum and vulnerable migrants such as Roma communities. We acknowledge the term is imperfect and that each of these communities may have discrete needs and experiences.

Inequalities, austerity and COVID-19

Pre-pandemic inequalities

Scottish government statistics indicate that pre-pandemic, people from minority ethnic (non-White British) groups in Scotland were more likely to be in relative poverty after housing costs compared with people from 'White British' groups (Scottish Government, 2019). This 'persistent poverty' of minority groups is evident in many intersecting domains (Bassel and Emejulu, 2018, p 36). For example, refugee and migrant groups are more likely to live in substandard housing and experience overcrowding (Pirie, 2020). Evidence indicates ethnic minorities in the UK are more reliant on the private-rental sector than the majority population and are thus at greater risk of rent arrears and eviction (Qureshi et al, 2020). These issues shape the health inequalities experienced by such groups.

Refugees and asylum seekers experience particular barriers and inequalities. In the UK, an individual seeking asylum receives £39.63 per week, with £3–5 extra allocated to pregnant women or children under the age of three years (UK Government, n.d.). Asylum seekers are therefore often reliant on the voluntary sector for additional support and are thus vulnerable to poverty (Sime, 2018; Saltmarsh, 2020). Those with rejected asylum claims and no recourse to public funds (NRPF) are vulnerable to destitution and face limited access to services (McKenna, 2018; McEwan et al, 2020; Poverty Alliance, 2020). Research also suggests that refugee and migrant groups experience particularly high levels of mental and physical ill health (Burchill, 2011; Balaam et al, 2016).

Austerity, gaps in provision and the voluntary sector's response

These social and economic inequalities are situated against a backdrop of austerity measures and cuts to public services in the UK. Scholars have argued that this 'culture of cuts' has led to a gap in provision for refugee and migrant families, which is unmet by public services (Bassel and Emejulu, 2018, p 45). Much literature has explored how voluntary sector organisations have become integral to filling this gap. Research shows voluntary sector workers often compensate for an absent state, providing support to refugee and migrant families (Balaam et al, 2016; DeVerteuil, 2017; Mayblin and James, 2019). The sector's role includes providing support and supplementing welfare, particularly for asylum seekers who are prevented from entering the labour market (Mayblin and James, 2019).

Research demonstrates that VSOs provide a valuable service to refugee and migrant families. In contrast to statutory services, they are often viewed as trusted sources of information and advocates for minority groups (Quinn, 2014). Voluntary practitioners supporting refugee and asylum-seeking women during pregnancy found they were often distrustful of statutory organisations (Balaam et al, 2016). Many refugee VSOs are small, local and volunteer-run (Phillimore and McCabe, 2010; Mayblin and James, 2019), offering safe and trusted environments which support the development of wellbeing and meet diverse needs (Vacchelli and Mesarič, 2020; Calò et al, 2021).

The voluntary sector has experienced well-documented challenges in recent decades. Research has explored the financial struggles many VSOs face in the context of austerity and funding cuts (Price, 2016; Goldstraw et al, 2020; Mesarič and Vacchelli, 2021). Capacity and financial constraints, paired with power imbalances favouring funders, create challenging conditions for organisations supporting refugee and migrant families. This is particularly true for smaller organisations. Despite offering important services that can be a lifeline, competitive funding streams often benefit larger VSOs that have the resources to submit successful bids (Goldstraw et al, 2020), leading to the contraction of smaller VSOs (Calò et al, 2021).

Despite competition over resources among migrant support groups (MacKenzie et al, 2012), voluntary sector practitioners working with refugee and migrant women have been shown to challenge policies and inequalities. Mesarič and Vacchelli (2021) found practitioners' understanding of policies and structural disadvantage is used strategically to secure funding and to challenge the hostile environment and neoliberal austerity policies.

Conversely, other research has explored how VSOs working in partnership with statutory services to support migrant families can shift criticism from the state (Paniagua and D'Angelo, 2017). By filling an unmet gap, the authors argue, the organisations inadvertently become complicit in the outsourcing of public services and abdication of the state's responsibilities. Other scholars have argued that the voluntary sector can be overly weak in contesting the state on behalf of beneficiaries (DeVerteuil, 2017).

The COVID-19 crisis and support for refugee and migrant families

Many VSOs were quick to mobilise in the face of COVID-19, credited with creative person-centred responses (Dayson and Damm, 2020; Bynner et al, 2021; Shakespeare et al, 2021), reaffirming the sector's reputation as 'flexible, responsive and innovative' (Harris, 2021, p 38). Research in Scotland with refugees and asylum seekers highlighted a reliance on the voluntary sector and minimal engagement with statutory services (Armstrong and Pickering, 2020; McBride et al, 2020). Research also evidenced fundamental changes in how VSOs provided support, often utilising technology in new ways (McMullin, 2021). A report about the pandemic's impact on vulnerable migrants in London highlighted a significant deterioration in health and increased reporting of inadequate housing (Lessard-Phillips et al, 2021). Evidence from England demonstrated that communities invested in 'integration' were better equipped to handle the pandemic, expressed through higher levels of social activism and more positive attitudes towards immigrants (Lalot et al, 2021). Existing research has demonstrated the importance of the voluntary sector during the pandemic, particularly in the absence of formal state support. This chapter aims to add to the literature on the voluntary sector's response to the COVID-19 crisis, with a particular focus on support for refugee and migrant families in a Scottish context.

Methodology

An exploratory approach was taken to the research. In order to understand the potential impact of the pandemic, a rapid literature review was undertaken into pre-existing vulnerabilities and inequalities experienced by refugee and migrant families in Britain (Pirie, 2020). A small empirical study was then conducted with nine individuals working at the frontline in VSOs with refugee and migrant families in Glasgow, Scotland. One organisation had a city-wide remit; the rest were community-based. All worked in communities with high levels of poverty and high numbers of asylum seekers, refugees and Roma families. Participants were recruited through existing contacts and direct contact with VSOs working with refugee and migrant families.

The interview guide was shaped by the findings of a rapid literature review (Pirie, 2020) and a report on the impact of COVID-19 on families, children and young people (Bynner et al, 2020). Qualitative semi-structured interviews were employed, providing participants some control over the discussion and enabling them to identify issues of importance to the families they supported (Mason, 2002). Interviews took place in May and June 2020, by phone or on Zoom, and lasted between 45 and 60 minutes. Interviews were transcribed verbatim and coded manually; an inductive thematic analysis framework was used from which an analytical framework was developed (Guest et al, 2012).

Findings

Flexibility and adaptability

VSOs were able to quickly mobilise and collaborate on the ground, adapting their work plans to meet high levels of need through emergency food provision and practical support: "Anything that we had done previously has been completely scrapped and our focus has been on working with other agencies [including a local mosque] and providing hot meals, hot food because that's the one thing that we can do" (Andrea, refugee support). Higher levels of poverty among refugee and migrant families left them more vulnerable to the impact of the pandemic and in greater need of support. For example, given high levels of digital exclusion among refugees and asylum seekers, the voluntary sector sought funds to help people access online learning and other provision during lockdown: "[An organisation] for young refugees across the whole of the UK have tried to work with corporate partners or raise money for phone data because young people just can't participate without data, and especially all this online group work that uses a lot of data" (Roselyn, refugee support).

One respondent explained that their organisation had to prioritise support based on the greatest need, and internet access was particularly challenging for those seeking asylum: "We've been looking at providing internet access for people as well, even that's limited. So, again we have to apply for that and we're prioritising asylum seekers because they are most likely to be financially unable to access things like that" (Danny, community work). VSOs' ability to quickly mobilise and adapt was contrasted with perceptions among participants of a slower response from the public sector. It was felt that the pandemic highlighted the crucial but often undervalued role the voluntary sector plays in supporting refugee and migrant families, particularly in the context of austerity and cuts to public services. "[T]he third sector have stood up and they've proved themselves that they're reliable and they're the ones that are doing the work on the ground. It's not the government, you know. Your day-to-day stuff, you know" (Grace, health and social care).

This study also found the competitive nature of funding in the voluntary sector, which is often a barrier to collaboration, was often temporarily overcome as organisations prioritised the immediate needs of vulnerable people: "There's certainly been a lot more pulling together of community resources and working together. I'd spoken to one community resource, and they were like it's a shame that it's taken a pandemic for us all to be talking to each other and working together" (Colin, health and social care).

Trust, empathy and connection

This study found that the trusting relationships, empathy and meaningful connections that voluntary sector workers develop with refugee and migrant communities were crucial to providing support during the pandemic. The highly local nature of grassroots organisations was highlighted: "It's hard to work in community work without thinking of places tied up with personalities and people ... although what we do is very like solidarity-based, a lot of the time you're just literally helping people" (Rachel, refugee support).

In the early days of the pandemic and lockdown, VSOs and local community-based groups emerged to provide practical and emotional support to vulnerable refugee and migrant families. Such groups were considered effective because they were trusted and rooted in communities: "they've got a reputation behind them" (Grace, health and social care). Furthermore, they played an essential role as trusted sources of information in a context of confusion, panic and misinformation. Refugee and migrant communities with limited or no English proficiency faced significant challenges in understanding public health guidance. VSOs sought to alleviate this by providing translation services themselves or applying for funding to have information translated into different languages. "We also recorded different messages with travel advice, what to do if you're experiencing symptoms and ... yeah, for people to have something valid and coming from people that they trust" (Catherine, housing).

Some participants felt that this represented the failure of the state to ensure refugee and migrant communities were treated equally, and that it was left to the voluntary sector to fill this void: "it's shifting a public duty on to the [VSO] or other third sector to try and explain what's happening" (Roselyn, refugee support). One worker from a grassroots organisation explained that her role changed entirely overnight because she was able to speak the language of the community she supports:

> 'Because I'm a Romanian speaker, my job changed, becoming more of a support role for the Romanian community, because that was a real, real challenge and the need went off the roof. ... So, I became a support worker along with my colleagues ... and that for me was a big jump because I had to learn so many things in such a short period of time.' (Catherine, housing)

Crucial 'bridge' between communities and statutory services

Participants emphasised the role of VSOs as advocates when engaging with statutory organisations. They explained that there is generally a need for this advocacy role due to refugee and migrant communities' mistrust of authority, but in the early stages of the pandemic it became a necessity. Many services stopped or became exceptionally difficult to access, and participants spoke of having to intervene to ensure people at risk were able to access social work and health visitors. This bridging role was also crucial to enable people with limited English proficiency to access basic care and public health guidance. In one example, a participant had been supporting a vulnerable woman seeking asylum who had no English proficiency and required emergency dental care: "I found myself sitting with three mobile phones in front of me, one to the individual, one to the translator ... well the individual was on speakerphone with me, one to the translator, and one to the dentist because she just didn't have a clue" (Grace, housing and social care). The same participant also had to organise translation of shielding letters. Patients had received instructions from GP practices but struggled to understand them as they had been translated via Google Translate.

At times, this work was emotionally draining and complex. A participant supporting the Romanian Roma community reflected on trying to help people who wanted to return home (or felt compelled to due to fear and confusion), and the repatriation of bodies given the disproportionately high mortality levels in the community: "You had babies getting born and you don't have a birth certificate and you can't travel without a birth certificate with a child. ... People that passed away, the repatriation of bodies to Romania, that was really challenging in this new context" (Catherine, housing). Such challenging work was considered even more difficult given the context of working from home without the support of colleagues: "You know, the idea that your living space becomes your workspace, and how people are able to make that transition. Particularly when you're potentially dealing with high levels of trauma" (Nick, health and social care). Indeed, VSO practitioners are often at risk of vicarious trauma due to the levels of secondary trauma they are exposed to through their varied and supportive roles (Waegemakers Schiff and Lane, 2019). Due to funding constraints, the necessary support is not always available. The support of colleagues alone is not necessarily enough, and there are instances where clinical supervision would be appropriate.

Navigating and challenging complex policy spheres

Finally, voluntary sector workers supporting refugees and asylum seekers had to engage with shifting policy contexts. Across the board, VSOs sought to mitigate the worst effects of policy decisions and the fact that many public sector-run services were stopped. One respondent explained that services were cut in the early days of the pandemic so only "critical level care" was available for home care services, and mental health provision was stripped away: "Mental health services, community mental health teams, and support has been kind of suspended indefinitely, or just cut with little to no warning. And a lot of people who don't have family support around have not been able to put anything else in place" (Nick, health and social care).

During the pandemic, VSOs had to deal with the practical implications of policy decisions taken by the Home Office, highlighting how closely related policy and practical work are when supporting asylum seekers.

One participant reflected on difficulties associated with giving supermarket vouchers to asylum seekers in place of normal food bank provision, because of worries this could be deducted from asylum support payments. Additionally, in response to asylum seekers being moved into hotels and having their asylum payments removed, VSOs worked collaboratively to investigate and challenge the legality of decisions:

> 'All the different integration networks in Glasgow coming together on that issue and other things around whether it was okay to take the money off people or whether it was lawful or whether ... So there's lots of movement there, if you like, as well as the kind of practical aid stuff that we're doing in the community groups.' (Rachel, refugee support).

In some cases, voluntary sector workers saw the highly fluid situation caused by the pandemic as an opportunity to challenge or work around punitive policies. One participant reflected on how VSOs began to explore how the damaging 'no recourse to public funds' policy could be challenged: "There was a big thing in this sector about kind of ending no recourse to public funds ... to take it as an opportunity from a policy perspective, to push things through" (Rachel, refugee support). This participant explained that as part of the temporary changes in rules, it was easier to "push through" Section 4[1] applications, helping people to receive financial support for basic living costs. This further demonstrates the skill set of voluntary sector workers, who, despite being often precariously employed, can engage with highly complex legal and policy contexts.

Discussion

Retreat of the state

Recent literature (Harris, 2021; Shakespeare et al, 2021) has argued that public services were, in many cases, slow to adapt their ways of working in the early days of the pandemic compared with the voluntary sector, despite having more sustainable funding and wider access to resources. Participants in our study supported this view, highlighting that many crucial services were suspended with implications for vulnerable communities. Voluntary sector workers therefore had to fill this gap, act as intermediaries between beneficiaries and statutory services, and provide crucial interpretation and translation. This adds further evidence to previous research findings which emphasise the crucial role of the voluntary sector as advocates when engaging with statutory organisations (Mayblin and James, 2019). Further, against the backdrop of more than a decade of austerity measures – with minimal support for asylum seekers in particular (Darling, 2016) – it was left to VSOs to provide direct support and provision, including mental health support, advocacy and food parcels. Such basic needs and human rights are the responsibility of the state, yet are often not met, particularly for vulnerable refugee and migrant communities.

Valuing the skill set and emotional labour of voluntary sector workers

Relatedly, our findings demonstrate the unique and valuable contributions of the voluntary sector in supporting refugee and migrant families. The existing trust and relationships between VSOs and local communities enabled workers to provide a service and address needs unmet by statutory providers. This builds on existing literature which demonstrates how emotionally demanding labour is taken on by voluntary sector workers with unique skill sets (Balaam et al, 2016). VSOs' adaptability, resilience and ability to quickly mobilise to meet the needs of refugee and migrant families during the period of crisis are key strengths of the sector. The sector's unique role and contribution needs to be acknowledged, supported and not taken for granted in future crises.

Collaboration and funding

Our findings highlight that VSOs channelled funding, staff and volunteer time into supporting refugee and migrant families in a crisis. Participants highlighted the positive collaboration between VSOs and with other organisations such as local mosques to provide culturally appropriate food and other practical support for families. As explored elsewhere in the literature, the voluntary sector has faced significant challenges for some time. Competitive funding processes require VSOs to bid against each other for funding to run support services (MacKenzie et al, 2012; Goldstraw et al, 2020). Yet despite micro-politics linked to competitive funding processes, collaboration is a key characteristic of VSOs successfully supporting refugee and migrant families (Price, 2016; Garkisch et al, 2017). Further, the pandemic arguably facilitated better collaboration within the sector. Longer term, however, significant changes to the funding of grassroots organisations which provide valuable frontline support to refugee and migrant families is necessary. Given how central the sector is to the state, ensuring it is funded sustainably should be a key policy priority.

Conclusion and implications

This study echoes findings from Mesarič and Vacchelli (2021) that voluntary sector practitioners strategically utilise their in-depth understanding of structural disadvantage and vulnerability to challenge austerity policies. Practitioners endeavour to improve the lives of refugee and migrant communities through their work on the ground while simultaneously lobbying for changes in policy and negotiating existing policy. The requirement to engage with complex legal and policy frameworks requires a particularly advanced skill set given the punitive and constantly evolving nature of migration and asylum policy under the current UK government. In Scotland, VSOs must work with and mitigate against policies that are imposed by the UK government, particularly given Scottish government constraints in influencing the material circumstances of asylum seekers living here. The evidence in this chapter has demonstrated that statutory services largely depended on VSOs to provide basic care and support to refugee and migrant communities in Glasgow, highlighting lessons for both local and national government. There is an urgent need to review policies relating to translation provision and other support for vulnerable people to access services, and to acknowledge the crucial bridging role that VSOs offer.

There are, of course, limitations to a small research study like this. Given the sensitivities around conducting research with vulnerable groups during the pandemic, our study engaged solely with workers in the voluntary sector and not refugee and migrant families directly. It is widely accepted that people with lived experience should be able to influence and shape research and policy making themselves (Quinn, 2014; Abdulkadir et al, 2016), and, accordingly, further research into the voluntary sector's role in supporting refugee and migrant families should involve these groups directly. For example, Quinn's (2014) study represents a positive example of utilising participatory research methods with asylum seekers and refugees. Such research should explore in greater depth the added barriers that refugee and migrant communities experience when trying to access statutory services. Careful consideration must be taken, however, to ensure the safety and wellbeing of participants due to the high levels of trauma experienced and varying levels of vulnerability. Measures to address issues such as the misuse and inadequacies of translation and interpreting services should be co-produced with communities and with the VSOs that support them.

Note

[1] Section 4 of the Immigration and Asylum Act (1999) refers to support available to those who have been refused an asylum claim to cover essential living needs.

References

Abdulkadir, J., Azzudin, A., Buick, A., Curtice, L., Dzingisai, M., Easton, D., Frew, C., Glinski, J., Holliday, D., Knifton, L., McLaughlin, D., Quinn, N. and Ramsay, D. (2016) *What Do You Mean, I Have a Right to Health? Participatory Action Research on Health and Human Rights*, [online], Available from: //strathprints.strath.ac.uk/58209/1/Abdulkadir_etal_IPPI_2016_What_do_you_mean_I_have_a_right_to_health.pdf [Accessed 14 March 2022].

Armstrong, S. and Pickering, L. (2020) *Left out and Locked down: Impacts of COVID-19 Lockdown for Marginalised Groups in Scotland*, [online], Available from: //scotlandinlockdown.files.wordpress.com/2020/12/scotlock_project_report_full_dec2020-2.pdf [Accessed 14 March 2022].

Balaam, M.-C., Kingdon, C., Thomson, G., Finlayson, K. And Downe, S. (2016) '"We make them feel special": the experiences of voluntary sector workers supporting asylum seeking and refugee women during pregnancy and early motherhood', *Midwifery*, 24: 133–40.

Bassel, L. and Emejulu, A. (2018) 'Caring subjects: migrant women and the third sector in England and Scotland', *Ethnic and Racial Studies*, 41(1): 36–54.

Burchill, J. (2011) 'Safeguarding vulnerable families: work with refugees and asylum seekers', *Community Practice*, 84: 23–6.

Bynner, C., McBride, M. and Weakley, S. (2021) 'The COVID-19 pandemic: the essential role of the voluntary sector in emergency response and resilience planning', *Voluntary Sector Review*, 13(1): 167–75.

Bynner, C., McBride, M., Weakley, S., Ward, S. and McLean, J. (2020) *The Impact of COVID-19 on Families, Children and Young People in Glasgow*, Glasgow: Children's Neighbourhoods Scotland.

Calò, F., Montgomery, T. and Baglioni, S. (2021) 'Marginal players? The third sector and employability services for migrants, refugees and asylum seekers in the UK', *VOLUNTAS: International Journal of Voluntary and Nonprofit Organizations*, [online], Available from: //link.springer.com/10.1007/s11266-020-00306-6 [Accessed 7 September 2021].

Darling, J. (2016) 'Asylum in austere times: instability, privatization and experimentation within the UK asylum dispersal system', *Journal of Refugee Studies*, 29(4): 483–505.

Dayson, C. and Damm, C. (2020) 'Re-making state-civil society relationships during the COVID 19 pandemic? An English perspective', *People, Place and Policy*, 14(3): 282–9.

DeVerteuil, G. (2017) 'Post-welfare city at the margins: immigrant precarity and the mediating third sector in London', *Urban Geography*, 38(10): 1517–33.

Garkisch, M., Heidingsfelder, J. and Beckmann, M. (2017) 'Third sector organizations and migration: a systematic literature review on the contribution of third sector organizations in view of flight, migration and refugee crises', *VOLUNTAS: International Journal of Voluntary and Nonprofit Organizations*, 28(5): 1839–80.

Goldstraw, K., Davidson, E. and Packham, C. (2020) 'Sustainable livelihoods analysis as a response to the crisis in the community and voluntary sector', *Illness, Crisis & Loss*, 28(3): 195–217.

Guest, G., MacQueen, K. and Namey, E. (2012) *Applied Thematic Analysis*, London: SAGE.

Harris, M. (2021) 'Familiar patterns and new initiatives: UK civil society and government initial responses to the Covid-19 crisis', *Nonprofit Policy Forum*, 12(1): 25–44.

Lalot, F., Abrams, D., Broadwood, J., Davies Hayon, K. and Platts-Dunn, I. (2021) 'The social cohesion investment: communities that invested in integration programmes are showing greater social cohesion in the midst of the COVID-19 pandemic', *Journal of Community and Applied Social Psychology*, 32(3), 536–54.

Lessard-Phillips, L., Fu, L., Lindenmeyer, A. and Phillimore, J. (2021) *Barriers to Wellbeing: Migration and Vulnerability during the Pandemic*, [online], Available from: www.doctorsoftheworld.org.uk/wp-content/uploads/2021/09/Barriers-to-wellbeing-09.21.pdf [Accessed 9 December 2021].

MacKenzie, R., Forde, C. and Ciupijus, Z. (2012) 'Networks of support for new migrant communities: institutional goals versus substantive goals?', *Urban Studies*, 49(3): 631–47.

Mason, J. (2002) *Qualitative Researching* (2nd edn), London: SAGE.

Mayblin, L. and James, P. (2019) 'Asylum and refugee support in the UK: civil society filling the gaps?', *Journal of Ethnic and Migration Studies*, 45(3): 375–94.

Mesarič, A. and Vacchelli, E. (2021) 'Invoking vulnerability: practitioner attitudes to supporting refugee and migrant women in London-based third sector organisations', *Journal of Ethnic and Migration Studies*, 47(13): 3097–113.

McBride, M., Feeney, E., Bynner, C. and McLean, J. (2020) *Refugee, Asylum Seeking and Roma Families during the COVID-19 Pandemic: Insights from Frontline Workers in Glasgow*, Glasgow: Children's Neighbourhoods Scotland.

McEwan, A., Whyte, C., Bujokova, E., Telling, H., Yoken, H., Abrams, L., Hamilton, M. and Bracke, M. (2020) *Gendering Covid-19: Economies of Care and Bodily Integrity. A Collective Essay*, Glasgow: Centre for Gender History, University of Glasgow.

McKenna, R. (2018) *From Pillar to Post: Destitution among People Refused Asylum in Scotland*, Glasgow: Refugee Survival Trust.

McMullin, C. (2021) 'Migrant integration services and coping with the digital divide: challenges and opportunities of the COVID-19 pandemic', *Voluntary Sector Review*, 12(1): 129–36.

Paniagua, A. and D'Angelo, A. (2017) 'Outsourcing the state's responsibilities? Third Sector Organizations supporting migrant families' participation in schools in Catalonia and London', *A Journal of Comparative and International Education*, 47(1): 77–90.

Phillimore, J. and McCabe, A. (2010) *TSRC Briefing Paper 33: Understanding the Distinctiveness of Small Scale Third Sector Activity*, Birmingham: Third Sector Research Centre.

Pirie, C. (2020) *Migrant Families and the COVID-19 Pandemic: A Review of the Literature on Pre-Existing Vulnerabilities and Inequalities*, [online], Available from: //childrensneighbourhoods.scot/wp-content/uploads/2020/12/CNS-lit-review-migrant-families-risk-factors-COVID.pdf [Accessed 1 December 2021].

Poverty Alliance (2020) 'National organisations & the impact of Covid-19: Poverty Alliance briefing, 22nd April 2020', [online], Available from: www.povertyalliance.org/wp-content/uploads/2020/04/Covid-19-and-national-organisations-PA-briefing-22-April.pdf [Accessed 6 May 2020].

Price, J. (2016) *Meeting the Challenge: Voluntary Sector Services for Destitute Migrant Children and Families*, Oxford: University of Oxford.

Quinn, N. (2014) 'Participatory action research with asylum seekers and refugees experiencing stigma and discrimination: the experience from Scotland', *Disability & Society*, 29(1): 58–70.

Qureshi, K., Meer, N., Kasstan, B., Hill, S. and Hill, E. (2020) *Submission of Evidence on the Disproportionate Impact of COVID-19, and the UK Government Response, on Ethnic Minorities in the UK*, Edinburgh: University of Edinburgh.

Saltmarsh, M. (2020) 'Charity sector scrambles to shield refugees as UK COVID-19 crisis deepens', [online], Available from: www.unhcr.org/uk/news/stories/2020/3/5e7a4d774/charity-sector-scrambles-to-shield-refugees-as-uk-covid-19-crisis-deepens.html [Accessed 6 May 2020].

Scottish Government (2019) 'Poverty and income inequality in Scotland: 2015–2018', [online], Available from: www.gov.scot/publications/poverty-income-inequality-scotland-2015-18/pages/8/ [Accessed 7 September 2021].

Shakespeare, T., Watson, N., Brunner, R., Cullingworth, J., Hameed, S., Scherer, N., Pearson, C. and Reichenberger, V. (2021) 'Disabled people in Britain and the impact of the COVID-19 pandemic', *Social Policy & Administration*, 56(1): 103–17.

Sime, D. (2018) 'Educating migrant and refugee pupils', in T. Bryce, W. Humes, A. Kennedy and D. Gillies (eds.) *Scottish Education* (5th edn), Edinburgh: Edinburgh University Press.

UK Government (n.d.) 'Asylum support – what you'll get', [online], Available from: www.gov.uk/asylum-support/what-youll-get [Accessed 7 September 2021].

Vacchelli, E. and Mesarič, A. (2020) 'Diversity as discourse and diversity as practice: critical reflections on migrant women's experiences of accessing mental health support in London,' *Identities*, 28(4): 418–35.

Waegemakers Schiff, J. and Lane, A.M. (2019) 'PTSD symptoms, vicarious traumatization, and burnout in front line workers in the homeless sector', *Community Mental Health Journal*, 55: 454–62.

8

The value and contribution of BAME-led organisations during and beyond COVID-19

Abigail Woodward, Beth Patmore, Gilli Cliff and Chris Dayson

Introduction

Pre-existing socioeconomic and racial inequalities among Black, Asian and Minority Ethnic (BAME) people have been amplified by the COVID-19 pandemic (Haque et al, 2021). The pandemic has revealed an urgent need to reinvest in BAME-led charities and specialist organisations which are often under-resourced and over-subscribed (Lingayah et al, 2020). This chapter draws upon qualitative data to explore the ways in which BAME-led organisations within the voluntary sector have responded to the pandemic, and how BAME communities have been supported. The data presented draws upon 15 stakeholder interviews with BAME-led VSOs and projects conducted across two larger qualitative studies during the pandemic. Presenting three UK place-based case studies, insights from Sheffield, Salford and Ealing illustrate how BAME-led voluntary sector organisations (VSOs) have reached, engaged with and identified the pressing needs of local BAME communities. Evidence reveals that these communities are typically deprived, have been historically underserved by health and care services, and have the added complication of being disproportionately affected by the pandemic in terms of health and socioeconomic impacts. The case studies provide evidence of the value and contribution that BAME-led VSOs make to wider systems of health, social care and other public services during crises through their distinctiveness, and use of adaptive and absorptive capacity.

Background: COVID-19 impact on BAME inequalities

A report exploring the devastating impact of COVID-19 on BAME communities in Great Britain found that BAME people are 'over-represented in COVID-19 severe illness and deaths' (Haque et al, 2021, p 2). The increased risk that BAME people have compared with the White population (Marmot et al, 2020a) is down to a multiplicity of factors, creating a complex relationship between ethnicity and health. As such, these inequalities pre-date the pandemic but have been exacerbated by the crisis. People across all ethnic minority groups are shown to have higher poverty rates than White people but rates among Bangladeshi, Pakistani and Black people are particularly high (Marmot et al, 2020b).

Evidence from Public Health England (2020b) shows that BAME people are more likely to live in deprived areas. Correspondingly, COVID-19-related mortality in England and Wales was reported as being nearly twice as high in the most deprived areas compared with the least deprived (Ayoubkhani et al, 2020). Socioeconomic factors are considered drivers of COVID-19 morbidity and mortality among BAME people. Such factors include an increased likelihood of living in households that are larger, overcrowded and multigenerational, and having an occupation working on the frontline, all of which significantly increases social contact and exposure to those infected with COVID-19 (Public Health England, 2020b; Haque et al, 2021). People from Black African, Black Caribbean, Pakistani and Bangladeshi backgrounds are shown to be particularly vulnerable to COVID-19 due to their occupation and work status which makes them more likely to be working outside their home in a face-to-face capacity. They are also likely to have less access to protection from personal protective equipment (PPE), making them 'more vulnerable than their white peers to COVID-19 infection and severity of disease' (Haque et al, 2021, p 9). Increased health inequalities have subsequently led to devastating socioeconomic impacts upon different ethnic minority groups, affecting how individuals are able to cope with and recover from the impact of COVID-19 (Ayoubkhani et al, 2020; Haque et al, 2021).

To counteract the impact of COVID-19, VSOs played an essential role in supporting BAME communities, but reductions in funding to this sector, even before the pandemic, meant significant losses to the amount of provision available across localities (Public Health England, 2020a). VSOs had to quickly absorb a major 'shock' to established ways of working when Britain went into a national lockdown in March 2020 (Dayson et al, 2021b). They readied themselves for a change to 'business as usual' by directing service users to telephone lines and websites, working remotely where possible (Dayson and Woodward, 2021) and adapting their services in light of restrictions on providing face-to-face provision. Organisations experienced a loss of income and uncertainty surrounding funding, combined with an increase in demand for services to meet emerging needs (Wilson et al, 2021). Micro and small BAME organisations were shown to be most affected by the threat of permanent closure due to a lack of support (Mathers et al, 2020), since they are 'almost exclusively dependent on volunteers or "goodwill" to keep the organisation going' (Murray, 2020, p 16).

A specific challenge across the board is how VSOs continue to meet the increasing demands upon services and how they move beyond 'crisis mode', to a state of 'business as usual'. Some of the most deprived and hardest-hit communities during the pandemic have experienced the greatest overall loss of funding over the last ten years (Marmot et al, 2020b). The pandemic has highlighted the urgent need to reinvest in BAME-led charities and specialist organisations which are often under-resourced and over-subscribed (Lingayah et al, 2020). Since March 2020, VSOs have had to prioritise certain aspects of their provision to cope with the emergency, often resulting in a reduction or loss of some social activities and groups. The pandemic has led to a situation of short-termism across the voluntary sector; that is, the inability to plan beyond the initial crisis, which impacts on organisations' ability to address many of the social and structural issues within BAME communities (Public Health England, 2020a).

Methodological approach

The three place-based case studies presented below draw upon data from 15 qualitative interviews with key stakeholders from BAME-led VSOs and projects (Sheffield n=5, Salford n=5, Ealing n=5). These were conducted as part of two larger qualitative studies during the pandemic, across 49 VSOs, and included fieldwork in the case study areas. As such, the case studies also draw upon some broader context from other interviews conducted with key stakeholders across the voluntary sector which have contributed to the analysis of data. The data have been selected to provide evidence of the value and contribution that BAME-led organisations and projects make to wider systems of health, social care and other public services during crises. The interview data were reanalysed for this chapter to explore the new research aim of how BAME-led VSOs in the three localities have responded to the pandemic.

The wider study in Sheffield looked at the role and contribution of VSOs in Sheffield during the COVID-19 pandemic and was funded by the Higher Education Innovation Fund (Dayson and Woodward, 2021). The study was conducted in two phases with the data presented below deriving from the first phase, between March and December 2020. The ten VSOs that took part in the study formed an 'engagement panel' and were identified in partnership with a local voluntary sector infrastructure organisation, who played an important coordination role. Due to the restrictions on face-to-face research during the pandemic, all interviews were conducted remotely using an online video conferencing platform. Semi-structured inteviews lasted between 45 and 60 minutes. The Sheffield case study also included a contribution from the Age Better in Sheffield programme, which collected interview data from a VSO with a large BAME focus, as part of a social and financial isolation project (Age Friendly Sheffield, 2020).

The data for Salford and Ealing are drawn from the study 'The value of small in a big crisis', which was funded by the Lloyds Bank Foundation for England and Wales. This larger qualitative study was designed to explore the distinctive contribution, value and experiences of smaller charities in England and Wales during the COVID-19 pandemic (Dayson et al, 2021b). The selection of the local authority areas (Salford and Ealing) and smaller charities was based on the original 'Value of Small' study conducted in 2017–18 (Coule et al, 2018). Between August and December 2020, researchers revisited key stakeholders from this study to explore how smaller charities responded during the pandemic, and the social and economic value of that response. Online and telephone interviews were conducted with employees and volunteers of smaller charities (Ealing n=6, Salford n=4) and local stakeholders (Ealing n=4, Salford n=4). Interviews were from 30 to 75 minutes in length.

For both qualitative studies, informed consent was obtained from all stakeholders and interviews were audio recorded using an encrypted dictaphone.

Insights from VSOs

Case study 1: Sheffield

Sheffield is a large city in South Yorkshire with a population of over 580,000. Around 19 per cent of Sheffield's population is BAME. VSOs in Sheffield reacted swiftly to the COVID-19 pandemic, finding practical steps to maintain contact with their service users remotely and then later, when possible, providing socially distanced contact. VSOs were often the first port of call (and last resort) for households across all communities. Food provision became an urgent priority during the first lockdown in March 2020 and one BAME-led mental health charity began to supply food parcels for the first time, delivering '1,500 meals' city-wide. A BAME grassroots organisation highlighted that the Roma community was particularly vulnerable to food insecurity and demand for food provision increased for this group.

With the pressing need to move services online, the magnitude of digital exclusion across Sheffield was highlighted. There were difficulties in reaching service users remotely due to limited access to technology. One BAME grassroots organisation relied heavily on telephone calls and where possible, utilised social networking platforms (WhatsApp and Facebook) as an interim to combat isolation among service users. The same VSO experienced a delay in setting up virtual social activities, instead turning their focus to addressing a range of other urgent needs exacerbated by the crisis. They adapted their employment support services to provide advice on the government furlough scheme and increased their unemployment support.

Older Asian women were among those experiencing increased levels of isolation due to loss of face-to-face activities and groups. A financial exclusion project worked in partnership across the voluntary sector to secure hardware and set up a virtual health and wellbeing group for older Pakistani women (Box 8.1).

Box 8.1: Online exercise class for Asian women

A project set up in a diverse inner-city district saw first-hand the negative impact of lockdown on older women in the Pakistani community:

'Naheed was typical, she missed the weekly group exercise sessions and seeing her friends. She was shielding due to severe asthma and was generally struggling through lack of mobility and social isolation. It was clear that what she needed most was to be exercising and to be around other people.' (Project coordinator)

Lots of legwork and determination were needed to enable nine women aged over 50 to get online for their first Zoom wellbeing group in October 2020. It became a mission to get women like Naheed online but there were considerable barriers: they needed hardware to access the technology, lacked digital skills and had language barriers as well as low levels of confidence. The message from the organisation was clear: "Don't wait for the perfect conditions or until everyone is ready; seize the moment and get people online now" (project coordinator). Free hardware was sourced through collaboration and good partnership working across the voluntary sector. No formal IT training was given but the younger generation within families were asked to provide help and the women were encouraged to support one another.

In response to the pandemic, partnership working across Sheffield was supported by a network of community 'hubs'. A BAME grassroots organisation acknowledged that they were already 'networked very well' with other BAME providers in Sheffield but joining the 'hubs' extended their network. The same representative explained that post-pandemic, they were being listened to more. Greater collaboration within the voluntary sector meant organisations such as theirs felt less 'isolated' and more 'supported', and the pandemic gave wider recognition to BAME groups among the public sector (BAME grassroots organisation). Similarly, another VSO said they are now more frequently asked to collaborate: "it's actually got us back on the agenda … my predecessor, she said … I could never even find the door to knock on much less get beyond the door to have these conversations" (BAME mental health charity). In response to the pandemic, thos charity became the community hub for the African and Caribbean community in Sheffield, a population which is very geographically dispersed across the city. They collaborated with two smaller BAME-led VSOs with the aim of trying to access additional resources and to support their work around suicide prevention, which had become more important since the pandemic began. They began coordinating the Sheffield Fraternal of Black Majority Churches, which has a reach of over 1,000 African Caribbean people. Through the churches, they connected with members to increase the uptake of COVID-19 vaccinations. They also accessed funding to recruit a communications officer to combat misinformation and improve the accessibility of information to different communities. At the same time, a communications group was established across the voluntary sector and public health in Sheffield which enabled information sharing. Elsewhere, one VSO with a focus on promoting health and wellbeing worked with Sheffield's Community Contact Tracing (CCT) project to deliver 'COVID-19 confidence sessions', which were supported by the local authority. The VSO made funding available to BAME groups in areas of high deprivation to deliver consistent messaging through 'COVID-19 champions' who were volunteers that were recruited and trained to support this activity.

Case Study 2: Salford

Salford is a city in the metropolitan borough of Greater Manchester and has a population of approximately 245,600. Around 14 per cent of Salford's population is from BAME groups. The Salford voluntary sector has a well-developed 'voice and influence' model. Central to this model is an infrastructure organisation that supports and values VSOs, and dedicated funding (Coule et al, 2018). In particular, the aim of this model is for the voluntary sector to be seen by the public sector as a trusted voice and collaborative partner for reaching so-called 'hard-to-reach' communities. During the pandemic, the infrastructure organisation facilitated BAME-led VSOs to raise the alarm concerning the needs of local BAME communities:

> 'What the [voluntary sector] can do is, to talk to their communities in a way that public sector organisations can't, so the trust is built. A message coming from them carries a lot more weight [than from someone outside of the community] ... to reach into those families and communities has to be via those organisations or with those organisations.' (VSO stakeholder)

Several BAME-led VSOs played a pivotal role during lockdown in relation to the translation and communication of messages concerning how to stay safe and workplace rights. These organisations translated key messages, using their contacts and networks within the communities most at risk.

These messages helped people to overcome "fear for their rights" and a scepticism towards "communication from officialdom" (local infrastructure organisation employee).

Digital exclusion made reaching service users challenging during lockdown. One VSO explained how the Black African community they served typically lacked access to digital technology or were older and not comfortable using technology or social media. In response, they arranged socially distanced meetings in public. However, this was not a straightforward solution in a tight-knit community where "everyone knows everyone" (Black African charity) and where the problems could be highly personal, involving finances, food insecurity and domestic violence. Other pre-existing issues exacerbated among this community related to the shift to 'home schooling' (Box 8.2), putting further strain on the ability of parents to pay electricity bills, and fund IT equipment: "Parents are complaining that they won't be able to keep the kid online because the electricity bill is so high for them to pay. For those that don't have IT like laptop or computer – where do they get that equipment from?" (Black African charity employee).

Box 8.2: Supporting parents and children during 'home schooling'

Following the suspension of their 'homework club', which was delivered face-to-face before the first lockdown, a charity which supports African asylum seekers helped 55 children by printing out schoolwork and posting it to families who either could not afford to print or lacked the means due to the closure of public libraries.

Many beneficiaries lived in areas of high deprivation which, along with language difficulties and digital barriers, impacted parents' ability to help their children with their homework. In addition, staff raised the issue of online safety for children who were studying at home due to the pandemic. The charity introduced training for parents during lockdown on how to protect their children from online predators and what to look out for.

The homework club works towards addressing some of the cultural and economic barriers facing African asylum seekers. Charity staff planned to revert back to face-to-face delivery when possible, but they predicted that the requirement to social distance would mean working in smaller groups, resulting in more volunteers who would need to be trained in safeguarding, and the need for more financial resources.

VSOs also worked to tackle health and social inequalities in Salford by devising innovative methods and schemes to limit the spread of COVID-19. A Yemeni community charity sourced and purchased radios to transmit prayers for the local Muslim community during the religious festival, Eid.

Their aim was to reduce COVID-19 transmissions in mosques, which posed a significant risk during this period. The charity identified a radio that enabled broadcasts of prayers and religious celebrations in the community. A local infrastructure organisation helped the charity secure funds to purchase the radios which were offered at a discounted price by an organisation in Bradford. By enabling the Muslim community to feel more connected, the charity increased their impact by supporting around 100 families and minimising the risk of COVID-19 transmission.

Another BAME-led VSO set up online activities to support the emotional and mental health of lesbian, gay, bisexual, trans, intersex and queer (LGBTIQ) people. This African grassroots charity supports approximately 500 LGBTIQ people of African heritage and other ethnic minority groups in Salford. In response to the pandemic, their volunteers ran virtual wellbeing activities to help members stay positive and feel supported. As with the Yemeni community charity, this charity also worked with their local infrastructure organisation to secure additional funding during the pandemic. They purchased essential goods including food provisions, household items and phone credit to improve both the physical and mental wellbeing of service users.

Case Study 3: Ealing

With over 352,000 residents, Ealing is one of the most populous London boroughs and over half (54 per cent) of Ealing's population belong to BAME groups. At the start of the COVID-19 pandemic, there was already a sense that many VSOs in the borough were stretched beyond capacity, with many struggling to obtain core funding as well as grants or contracts for specific services. This was in part attributed to the prevalence of large national charities who, according to one BAME-led information and advice provider, 'have a monopoly in the area', with many small organisations being 'squeezed out' of consortiums that were formed to deliver commissioned services. This issue was particularly acute for Ealing's BAME-led organisations, most of whom are small and rely on significant input from volunteers.

Despite the challenges, and in the face of rising need and demand for support, Ealing's BAME-led organisations responded swiftly and effectively following the outbreak of COVID-19 and lockdown. They were able to adapt their provision to provide targeted interventions such as telephone befriending services, delivery of food and medicine to the most vulnerable and support to parents through assisting children and young people to access and complete schoolwork. VSOs also provided information, advice and guidance on issues such as housing and organising burials. Providing reactive support brought additional benefits since VSOs were out in communities during the pandemic (delivering food) and were able to identify wider needs such as the poor housing conditions people were living in, which included people in unsuitable or overcrowded accommodation.

Staff and volunteers who speak different languages were able to help clients with little or no English access key public services, helping to "meet needs that can't be met elsewhere" (VSO supporting Black African immigrants). Language skills meant BAME-led VSOs played a pivotal role in communicating government messages about COVID-19. This was made possible because they are trusted and seen as being well-informed and therefore could correct misinformation and promote 'myth busting'. They were also able translate public health messages into many languages and into more accessible messaging. Once they had translated the information, they had the connections to get messages out quickly. One VSO that supports Black African refugees set up a WhatsApp group and a Freephone number to get advice out to their clients, many of whom were shielding. A BAME umbrella organisation sent out SMS and WhatsApp messages to more than 600 service users in multiple languages with the aim of countering conspiracy theories and correcting misinformation about COVID-19, including cures (Box 8.3).

Box 8.3: The importance of understanding culture

A BAME umbrella organisation that worked with people from a wide range of communities including Syrians, Somalians, Nepalese, Afghans and different Sikh communities understood the importance of cultural background. By taking the time to get to know and understand the different people and groups that came to them for support, they were able to respond appropriately to needs as they arose during the pandemic. For example, they gained insights into how misinformation about COVID-19 was being transmitted and therefore how best to get accurate information out to communities: "A lot of people come from cultures where information travels fast, as do fears" (staff member).

In one case, they found that some of their Syrian service users were not leaving the house during the early days of the pandemic. Through careful engagement, they learnt that this was because they had experienced chemical warfare and so when they heard that COVID-19 was 'in the air' they assumed it came with the same risks.

BAME-led VSOs felt their work had been more visible during the pandemic and, perhaps, better understood by the public sector and larger mainstream VSOs: "During COVID we were recognised [for] our contribution. With funding, we have to be recognised. With representation, we have to be recognised" (VSO supporting Black African refugees). Moving forward, the same organisation hoped this would mean they would be invited to become more centrally involved in the design and delivery of services from the very beginning, saying "ethnic minority groups must be able to lead on the whole piece". While they felt their work had gained recognition, they need funding to follow if real progress is to be made during the recovery from the pandemic.

Discussion and conclusion

This chapter has presented evidence surrounding the value and contribution of BAME-led organisations during the COVID-19 pandemic to support the needs of diverse and vulnerable communities. Their response was fast and flexible, demonstrating high levels of 'resilience' through their *absorptive* and *adaptive* capacity (Dayson et al, 2021a). This was evident in how they responded to the shock of lockdown by staying open and present in communities when many other types of organisations shut down, and then, in how they adjusted their provision and developed innovative ways to provide support as the pandemic progressed. While VSOs in general are shown to have done this in one form or another (Dayson et al, 2021b), the role played by BAME-led VSOs was distinctive in a number of ways.

BAME-led organisations were able to reach communities and undertake activities that were beyond the scope of the wider health and care system. They were uniquely placed to reach BAME people and to address the pressing needs within some of the hardest-hit communities across Britain. With the pandemic compounding inequalities further, even greater pressure has been put on BAME groups who were already at higher risk of poverty (JRF, 2021). Across the three place-based case studies presented, one of the most important roles fulfilled by BAME-led VSOs was the communication of public health messages relating to the pandemic, supplementing the work of mainstream health and care providers. VSOs supporting BAME communities were better equipped than parts of the public sector and mainstream VSOs to translate communications published by the UK government into different languages, to ensure that important messages were reaching non-English-speaking people.

Cultural awareness and understanding of BAME communities was vital for combating misinformation relating to the vaccine and transmission of COVID-19. Between December 2020 and January 2021, lower COVID-19 vaccination rates were found among ethnic minority groups in the UK, with vaccine hesitancy being highest among Black, Bangladeshi and Pakistani populations compared to people of White ethnicity (Razi et al, 2021). The spread of misinformation regarding the vaccine is said to have played a significant role in vaccine hesitancy. Wider evidence suggests that some ethnic groups were subjected to rumours that they were 'being targeted to test the vaccine, or the vaccine was being used as a way to harm them' (Lockyer et al, 2021, p 7). Improving the vaccine take-up among BAME groups continues to be high on the agenda across the UK, an issue that BAME-led VSOs in Sheffield, Salford and Ealing have been working on.

The innovative ways in which organisations strived to try and overcome these issues is evident through the examples provided in Sheffield where additional funding has been accessed to support the CCT project and for one BAME-led VSO to establish a communications role. In Salford and Ealing, there was recognition that messages conveyed by BAME-led organisations can carry more weight and reach their intended audience more effectively. These findings suggest that BAME-led VSOs are more trusted within BAME communities. Their cultural understanding and awareness mean they are also best placed to know what the most effective communication mechanisms are.

With opportunities for face-to-face communication severely restricted, BAME communities in Sheffield and Ealing were contacted through social networking platforms such as WhatsApp, which appeared to be more accessible than other forms of digital communication. Such platforms assisted in conveying important messages and addressing misinformation, and in combating feelings of isolation, especially among those who were otherwise excluded. Effective and meaningful digital communication was at the heart of keeping those who were considered harder to reach informed and connected.

Some BAME-led VSOs reported feeling more recognised and supported by the public sector during the pandemic. These findings reveal a distinctiveness surrounding the type of targeted provision that BAME-led organisations offer and the value that they add. Macmillan (2013, p 39) explains that when investigating the distinctive qualities and contributions of what he terms 'the third sector', part of this is about discovering what is 'special' as well as why 'specialness' matters. Distinctiveness within the voluntary sector may arise through specific values which when enacted may differ to those of other sectors. During 'difficult times', distinctiveness can become strategically more important 'because it may help third sector organisations in the increased competition to sustain and secure otherwise constrained resources' (Macmillan, 2013, p 45).

Through their response to the pandemic, BAME-led VSOs have been successful in proving their distinctiveness from other parts of the sector, demonstrating that they can be 'better than comparable entities, and worthy of preservation or increased attention and resource' (Macmillan, 2013, p 51). It has been suggested that smaller VSOs lack clarity over their role in the recovery from the pandemic because future funding is so precarious (Dayson et al, 2021b). In recognition of their unique position, small amounts of specific funding have been made available to BAME-led VSOs to support them in countering the negative impacts of the pandemic, but this is mostly short term and has been against a backdrop of funding losses over the last ten years (Marmot et al, 2020b). The challenge will therefore not necessarily be about how BAME-led organisations maintain their distinctiveness and uniqueness beyond the crisis but rather, how to ensure they continue to be valued, particularly by the health and care system. This will largely be reliant upon effective, cross-sectoral collaboration to ensure that those who were seldom heard prior to the pandemic can remain a primary concern moving forwards.

Acknowledgements

We are grateful to the valuable contributions made by Sofeena Aslam at SOAR and colleagues at 'Age Better in Sheffield', and to Leila Baker and Katie Turner who collected and analysed data for the Ealing case study.

References

Age Friendly Sheffield (2020) 'Digital exclusion in multi-generational households – a story of dedication and empowerment', [online], Available from: //agefriendlysheffield.org.uk/news-and-blogs/digital-exclusion-in-multi-generational-households-a-story-of-dedication-and-empowerment/ [Accessed 25 February 2022].

Ayoubkhani, D., Nafilyan, V., White, C., Goldblatt, P., Gaughan, C., Blackwell, L., Rogers, N., Banerjee, A., Khunti, K., Glickman, M., Humberstone, B. and Diamond, I. (2020) 'Ethnic-minority groups in England and Wales – factors associated with the size and timing of elevated COVID-19 mortality: a retrospective cohort study linking census and death records', *International Journal of Epidemiology*, 49(6): 1951–62.

Coule, T., Patmore, B. and Bennett, E. (2018) *The Value of Small: In-Depth Research into the Distinctive Contribution, Value and Experiences of Small and Medium-Sized Charities in Salford*, Sheffield: Sheffield Hallam University.

Dayson, C. and Woodward, A. (2021) *Capacity through Crisis: The Role and Contribution of the VCSE Sector in Sheffield during the COVID-19 Pandemic*, Sheffield: Sheffield Hallam University.

Dayson, C., Bimpson, E., Ellis Paine, A., Gilbertson, J. and Kara, H. (2021a) 'The "resilience" of community organisations during the COVID-19 pandemic: absorptive, adaptive and transformational capacity during a crisis response', *Voluntary Sector Review*, 12(2): 295–304.

Dayson, C., Baker, L., Rees, J., Bennett, E., Patmore, B., Turner, K. and Terry, V. (2021b) *The 'Value of Small' in a Big Crisis: The Distinctive Contribution, Value and Experiences of Smaller Charities in England and Wales during the COVID 19 Pandemic*, Sheffield: Sheffield Hallam University.

Haque, Z., Becares, L. and Treloar, N. (2021) *Over-Exposed and Under-Protected: The Devastating Impact of COVID-19 on Black and Minority Ethnic Communities in Great Britain*, [online], Available from: www.runnymedetrust.org/uploads/Runnymede%20Covid19%20Survey%20report%20v3.pdf [Accessed 25 February 2022].

Joseph Rowntree Foundation (JRF) (2021) *UK Poverty: 2020/21 The Leading Independent Report*, [online], Available from: www.jrf.org.uk/report/uk-poverty-2020-21 [Accessed 25 February 2022].

Lingayah, S., Wrixton, K. and Hulbert, M. (2020) *Home Truths: Undoing Racism and Delivering Real Diversity in the Charity Sector*, [online], Available from: www.tnlcommunityfund.org.uk/media/insights/documents/ACEVO_Voice4Change_home_truths_report_v1.pdf [Accessed 25 February 2022].

Lockyer, B., Islam, S., Rahman, A., Dickerson, J., Pickett, K., Sheldon, T., Wright, J., McEachan, R. and Sheard, L. (2021) 'Understanding COVID-19 misinformation and vaccine hesitancy in context: findings from a qualitative study involving citizens in Bradford, UK', *Health Expectations*, 24(4): 1159–68.

Macmillan, R. (2013) '"Distinction" in the third sector', *Voluntary Sector Review*, 4(1): 39–54.

Marmot, M., Allen, J., Goldblatt, P., Herd, E. and Morrison, J. (2020a) *Build Back Fairer: The COVID-19 Marmot Review. The Pandemic, Socioeconomic and Health Inequalities in England*, [online], Available from: www.health.org.uk/sites/default/files/2020-12/Build-back-fairer--Exec-summary.pdf [Accessed 25 February 2022].

Marmot, M., Allen, J., Boyce, T., Goldblatt, P. and Morrison, J. (2020b) *Health Equity in England: The Marmot Review 10 Years On*, [online], Available from: www.instituteofhealthequity.org/resources-reports/marmot-review-10-years-on/the-marmot-review-10-years-on-full-report.pdf [Accessed 25 February 2022].

Mathers, A., Richardson, J., Vincent, S., Chambers J. and Stone, E. (2020) *Good Things Foundation COVID-19 Response Report*, [online], Available from: www.goodthingsfoundation.org/insights/covid-19-response-report/ [Accessed 25 February 2022].

Murray, K. (2020) *Impact of COVID-19 on the BAME Community and Voluntary Sector: Final Report of the Research Conducted between 19 March and 4 April 2020*, [online], Available from: www.ubele.org/publications [Accessed 25 February 2022].

Public Health England (2020a) *Beyond the Data: Understanding the Impact of COVID-19 on BAME Groups*, [online], Available from: //assets.publishing.service.gov.uk/government/uploads/system/uploads/attachment_data/file/892376/COVID_stakeholder_engagement_synthesis_beyond_the_data.pdf [Accessed 25 February 2022].

Public Health England (2020b) *Disparities in the Risk and Outcomes of COVID-19*, [online], Available from: //assets.publishing.service.gov.uk/government/uploads/system/uploads/attachment_data/file/908434/Disparities_in_the_risk_and_outcomes_of_COVID_August_2020_update.pdf [Accessed 25 February 2022].

Razai, M. S., Osama, T., McKechnie, D. G. J., Majeed, A. (2021) 'Covid-19 vaccine hesitancy among ethnic minority groups' *BMJ*, 372: n513.

Wilson, S., Bilbrough, A.C. and Chahal, K. (2021) *Community-Based Responses to Covid-19 in Birmingham: Insights and Experiences*, Birmingham: Birmingham City University.

9

The impact of the COVID-19 pandemic on advocacy work of voluntary sector organisations in Wales

Elizabeth Cookingham Bailey, E. Katharina Sarter and Vita Terry

Introduction

Preliminary research shows that the pandemic has worsened inequalities for the most precarious, vulnerable and marginalised members of society (British Academy, 2021). Among some of those disproportionately impacted by the COVID-19 pandemic in the UK are members of the Black, Asian and Minority Ethnic (BAME) community (Bhatia, 2020). The pandemic has increased social, economic and health inequalities for this group, particularly for those with linguistic barriers (Otu et al, 2020). The additional impact on minority and migrant women in specific in terms of accessing public services during the pandemic has also been substantial (Germain and Yong, 2020). This exacerbates the difficulties these groups already face in accessing public services.

Voluntary sector organisations (VSOs) play a vital role in advocating for these groups to access better services, and where needed, acting as alternative sources of provision (Mayblin and James, 2019). Given these key roles, this project sought to determine how the advocacy work of voluntary sector groups was impacted by the pandemic. This focused particularly on VSO work on behalf of marginalised groups, particularly refugees and asylum seekers, as well as targeted work with the BAME community. More specifically, this study analysed the impact of the pandemic and the aligned government restrictions which limited the ability of VSOs to meet users in person and provide support services. This study focused on advocacy for marginalised groups in the Welsh voluntary sector, highlighting the experiences of VSOs working in a devolved nation.

Understanding advocacy

There are a variety of ways of understanding the advocacy functions of VSOs working with marginalised groups. One of the key roles of small and medium-sized VSOs is *individual advocacy*, helping individuals to secure their rights and entitlements from statutory agencies (Henderson and Pochin, 2001). It may also involve *community advocacy*, or *community development* work, which focuses on a common issue within a community (Henderson and Pochin, 2001). These can both feed into *political advocacy*, which highlights the views of individuals and communities for governments (Marwell, 2004; Almog-Bar and Schmid, 2014). Many organisations may not define individual and community advocacy as part of the larger political environment. However, political advocacy is a means of directing the focus of decision makers towards key issues. VSOs that understand the nuances of the lived experience of groups can help identify the most important issues for policy makers to focus on (Mosley, 2010). Therefore, while advocacy is seeking to influence policy, it may not be seeking to achieve a specific political aim, such as lobbying activities (Visser, 2016); rather, it may be seeking to achieve broader social change which VSOs may not define as advocacy (Andrews and Edwards, 2004; Balassiano and Chandler, 2010; Shelia McKehnie Foundation, 2018). The types of change that particularly small charities can bring about are improving access to services and individual confidence, impacting policy, and ensuring it is put into practice, trialling new means of delivering services and shifting the discourse or narrative around an issue (IVAR, 2020). This research will seek to reinforce how VSOs define their advocacy activities and whether that has changed during COVID-19.

This also requires understanding the relationship of advocacy activities with other VSO activities. Delivery of key services for vulnerable groups is often linked to advocacy work (Cookingham Bailey, 2021), where organisations have developed *multi-purpose hybridity* (Minkoff, 2002; Hasenfeld and Gidron, 2005; Evers, 2020). This means that social movement and non-profit activities may be mixed in one organisation, particularly those serving BAME groups (Minkoff, 2002; Ware, 2013). One way to categorise the activities of these organisations is by the degree to which advocacy could be seen to be *core* or *peripheral* within an organisation (Child and Grønbjerg, 2007). This will depend on whether the advocacy work develops out of the day-to-day operations of the VSO or whether it is the specific aim of the organisation. The boundary between service-orientated and advocacy-orientated VSOs is therefore quite blurred (Fyall and McQuire, 2014; Cookingham Bailey, 2021). This research sought to further explore these links between service delivery and advocacy in VSOs working with vulnerable and marginalised groups with a variety of needs.

Traditionally, VSO advocacy activities in the political arena involved lobbying or campaigning activities, invitations to respond to consultations or sitting on government committees on relevant issues (Mosley, 2010). These functions have been discussed as more *formal* advocacy functions as opposed to those focused on the more *informal* functions around empowerment, community development and awareness raising (Cambridge and Williams, 2004). As part of this, these VSOs provide a platform for the voices of marginalised groups and empower them to engage in political activities (Cambridge and Williams, 2004; Almog-Bar and Schmid, 2014). This is determined by the degree to which VSOs are *insiders* who might receive government funding and/or have regular access to contribute to political debates (Fyall and McQuire, 2014). With insider groups, there is a concern around reliance on government funding and restrictions on the ability of VSOs to critique government actions (Arvidson et al, 2018). Alongside this, VSOs might also be *outsiders* who use more grassroots movement and public education to raise awareness (Fyall and McQuire, 2014). VSOs may end up using a mix of insider and outsider strategies which may depend on their area of focus (Andrews and Edwards, 2004). To add to the existing literature in this area, this chapter explores the relationship between VSOs and state-based organisations during the pandemic. It aids understanding of how the pandemic impacted on VSO activities by focusing on the delivery of services for the state, engagement in political discussions and awareness raising activities with state-based organisations.

Providing marginalised individuals with a voice and means to access essential services are key components of advocacy work. One of the aspects of advocacy with individuals who might feel marginalised by state systems and functions is to build up trust (Cambridge and Williams, 2004; Cookingham Bailey, 2021) and social capital (Cookingham Bailey and Terry, 2021). This means building *trust between individuals* (for example, victims of domestic abuse and voluntary sector case workers) or *between groups* (for example, new migrant communities and the VSO). This is based on VSOs building *legitimacy* in these communities (Suchman, 1995), which is often about setting themselves apart from state-based organisation (Buckingham, 2010). It is frequently also about VSOs being adaptable, flexible, holistic, adjusting services to the variety and complex needs of marginalised individuals (Cookingham Bailey and Terry, 2021). This was seen in the pandemic with VSOs working with refugees and asylum seekers, expanding services to include provision of basic necessities (for example, food, bedding), translation of official documents and regular mental health check-ins.

Early research on the pandemic has shown that VSOs, like all service bodies, had to innovate and engage with new digital technologies to reach vulnerable clients. Prior to the start of the pandemic, VSOs were introducing more technology into service delivery and advocacy work as a means of driving *organisational efficiency* and *improving the experience for service users* (IVAR, 2019). The pandemic has resulted in many VSOs engaging in these new technological forms of delivery to meet the needs of users while finding ways to ensure services remain inclusive for those with digital barriers (IVAR, 2021). Research has shown that digital exclusion has been a key issue among vulnerable members of society (Beaunoyer et al, 2020). This research sought to explore how VSOs shifted organisational activities to build trust and ensure inclusivity when face-to-face options were limited and digital options were increasingly the norm.

Methods

This study looked at how the pandemic impacted individual, community-level and larger political advocacy for marginalised groups. Additionally, it examined how the need for increased services and personal advocacy impacted the balance of activities. It addressed the following research questions:

- How did the daily activities change for those employed in the VSOs regarding the services they deliver?
- How did the VSOs' larger advocacy activities with statutory bodies, local governments and regional governments change because of the restrictions?
- How did the immediate needs of service users for informal advocacy impact on the capabilities of the VSO to engage in more formal political advocacy work?
- How did funding changes impact the organisational capacity for advocacy activities?

Five case studies were used to understand how service delivery activities and advocacy activities worked before the pandemic and have changed since. Cases were selected to cover a range of sub-areas within the advocacy sector which represented the core marginalised groups most impacted by the pandemic and the resulting lockdowns. VSOs that engaged in advocacy work with asylum seekers and refugees, survivors of domestic violence, homeless or vulnerably housed individuals, and/or BAME communities (focusing on work relating to young people, education, mental health and older people) were selected. Using the selection criteria, the cases were identified using three potential routes. First, using gatekeepers known to the researchers within the advocacy community and the larger voluntary sector of Wales. Second, based on recommendations from the Welsh Council for Voluntary Action, particularly identifying VSOs who were part of existing councils and committees working with the Welsh government. And third, using the charity registry for England and Wales.

VSO 1 was the largest organisation working across all of Wales on advocacy for older people. This included some work in the BAME community. VSO 2 was a medium to large organisation working primarily across south and west Wales on domestic abuse, primarily within the BAME community. VSO 3 was a medium to large organisation working mostly in north and south Wales with BAME young people and their families. This included some work with older members of the community. VSO 4 was a small community centre serving the BAME and Roma communities with strong youth work programmes based in south-east Wales. VSO 5 was a small organisation serving asylum seekers and refugees also based in south-east Wales. The variety in size, and where possible geography, allowed for a richer picture around collaborations with different levels of governments.

Six semi-structured interviews were conducted with nine individuals over virtual platforms and recorded with consent of interviewees. Respondents were also sent information about the project and consent forms prior to the interviews. This project was reviewed and approved by the Faculty of Creative Industries ethics champions at the University of South Wales. Respondents and case study organisations will remain anonymous. Where possible, interviews were conducted with multiple VSO employees with no more than two respondents and two interviewers. With VSOs 3 and 5, only one member of the organisation was available. These interviews sought to get a sense of the structure, activities and scope of the VSOs. They also sought to see how the VSO interacted with other VSOs in the advocacy sector as well as with various statutory and political bodies. Then respondents were asked to discuss how aspects of the VSO, its work and the work of the staff changed because of COVID-19. Respondents were also asked to reflect on what could be learnt and taken forward from the pandemic for the future. The resulting interview transcripts were then coded thematically around responses to the core research questions.

In terms of limitations, the interviews were only conducted at one point in time during the pandemic (summer 2021), which provides a snapshot of that moment. Additionally, given the constraints of social distancing regulations, interviews were conducted online which means that some of the nuances of body language were lost as well as the opportunity to speak to respondents in their own context. Finally, as interviews were semi-structured, this allowed respondents flexibility in their responses, but also meant some divergence from the core topics under discussion, which required keeping a close eye to relevance in the analysis of the data.

Findings

Defining advocacy

To explore how advocacy activities changed, it was important to first determine how respondents understood advocacy. Multiple respondents noted that in work with marginalised groups, the day-to-day support activities led to identifying issues that fed into political advocacy at the governmental level. Respondents saw their roles as fighting for the rights of their clients, particularly around accessing statutory services, and in the longer term, empowering their clients to engage in political action themselves.

Respondents also noted the importance of engaging in preventative activities in the community to tackle key issues around domestic violence. This aligns to ideas of community advocacy, or as VSO 1 described it, 'group advocacy', where a common issue to a large group was taken on by the organisation. Multiple respondents noted that core to fighting for the rights of clients was highlighting the voices of marginalised groups, and sharing their experiences with local government and the larger Welsh government. In some cases, this was through consultations, or strategy meetings, that VSOs were invited to contribute to as experts in the experiences faced by their clients, particularly during COVID-19. The data on client issues collected by these VSOs was fed into advocacy networks and discussions about the formulation of policy.

To provide context to how their work changed during the pandemic, VSOs explained that their advocacy work was usually based around a mix of information sharing and awareness raising through networks and existing relationships, particularly with statutory bodies. VSOs 4 and 5 relied on their established networks to access and circulate information about issues impacting their service users which was challenging when statutory agencies were slow to respond during the pandemic. VSO 4 held a series of online forums during the pandemic bringing together community leaders and statutory organisations around a key issue such as health and education as an alternative way of reaching partners. This allowed groups to share concerns and highlight strategies for supporting service users through the pandemic. Multiple respondents noted that an important factor in successful advocacy working during the pandemic was sharing of experiences through networks of common practice within the advocacy sector.

Barriers to statutory services

VSOs repeatedly mentioned the barriers faced by their marginalised clients in accessing core services during the pandemic. VSOs 2 and 5 noted delays from the Home Office regarding decisions on asylum seeker cases and on housing. This meant that VSOs had to fill in many of the statutory gaps. The challenge was being able to access contacts within statutory organisations during the lockdowns: "You find this hard, much harder to access any service because everybody's you know ... you ring out some numbers and nobody answers, and it just doesn't go anywhere. Or you ring up and they say, Oh, he's working from home. I got contact in silence" (Respondent, VSO 5). This was particularly challenging where social distance requirements reduced the amount of direct contact and face-to-face advocacy. This was particularly important for VSOs that worked with migrants with language barriers. Language barriers also impacted on client ability to engage with digital alternatives for advocacy check-ins and signposting of resources. Multiple VSOs worked with client groups to provide videos and translated documents outlining government guidance around lockdowns and social distancing. These service users relied on trusted relationships with the VSOs to review documents.

Having VSOs that recognised the need to provide these alternatives was essential to building trust and buy-in for public health policies. VSOs 2 and 5 noted that loss of regular direct face-to-face contact meant clients were at greater risk of isolation, particularly among refugees and victims of domestic violence. Both VSOs had to continue to run some limited in-person support work to check in on vulnerable clients. However, VSOs 1, 3 and 4 were also concerned about the loss of face-to-face check-ins and structured activities for young and old client groups. Digital exclusion was a barrier for most groups that VSOs worked with, which compounded these issues. VSO 3 noted that among the client groups, young people and refugees were living in homes with a limited number of devices and poor Wi-Fi.

Changing ways of working

Within VSOs, ways of working changed because of COVID-19. The increased demands from clients, and the reduced number of volunteers owing to stay-at-home orders, meant that individual advocacy by all staff took prominence: "Everyone right from management, you know, to our support workers, everybody was working … most people are like managers became support workers as well, providing that support. Advice workers were support workers … the receptionist, you know, also became support workers" (Respondent, VSO 2).

The increase in individual advocacy and support for service delivery was alongside regular activities such as fundraising, organisation strategy, safeguarding and broader political advocacy activities. VSOs 1 and 2 were frequent contributors to advocacy networks and Welsh government policy meetings but they noted that the number of meetings had increased substantially during the pandemic. This was partially driven by the increased need to communicate the issues on the ground but also the ease of setting up online meetings. VSO 3 also noted being able to see more clients online in a day compared with pre-pandemic in person. This had benefits, but many VSOs still expressed concerns about the mental health of clients from online contact and the impact on the wellbeing of advocacy workers from the increased volume of client meetings.

Core to the success of political advocacy work of these VSOs seemed to be strong and open relationships with local governments, particularly in the south-east, and an active interest from the Welsh government in bringing specialists on marginalised issues to the policy table. Most of the VSOs relied to some degree on both local and Welsh government funding for their service and advocacy activities. VSO 1 noted that despite being funded by the Welsh government for their advocacy work, they still felt that they were able to maintain their independence and bring key evidence to the table to ensure social justice issues were dealt with: "where we need to, we do work, or we sometimes have to challenge" (Respondent 1, VSO 1). They felt this was possible owing to their long-standing relationship with the government and their role as an insider. However, they also felt they could do this with health boards and local authorities, where there was no official partnership, where they could use their legitimacy as an established VSO to engage in outsider strategies as well.

While the smaller and medium-sized VSOs noted concerns for the future and the general trends to greater precarity, they found that there were several funding opportunities available to them from the Welsh government during COVID-19. Primarily, the funding was to cover expenses related to service delivery during the pandemic, such as for personal protective equipment (PPE) or small amounts of money to cover food parcels. Additionally, funding was easy to obtain for white goods, bedding or other personal items to give to vulnerable individuals during the lockdowns. This reliable government funding was essential as other forms of charitable funding were quite mixed, with VSO 3 having an increase in local community donations owing to the crisis as compared with income losses in VSO 2 from fundraising events that were cancelled.

Learning and innovation from the pandemic

There were several challenges from the pandemic, but VSOs noted that there were significant benefits. The increased inclusion of VSOs of all sizes in both statutory organisation and governmental decision making was a positive. Most VSOs felt they were brought to the policy table more frequently throughout the pandemic to give views on issues impacting vulnerable groups. This strengthened the insider positions of VSOs 1 and 2 who were already in those discussions, but VSO 3 also found there was an increase in their participation in political advocacy. The smaller VSOs stated that the statutory sector "suddenly discovered we're out there" (respondent, VSO 5), which led to "recognition of our value" (respondent 2, VSO 4). Both VSOs noted that the benefits were owing to their extensive networks and "relational and organic approach" (respondent, VSO 5), which allowed them access to people they would not otherwise be able to reach. Many argued that the future of advocacy work might be smaller VSOs working closely together sharing information and forming networks to inform policy and statutory strategy.

Although many VSOs noted that technology was a barrier to various clients accessing services, it also provided them with opportunities for innovation and creative thinking. As groups got used to online meeting systems like Zoom, it provided new opportunities for organisations to share volunteers more widely across regions and to check in on clients. WhatsApp became an important communication tool for VSOs during the pandemic. It allowed clients to securely share documents with support workers allowing them to advocate on the client's behalf with other services. It also provided a tool for quickly sharing information among networks. VSO 3 set broadcast lists to pass on information quickly without compromising personal information of clients, which was a concern among the young people they worked with. Alongside advocating for government communications relating to public health to be available in a wider range of languages, VSO 3 also asked for social media compatible information about lockdowns and vaccines. This allowed VSOs to promote those materials as part of their function as trusted conduits of information to and from the government.

Discussion

The pandemic led to important changes in the daily operation of activities in the case study VSOs. The boundaries between service delivery and advocacy (Fyall and McQuire, 2014; Cookingham Bailey, 2021) became even more blurry. Many of the respondents noted the essential (and increased) importance of service delivery and informal advocacy to provide the evidence base for political-level advocacy, supporting Almog-Bar and Schmid (2014) on the relationships between these layers. Respondents defined their advocacy work prior, and during, COVID-19, around fighting for client rights and empowering them being a clear representation of individual advocacy (Henderson and Pochin, 2001). The pandemic strengthened the entanglement of service delivery and advocacy in these VSOs. The workload of staff leaned heavily towards support work owing to the increase in needs during the pandemic, but this better informed understanding of the issues to take forward with policy makers and statutory bodies. Funding opportunities increased during the pandemic around service delivery needs, which helped to balance the increase in activity in that area.

The insider roles of VSOs (Arvidson et al, 2018) in contributing to government consultation and committees were strengthened owing to demands for information on the impact of the pandemic on marginalised groups. It allowed smaller groups, who could not engage in those strategies prior to the pandemic, more access points, with decision makers reaching out and 'discovering' them. All the VSOs in the study increased usage of 'outsider', grassroots strategies (Fyall and McQuire, 2014), to educate both the larger community and public services about service gaps. The smaller VSOs noted the importance of both collaborative and relational working which relied on established social capital and trust with partners (Cambridge and Williams, 2004; Cookingham Bailey, 2021; Cookingham Bailey and Terry, 2021). The responses of VSOs seem to support the importance of small organisations working together as networks to achieve social change (Shelia McKehnie Foundation, 2018; IVAR, 2020).

Technology aided this, in line with work conducted by VSOs prior to and at the start of the pandemic (IVAR, 2020; 2021). It also reinforced concerns about digital exclusion of vulnerable groups (Beaunoyer et al, 2020). Video meetings allowed support workers to engage with a greater number of clients and more efficient allocation of volunteer resources based on need. Alongside this, messaging services (for example, WhatsApp) provided a way of sharing sensitive data securely and quickly to help meet client needs. However, in both cases this relied on existing trusted relationships between clients and support workers. VSOs also noted that with the most sensitive cases, there was no proper substitute for face-to-face meetings. Going forward, some degree of blended approach would also be essential with vulnerable groups with language and technological barriers, but also where issues can only be identified effectively with face-to-face meetings, such as domestic violence or mental health concerns.

There are several implications from this work and key learning points. For these VSOs, the pandemic reinforced the precarity both of marginalised groups and the organisations themselves. New technologies provided opportunities for greater connection but owing to gaps in client access, they cannot be the only tool used to reach vulnerable groups. Digital technology worked where there were established relationships of trust. This meant organisational responses were limited by staffing capacity with many staff taking on multiple roles to maintain some face-to-face contact and ensure the most vulnerable did not fall between the cracks. Once again, this highlighted the need for more funding for advocacy and support work.

VSOs noted that it was likely that the special funding set up during the pandemic would be short-lived, even though demand for services would remain high, leading to limited future resources. This will place continued importance on relational and collaborative approaches to working noted by the respondents, drawing on personal relationships and networks to access support for service users, owing to the complexity of needs of clients and resource limits of individual VSOs. The local networks provided an opportunity for VSOs to engage in outsider strategies and push for social change. Additionally, the profile of many smaller and medium-sized VSOs has been raised at the political level, increasing the number of insider organisations brought in for consultation. The challenge going forward will be for smaller VSOs to meet the time-consuming requirements of contributing regularly to political discussions given their organisational and financial constraints.

This study shows the value of VSOs to marginalised communities during the pandemic as they were seen as a trusted source of support and stability. VSOs continued to operate during the pandemic, and in many cases increased operations, while statutory partners restricted services. This support proved essential for vulnerable individuals in precarious situations where a break in service could be life-altering.

References

Almog-Bar, M. and Schmid, H. (2014) 'Advocacy activities of nonprofit human service organisations: a critical review', *Nonprofit and Voluntary Sector Review*, 43(1): 11–25.

Andrews, K.T. and Edwards, B. (2004) 'Advocacy organizations in the political process', *Annual Review of Sociology*, 30: 479–506.

Arvidson, M., Johansson, H. and Scaramuzzino, R. (2018) 'Advocacy compromised: how financial, organizational and institutional factors shape advocacy strategies of civil society organizations', *Voluntas*, 29(4): 844–56.

Balassiano, K. and Chandler, S.M. (2010) 'The emerging role of nonprofit associations in advocacy and public policy: trends, issues and prospects', *Nonprofit and Voluntary Sector Quarterly*, 39(5): 946–55.

Beaunoyer, E., Duprere, S. and Guitton, M.J. (2020) 'Covid-19 and digital inequalities: reciprocal impacts and mitigation strategies', *Computers in Human Behavior*, 111: 106424.

Bhatia, M. (2020) 'Covid-19 and BAME group in the United Kingdom', *International Journal of Community and Social Development*, 2(2): 269–72.

British Academy (2021) *The COVID Decade: Understanding the Long-Term Societal Impacts of COVID-19*, London: The British Academy.

Buckingham, H. (2010) *Hybridity, Diversity and the Division of Labour in the Third Sector: What Can We Learn from Homelessness Organisations in the UK?*, Birmingham: Third Sector Research Centre, University of Birmingham.

Cambridge, P. and Williams, L. (2004) 'Approaches to advocacy for refugees and asylum seekers: a development case study for a local support and advice service', *Journal of Refugee Studies*, 17(1): 97–113.

Child, C.D. and Grønbjerg, K.A. (2007) 'Nonprofit advocacy organizations: their characteristics and activities', *Social Science Quarterly*, 88(1): 259–81.

Cookingham Bailey, E. (2021) 'Advocacy and service delivery in the voluntary sector: exploring the history of voluntary sector activities for new minority and migrant groups in East London, 1970s–1990s', *Voluntas*, 32: 1408–18.

Cookingham Bailey, E. and Terry, V. (2021) *What about the Migrants? An Exploration of Organisational Change in an Asylum Seeker and Refugee Voluntary Sector Organisation* Social Policy Association Conference, University of Swansea, 18 August.

Evers, A. (2020) 'Third sector hybrid organisations: two different approaches', in D. Billis and C. Rochester (eds.) *Handbook on Hybrid Organisations*, Cheltenham: Edward Elgar Publishing.

Fyall, R. and McQuire, M. (2014) 'Advocating for policy change in nonprofit coalitions', *Nonprofit and Voluntary Sector Quarterly*, 44(6): 1274–91.

Germain, S. and Yong, A. (2020) 'COVID-19 highlighting inequalities in access to healthcare in England: a case study of ethnic minority and migrant women', *Feminist Legal Studies*, 28: 301–10.

Hasenfeld, Y. and Gidron, B. (2005) 'Understanding multi-purpose hybrid voluntary organizations: the contributions of theories on civil society, social movements and non-profit organizations', *Journal of Civil Society*, 1(2): 97–112.

Henderson, R. and Pochin, M. (2001) *A Right Result?: Advocacy, Justice and Empowerment*, Bristol: Policy Press.

IVAR (2019) *Start Somewhere: An Exploratory Study into Making Technology Imaginable and Usable for Small Voluntary Organisations*, London: Institute for Voluntary Action Research.

IVAR (2020) *Small Charities and Social Change*, London: Institute for Voluntary Action Research.

IVAR (2021) *Response to Change: How Small Voluntary Organisations Are Using Tech*, London: Institute for Voluntary Action Research.

Marwell, N.P. (2004) 'Privatizing the welfare state: nonprofit community-based organizations as political actors', *American Sociological Review*, 69: 265–91.

Mayblin, L. and James, P. (2019) 'Asylum and refugee support in the UK: civil society filling the gaps?', *Journal of Ethnic and Migration Studies*, 45(3): 375–94.

Minkoff, D.C. (2002) 'The emergence of hybrid organizational forms: combining identity-based service provision and political action', *Nonprofit and Voluntary Sector Quarterly*, 31(3): 377–401.

Mosley, J.E. (2010) 'Organizational resources and environmental incentives: understanding the policy advocacy involvement of human service nonprofits', *Social Science Review*, 84(1): 57–76.

Otu, A., Ahinkorah, B.O., Ameyaw, E.K., Seidu, A.-A. and Yaya, S. (2020) 'One country, two crises: what Covid-19 reveals about health inequalities among BAME communities in the United Kingdom and the sustainability of its health system?', *International Journal for Equity in Health*, 19: 189.

Shelia McKechnie Foundation (2018) *Social Power: How Civil Society Can 'Play Big' and Truly Create Change*, London: Shelia McKechnie Foundation.

Suchman, M.C. (1995) 'Managing legitimacy: strategic and institutional approaches', *The Academy of Management Review*, 20(3): 571–610.

Visser, A. (2016) 'Complex non-profit collaboration: a case study of the advocacy initiative', *Project Management Research and Practice*, 3: 5121.

Ware, P. (2013) *'Very Small, Very Quiet, a Whisper …' – Black and Minority Ethnic Groups: Voice and Influence*, Birmingham: Third Sector Research Centre, University of Birmingham.

10

Community ownership of physical assets in changing times: the context of opportunities in the pandemic

Carina Skropke

Introduction

Community buildings are woven into the fabric of British life. From community centres and village halls to sports facilities and community shops, it is hard to overstate their variety and function. And yet, the COVID-19 pandemic has fundamentally changed the context for the community organisations that own these physical assets. There are continuing uncertainties about how these assets can be used to benefit local communities (for instance, through facilitating the provision of services) as they might have done prior to the outbreak of COVID-19. Additionally, it is unclear how income streams will be generated in this context in order to cover the running costs of these facilities as well as the organisations owning them. New business models may be needed to account for the maintenance of the property and to meet community needs in the post-COVID-19 'new normal' (Langdale et al, 2021; Wilson et al, 2021). Recent research exploring the impacts of the pandemic on village halls in England (Archer and Skropke, 2021) highlights an emerging polarisation in financial positions and widespread loss of staff and volunteers, while also showing the central role these assets played on the frontline of the COVID-19 outbreak. But such research shows only a partial, and largely quantified, picture of effects, and little about how these organisations are responding in practice.

There have been several shocks in the past decades which have significantly changed the operational contexts for community organisations owning physical assets which are used for community purposes; however, none of these crises have changed the practical usage of these assets as drastically as the COVID-19 pandemic, changes which are important to capture. We are yet to see which roles community-owned assets may play in the remaking of the social and economic lives in their communities.

In this chapter, I explore the question of how organisations that own physical assets have responded in practice to the changed context in which they work, drawing from doctoral research on community ownership of physical assets and the processes of their maintenance physically and symbolically as assets during the major crisis of a pandemic – in particular, in case of not being able to use them when needed the most. The research concentrates on the immediate impact of the pandemic and related consequences on the organisations and explores the organisational perspectives. The chapter explores the opportunity context of these community organisations during the pandemic which is comprised of i) the material and non-material resources available to those organisations, for example financial income streams, skills and capacities in their communities, or networks and connections; ii) the organisations' ability to make use of the resources by discovering, activating and mobilising these; and iii) steering the usage of these to benefit their local communities and contribute to maintaining the organisations, their activities and the assets they own.

The chapter progresses as follows. Firstly, an introduction to community ownership of assets is offered, discussing the relevant policy context and definition applied in this chapter. After describing the study's methods, the impacts of the pandemic on community organisations owning physical assets and changes in the opportunity context will be delineated by exploring the increased dilemmas of these organisations owning and managing assets during the crisis, the resulting sentiment and perceptions by actors involved and highlighting the reassertion of the significance of communities in space caused by the pandemic. The chapter will conclude with an outlook for future research and looming difficulties organisations may face in the aftermath of the pandemic.

Community ownership: origins and definitions

Community ownership is not a new phenomenon in the UK, with a long-standing history rooted in the ideas of community and mutual aid (Wyler, 2009; Moore and McKee, 2012; 2014). Nonetheless, its political relevance has only recently re-emerged alongside increased academic interest. Since the commissioning of the 'Quirk Review' (Quirk et al, 2007), public discussions have flourished and political attention was given to legislative issues concerning the transfer, ownership and management of assets by community organisations, accompanied by academic investigations into the associated practices and processes of 'doing' community ownership. This research applies a definition of community-owned assets which describes physical structures, such as buildings, which are controlled by community groups comprised of local residents. Although the term 'ownership' may rather refer to a clearly defined legal status, the working definition covers organisations which are responsible for their 'owned' assets in several respects, such as financial and managerial.

Major cuts in public budgets have accelerated asset disposal by public bodies (Hancox, 2019). The changes in ownership have affected the price of accessing resources; privatisation of public spaces and a demand for residential and other forms of development outstrips supply and drives up prices for finite resources such as space. This is likely to increase the exclusion of communities from spaces they value (Bayliss, 2014; CMA, 2016). The recent rise in 'community ownership' is one response to this, as groups seek continued access to valued spaces and services in the face of broader privatisation processes.

It is assumed that community ownership of assets is a means to revive community empowerment, autonomous and participative decision making, addressing local needs, generation of wellbeing, community cohesion and compensating shrinking welfare service delivery (Quirk et al, 2007; Aiken et al, 2016; Hobson et al, 2019). Hence, there have been several attempts to systematically investigate the occurrence of community ownership. However, the lack of available data and the scattered nature and contexts of organisations engaged in ownership impede the generation of a comprehensive categorisation and analysis. The organisations owning physical assets manifest in various forms, pursuing various activities, and emerge in various socio-spatial contexts, making them distinctly heterogeneous.

Academic investigations have rarely challenged the largely positive political narrative on the transfer of physical property into community ownership, even though ownership, management and maintenance impose costs on communities and community organisations that they may not necessarily be able to meet. This positive portrayal is reflected in the use of the term 'asset' to describe the physical property which is transferred, irrespective of whether the property is or becomes a liability to the new owner depending on the capacities to use and maintain the property. This depends, in part, on wider socioeconomic and socio-material conditions in which the organisations are embedded and the opportunity context that this provides. The opportunity context for community organisations owning physical assets in this study is defined by the available resources in terms of material as well as non-material assets, and their ability to make use of them to benefit for their communities, to maintain the assets, the activities and organisations generally under prevailing contextual circumstances. The more resources available to the community organisations, the higher the likelihood of them being able to maintain and successfully run physical assets for and on behalf of communities. This is valid for financial and material resources as well as for immaterial resources such as acceptance and uptake. Legitimacy of the organisations and their actions depends on this acceptance and facilitates more opportunities to be realised and efficiently used. However, as the pandemic has impacted on the availability of human assets, skills and spaces to use for the provision of services and community activities and yet affected the financial and material resources available, the operational realities for organisations owning assets has fundamentally changed.

The income-generating potential of these organisations has been shown to vary from organisation to organisation. As Aiken et al (2011) emphasise, already prior to the pandemic, 'support is needed in developing the skills required to manage assets effectively'. This highlights the emerging trade-off between the required financial sustainability to maintain physical assets on the one hand and delivering community benefits on the other. The former increasingly forces organisations to generate income streams and incorporate economic activities into their core practices at the cost of community benefits.

Study methods

This chapter relates the findings from part of a larger PhD research investigating more broadly the issue of community ownership of physical assets and the impact of COVID-19. Here, I concentrate on the findings relating to the immediate impacts of and response to the pandemic by community organisations owning physical assets. In this research, an inductive approach is applied in order to analyse the gathered qualitative data from various sources. The data has mainly been acquired by conducting 18 semi-structured interviews with organisational representatives in nine different local manifestations of community organisations owning assets between October 2020 and April 2021. Because the pandemic restricted full access to these organisations and participants, the interviews are complemented by social media content as an additional source of information. In contrast to other qualitative methodologies, an inductive research approach does not begin with a certain theory or assumption, but rather with a certain research problem, and explores what emerges as being important in order to address this problem and related questions (Bitsch, 2005). Therefore, a focus of the analysis has been the impact of the pandemic on community organisations owning physical assets and their opportunity context.

The cases for this research were selected using national quantitative data applying a sampling criterion which maximised the diversity in cases; selection varies in relation to key indicators such as geographical location, rurality, urbanity, economic profile and type of asset. Community assets were affected differently by the pandemic and the related restrictions, ranging from full closure to only minor limitations in daily operations. The sample includes community centres, a village shop, sports and education facilities, adventure playground and outdoor spaces as well as an arts centre.

Analysis took the form of coding the qualitative interview data and has revealed many shared experiences and perceptions cutting across background characteristics. The findings presented here are of a preliminary nature as the research study continues. The quotes in the following sections are taken directly from the data produced during the research.

Findings

The pandemic forced communities to socially distance and prevent, if possible, interaction with individuals outside their own households. This has decisively changed the opportunity context for community organisations running physical assets for and on behalf of their communities, having been compelled to close buildings and community assets as the pandemic unfolded. The three dimensions of the opportunity context were under continuous change as the pandemic altered the available resources, the organisations' ability to discover and mobilise these, and to make use of these to benefit their communities under the prevailing conditions of the pandemic-related restrictions.

The physical assets being valued by communities are usually utilised to respond to local needs and for community activities. However, the pandemic took away this decisive characteristic which differentiates these organisations from other third sector and voluntary organisations: the availability and self-determined use of a physical asset which they own.

Whereas one participating community organisation, a football club, had to fully close and was not allowed any activities at the premises for the peak of the pandemic, another participating community, a village shop, was allowed to remain fully open as it was deemed as essential shopping and only had to adjust its internal layout and management. Other cases have been able to offer various activities, depending on the stage of the pandemic, for example during national lockdowns or multi-tiered restrictions, and their ownership of outdoor spaces.

Irrespective of the context and closure, the meaning and impact of social distancing measures on communities and in particular those organisations offering physical spaces for individuals to meet and provide a sense of community has been exceptional. Conflicts and difficulties which were present prior to COVID-19 have been amplified and threatened the previous achievements made by community groups stepping up and stepping in to respond to local needs and compensate for a lack of public service provision.

The following section will elaborate on how the pandemic impacted on the organisations' situations and their ability to maintain activities and support for their communities, and the emerging difficulties as the pandemic has amplified pre-existing challenges and caused a sharp rise in conflicts for communities.

Dilemmas in managing assets in the pandemic

One of the main trade-offs facing community organisations owning assets relates to on the one hand financial and legal responsibilities and on the other hand serving their communities and fulfilling their social mission. This trade-off has been magnified due to COVID-19 as lost income streams are threatening the existence of these organisations. Although important emergency funding has been provided by central government and foundations (Archer and Skropke, 2021), the organisations are not only responsible for their community, in some cases for staff as well, but also for their premises, which includes the maintenance and security of buildings being used. This poses additional challenges in terms of resources, necessitating alternative solutions and financial models. Rather than concentrating on their core aims and ambitions of providing support during times of crises, the organisations are now focusing internal capacity on securing funding. Organisational representatives involved at a strategic level have already begun to worry about the future, in particular raising concerns about how to continue business and social activities when furlough, business support and emergency funding streams end.

> 'I mean ... at the moment we have got the retention scheme and how that will look if it finishes obviously that's goings to put extra difficulties and strains ... And what we have put in place now is like an extra tier of senior managers and staff to look for opportunities for funding. We all need to help out with that now. It's so crucial, even if there is only a small award, it could make the difference between either keeping a member of staff or paying a bill.'

These conditions may require community organisations to increasingly integrate revenue-generating activities. They are seeking to increase commercial income from their operations. In contrast to non-owning organisations, however, the ability to financialise their physical assets enables the community organisations not only to secure their own funding base but also ensure a value-driven approach coupled with self-determined decision making on how and by whom their assets are being used.

> 'We have still been able to have a little bit of trading income. Actually, it has kind of made us look at the whole asset in a slightly different light. Like how can we hire this out to people who might want it? I mean, we're still doing our community work, but if you can hire the whole of the space out for the other times that we are not doing the bits we are already doing, then actually we have got quite a good model there. Like I said, we can't do everything. And if I'm bringing in the right companies that are offering activities for community as well. But they are going to run it and do it and we just hire them the space then, yay.'

Whereas social entrepreneurs or social businesses may engage in commercialised activities from the very beginning, the community organisations in this research have been urged subsequently to engage in income generation due to a lack of funding and the effects of the pandemic, and altered their opportunity context in so far as the lost income streams change the organisations' initial resource basis and consequently impacts on the internal ability to mobilise resources to benefit their local context.

> 'And at the end of the day, if a building becomes surplus to the requirements, then it's a potential income stream should we need it. And it is you know we have also sat at the back of it, if it would force us to sell, to finance what we are doing, then we will. It's just we haven't got in that position. Fingers crossed we won't get in that position.'

Although the combining of revenue generation and social mission is nothing new, there has not been extensive research on how the compulsion to engage in revenue-generating activities impacts on the balancing of social and financial interests and the community organisation's identity.

The changed resource basis has left the organisations in an unknown situation, which affected their usual way of working and their ability to steer their activities to benefit their communities. Actors involved were also affected by the pandemic on an individual level which left them with increasing worries.

Sentiment, perceptions, challenges

The general sentiment was characterised by a lack of confidence, and increased uncertainty and exhaustion caused by the increased workload and diminished resources.

Optimism for the near-term future was largely absent, but the interviewees emphasised their overarching aim to undertake all necessary actions for the community organisations to survive, maintaining access to their assets and supporting their communities with what is needed.

The interviews revealed a high level of uncertainty about the long-term picture, and even in short-term assessments of their organisation's future and planned developments.

> 'I think that at this point it is impossible to predict what the consequences in the long term are of the pandemic. And I think the first thing is, we know all this when things might get back to normal and my guess is that's going to be a long, long time away. ... but to go back to normal I just think it's impossible to predict and I just think that in terms of the economy, and in terms of jobs, in terms of health, in terms of changes in people's own lives. ... A lot of people

have been touched by this and I just think with trying to think like things through what we will do at the moment is far too early really.'

While interviewees gave the impression of hopelessness and difficulty in coping with prevailing uncertainties, the organisations have not failed to take action. A step-by-step mentality has helped the organisations to remain agile and be able to respond to new emerging needs caused by the pandemic. Although many have been forced to close their premises, some have made effective use of these to organise emergency responses; among other things, spaces have been used for storage to arrange food delivery systems to mitigate food poverty; others have used the spaces to prepare and provide online services to reach out to their communities and facilitate participation during lockdown and social distancing. This corroborates recent research showing the important role these assets played in marginalised communities in fighting COVID-19 (Archer and Skropke, 2021; Langdale et al, 2021). The new circumstances have required the staff and volunteers, as well as the structures the organisations are constituted through, to be more flexible. Although many of the organisations had become more formal in order to take on ownership of assets, the internal structures and processes have often remained less formal and facilitate solutions to be deployed quicker than other organisations, such as public bodies. "We can change quite quickly, and we can respond. And that might be something that we weren't anticipating doing but we're quite lucky that we got really great staff and that are keen to help."

The pandemic has also offered organisations owning their buildings to make use of the down time for internal refinement, to reflect more deeply on their work and to undertake refurbishment works. "In a way, I do think COVID's give us, it has given us the opportunity to assess everything as well." "When we went in when it was closed, I said to 'Let's get the hall decorated'. Because it's our only chance, we had such a high footfall during the week, we can't get a decorator in."

By discussing the current situation and actions being taken and general visions rather than directly asking for an assessment for the near- or long-term future, the interviewees were able to express plans and visions irrespective of the situation during national lockdowns and uncertainty this brought. All interviewees were convinced of their organisation's ability to survive irrespective of the emerging challenges. "We have got some long-term plans, we want to improve, we want to strive, we want to get forward together."

Despite an underlying confidence, the community organisations face increased challenges within their organisations and their communities. These range from emotional and mental health-related difficulties as individuals locally struggle with the isolation and a lack of clarity on how and when to expect the situation to get better, to more practical issues facing the organisations such as losing income streams, diminishing financial reserves and an increased workload. The opportunity context has been affected as the resources available have been reduced overnight and new innovative ways had to be developed to facilitate an optimal use of what is left. The organisations' ability to use the remaining resources and mobilise what is needed to benefit and support their communities has enabled them to continue engagement and the provision of support. However, the community organisations in this study face increasingly conflicting situations as limited resources cannot be stretched endlessly to meet the needs present and emerging in communities.

Community assets: reasserting the significance of communities 'in space' – the changed opportunity context

The pandemic has drastically changed the opportunity context for community organisations, not only in terms of the financial viability and urgent need for developing alternative business models, but also ongoing challenges in ensuring civil participation in generating and creating community space. The individuals involved in running the organisations studied have become increasingly worried about the ability to support and reinvigorate communities as lockdowns and social distancing measures have had far-reaching effects.

In contrast to the financial crisis of 2008–09 which caused a significant increase in community-owned assets, the pandemic may represent a greater existential threat. The financial crisis led to the decision of national government to implement austerity, decreasing public spending on welfare service provision which amplified political devolution processes. These in turn led to the third sector and civil society being increasingly asked to take over key local spaces.

The pandemic, however, represents an altogether different shock to the system. It has taken away the ability to collaboratively generate alternative spaces which may be used differently than privatised, for-profit spaces and has forced people to isolate, at least physically. Despite enforced separation, civil society and pre-existing social infrastructure have systematically been used to develop responses by compensating for the prohibited physical interaction via distanced activities, online tools and delivery models which have become very effective in responding remotely to social and economic issues.

During the peak of the pandemic, interviewees were increasingly worried about their ability to remake community, the strength of relations within and among community members and to retain the condition of their buildings as assets. One interviewee even questioned the sustainability of ownership altogether: "One will ever want a physical building again?"

Although the physical resources have been taken away from the organisations, these used their non-material resources of access to the local community and their networks to continue using any available opportunity to react to local needs. Despite being confronted with existential threats to valued community assets, the interviewees highlighted a wave of civic engagement and how the pandemic has reasserted the significance and relevance of these assets to people's lives. "So, appreciation [and] value has increased. You don't realise you're going to miss something till it's gone. You don't appreciate something's value until you haven't got it anymore. People. When I do see people just in the street, they can't wait for us to open again." This may be able to reverse the ongoing and amplified negative trend of decreasing voluntary engagement and diminishing available resources. Engagement has recently increased, at least for parts of the voluntary sector, again (ONS, 2017; NCVO, 2021).

> 'I think the feedback is, when the building was shut during COVID, people and community members would stop here and they were really concerned what is happening, you know is it closing down? That was, it gave you the opportunity to see the other side of it – that if it wasn't there and it wasn't in existence it would be missed.'

The increased awareness may be an opportunity which can be put to use by existing community organisations. By integrating civil engagement and solidarity which has formed, for example, via mutual aid groups, momentum may be kept and catalysed in the long term. However, it is as yet unclear how and in which ways community organisations can leverage this.

Discussion and conclusion

The proclamation of the so-called Freedom Day on 19 July 2021 meant that, for the foreseeable future at least, all distancing and containment measures were withdrawn in England. Therefore, community organisations were allowed to fully reopen their premises without any limitations. In so far as the situation continues, what remains unclear is the role community organisations owning physical assets will play in the remaking of social life. The recent pandemic-related developments, however, demonstrate that normality may be increasingly distant and suggest a long way from 'normality' for community organisations.

The pandemic has impacted on the organisations' situations in various ways, leaving them with rather pessimistic sentiments due to increased levels of uncertainty. In contrast to other organisations, those owning physical assets were left unsure when they could reopen, and how to maintain their assets during the period of closure and social distancing measures. This directly impacted on their confidence about future sustainability in the aftermath of the pandemic. Nonetheless, the organisations have managed to maintain connections to their local communities and tried to provide urgently needed support. By adopting increasing mixed financial and operational forms, sustainability may be assured. However, this may alter the organisations' identities and affect perceived legitimacy among local users and residents. In sum, all this affects the organisations' opportunity context: on the one hand, the available resources are reduced and are feared to further diminish, and on the other hand, the prevailing conditions under which organisations operate continuously change and affect their ability to make use of the available resources to benefit their communities and to maintain the buildings and activities.

Irrespective of the increasingly challenging circumstances for organisations owning physical assets, the meaning and importance of community spaces has become ever more apparent. The significance of community 'in space' has been reasserted through the pandemic, and the potential to remake our social and economic lives has become more urgent. The broad picture of community-owned assets pre-COVID-19 suggests that this model was more prevalent in affluent areas; however, localities equipped with fewer resources may be in greater need for support to remake social ties and infrastructure. It is not a level playing field for organisations owning assets – some will be in a stronger position than others depending on their context of available opportunities and their ability to use these.

Existing organisations and community assets will become increasingly pressurised by diminishing resources in combination with ever more increasing needs. The lack of social support infrastructure, funding schemes and economic and social prospects for residents may even worsen the prospects for these areas. Considering these threats to local social infrastructures, the government continues to support the idea of community ownership of assets (GOV UK, 2021). However, the nature of this support will further devolve responsibilities towards local communities and in turn amplify the pressures of an economic reality on these community organisations, as they need to raise money to continue to run the assets and their organisation after the acquisition. Physical assets and spaces will become available; the question now is how community ownership may be facilitated to meet the needs of the communities and contribute to the remaking of society in a post-COVID-19 world. This is a particular issue in areas where there are fewer community-owned assets, but where these may be needed the most. What is lacking is a support scheme to not only provide financial resources but also to strengthen communities and community organisations' ability to use these to benefit their local context. Also, the pandemic offers the opportunity as a major disruption of economic practices, predominant structures and perception of governmental responsibilities to sustainably change these towards actively shaping inclusive societies. If these opportunities, however, remain unused, the pressures on the finances of assets and the push to increasingly devote organisational capacities to securing funding and financial income streams may limit that space for this 'remaking' to take place.

The difficult reality of community-owned assets may need more attention than is acknowledged in current public discourse. Whereas community approaches are generally praised as solutions to urgent societal challenges, the government continues to support the idea of community-owned assets. However, the complexity these endeavours entail and the level of support beyond financial investment which is needed to facilitate successful addressing of existing and emerging social problems are still neglected. The opportunity context the community organisations encounter is not only defined by the (financial) resources available, but also by non-material resources such as volunteers, skills, capacities and motivations. In particular, the organisations' ability to identify and mobilise and make use of these resources to really benefit their communities is decisive in making a difference. This dimension, however, remains unattended, and it is yet to be seen how far the post-COVID-19 new normal may alter the prevailing conditions under which community organisations need to operate and cope with in order to maintain assets and their activities.

References

Aiken, M., Cairns, B., Taylor, M. and Moran, T. (2011) *Community Organisations Controlling Assets: A Better Understanding*, [online], Available from: //www.jrf.org.uk/report/community-organisations-controlling-assets-better-understanding [Accessed 20 May 2019].

Aiken, M., Taylor, M. and Moran, T. (2016) 'Always look a gift horse in the mouth: community organisations controlling assets', *VOLUNTAS: International Journal of Voluntary and Nonprofit Organizations*, 27(4): 1669–93.

Archer, T. and Skropke, C. (2021) *The Impact of Covid-19 on Village and Community Halls in England*, [online], Available from: //www4.shu.ac.uk/research/cresr/sites/shu.ac.uk/files/impact-of-covid-on-village-halls-final-report-2021.pdf [Accessed 2 September 2021].

Bayliss, K. (2014) 'The financialization of water. Review of radical political economics', *Review of Radical Political Economics*, 46(3): 292–307.

Bitsch, V. (2005) 'Qualitative research: A grounded theory example and evaluation criteria', *Journal of Agribusiness*, 23(245-2016-15096): 75–91.

CMA (2016) *Energy Market Investigation*, [online], Available from: //assets.publishing.service.gov.uk/media/5773de34e5274a0da3000113/final-report-energy-market-investigation.pdf [Accessed 30 September 2021].

GOV UK (2021) *Community Ownership Fund: Prospectus*, [online], Available from: www.gov.uk/government/publications/community-ownership-fund-prospectus/community-ownership-fund-prospectus [Accessed 21 September 2021].

Hancox, D. (2019) 'Great British sell-off: how desperate councils sold 1.9bn of public assets', [online], Available from: www.theguardian.com/cities/2019/mar/05/great-british-sell-off-how-desperate-councils-sold-91bn-of-public-assets [Accessed 19 September 2021].

Hobson, J., Lynch, K., Roberts, H. and Payne, B. (2019) 'Community ownership of local assets: conditions for sustainable success', *Journal of Rural Studies*, 65: 116–25.

Langdale, E., MacMillan, R., O'Flynn, L., Oxborrow, L. and Wilson, M. (2021) *Community Responses to COVID-19: Community Hubs as Social Infrastructure*, [online], Available from: //localtrust.org.uk/wp-content/uploads/2021/08/COVID-19-Briefing-13-FINAL-1.pdf [Accessed 14 September].

Moore, T. and McKee, K. (2012) 'Empowering local communities? An international review of community land trusts', *Housing Studies*, 27(2): 280–90.

Moore, T. and McKee, K. (2014) 'The ownership of assets by place-based community organisations: political rationales, geographies of social impact and future research agendas', *Social Policy and Society*, 13(4): 521–33.

NCVO (2021) *Latest Research Reveals Mixed Impact of Pandemic on Volunteering Numbers Despite More Positive Outlook, Increased Diversity and Rise of the Digital Volunteer*, [online], Available from: www.ncvo.org.uk/about-us/media-centre/press-releases/2810-latest-research-reveals-mixed-impact-of-pandemic-on-volunteering-numbers-despite-more-positive-outlook-increased-diversity-and-rise-of-the-digital-volunteer [Accessed 30 September 2021].

ONS (2017) *Billion Pound Loss in Volunteering Effort*, [online], Available from: www.ons.gov.uk/employmentandlabourmarket/peopleinwork/earningsandworkinghours/articles/billionpoundlossinvolunteeringeffort/2017-03-16#footnote_3 [Accessed 22 September 2021].

Quirk, B., Thake, S. and Robinson, A. (2007) Making Assets Work: The Quirk Review of Community Management and Ownership of Assets, [online], Available from: //library.uniteddiversity.coop/Community_Assets/Makingassetswork.pdf [Accessed 15 August 2021].

Wilson, M., McCabe, A., Paine, A.E. and Afridi, A. (2021) *Community Responses to COVID-19: Potential and Limits of Community Power in a Pandemic*, [online], Available from: //localtrust.org.uk/wp-content/uploads/2021/05/COVID-19-Briefing-12.pdf [Accessed 30 September 2021].

Wyler, S. (2009) *A History of Community Asset Ownership*, [online], Available from: www.communityplanning.net/pub-film/pdf/AHistoryofCommunityAssetOwnershipsmall.pdf [Accessed 27 March 2021].

11

The impact and effect of COVID-19 on BAME-led voluntary sector organisations: resilience and new ways of working

Karl Murray

Introduction and context

This chapter seeks to examine the impact and effect of COVID-19 on Black, Asian and Minority Ethnic (BAME)-led voluntary sector organisations (VSOs) in the UK during the first year of the pandemic.[1] The chapter focuses on frontline organisations providing services to the ethnic and cultural communities they serve. The need for this focus, and the research that has informed this chapter, sits within a context of long-standing concerns about the presence of BAME-led VSOs within the broader charity and community sector (V4CE, 2014). This has led Lingayah et al (2020) to argue that the over-representation of BAME frontline staff attests to the racism that exists more widely in society. It was not, as they put it, 'coincidental but a result of the ways in which racism is embedded in our socio-economic arrangements' (p 5). Between March and May 2020, for example, 36 per cent of critically ill COVID-19 patients were from an ethnic minority group, despite representing only 13 per cent of the general population (PHE, 2020a). This over-representation was most prominent in the healthcare profession, where BAME workers are disproportionately employed in frontline positions as nurses, porters and ancillary workers, which placed them in the eye of the pandemic storm. Evidence showed that Indian and Black African men are 150 per cent and 310 per cent respectively more likely to be working in frontline capacities than White British men, while Indian women are 25 per cent and Black African women 130 per cent more likely than White British women to work in these roles (Platt and Warwick, 2020).

To understand the impact of COVID-19 on BAME-led organisations is to understand the conditions that shape and inform discourse and practice in living within an environment that Hall (1984) described as 'exclusively concerned with forms of political domination or disadvantage, based on the exploitation of racial distinctions' (p 307). Here, the presence and construction of social formations, he argues, need to be understood not just in binary class reductionism but in 'how different racial and ethnic groups' have been 'inserted historically, and the relations which have tended to erode and transform, or to preserve these distinctions through time—not simply as residues and traces of previous modes, but as active structuring principles of the present organization of society' (p 341). This helps us to understand, to some degree, the concerns that were being expressed by BAME communities at the outset of the pandemic to explain the disproportionate impact the virus was having on those from a BAME background.

In order to better understand the concerns of the BAME communities, and therefore the impact on BAME-led organisations, we need to understand the concerns that gave rise to BAME-led organisations feeling left behind and the responses of funders, for example, to their plight. For this, the chapter will first need to look at some of the challenges and concerns at the start of the pandemic and responses to them, especially the role of BAME-led VSOs. However, ahead of this we will offer some insights as to the research approaches that have informed this chapter. Second, we will consider some of the direct impacts on programmes and the sustainability of BAME-led organisations, especially the role of funders during this period. Third, we consider implications for BAME-led organisations as we head towards recovery. Finally, we conclude with some thoughts on the implications for research and practice within the voluntary and community sector against the backdrop of Hall's (1984) observation of racism operating as an 'external function' in favour of those most benefiting, and one which speaks to the 'dominated' (that is, those most impacted on).

The research approaches

In the writing of this chapter, I draw specifically on a wide body of research that I have directly conducted as lead researcher and author or as part of a team (Murray, 2020a; Murray, 2020b; Nazroo et al, 2020; Murray and Rolston, 2020; Murray, 2020c; Murray, 2020d). All our research focused on the impact of COVID-19 on the voluntary sector though with a specific lens on BAME-led VSOs, which we define as those with 51 per cent of their management board/committees who are from BAME communities. The approaches consisted of a mix of qualitative and quantitative analyses, with an emphasis on qualitative interviews and dialogue. The approach included structured interviews, focus groups, an online survey conducted with Survey Monkey and a desk-based literature search.

Responses to the first Ubele Report (Murray, 2020a) came from 165 responding organisations, of which 137 were BAME-led; 87 respondents to the national mapping of BAME mental health services (Murray, 2020b); the deep dive follow-up report, which was based on 34 structured interviews with respondents who had taken part in the initial survey in April (Murray, 2020d); 53 structured one-to-one interviews conducted as part of the GLA rapid review, which looked at the nine protected characteristics under the Equality Act 2010 – though focused on the impact on individuals rather than voluntary sector organisations for primary materials (Murray and Rolston, 2020). At the heart of the research approach was the need to hear the voices of those directly impacted by the crisis, to hear from directors and trustees overseeing the leadership and development of their organisations as well as those receiving services as beneficiaries, policy makers and funders. The latter two groups of stakeholders involved a series of conversations, some of which were structured around presentations, while others were one-to-one interviews and discussions (that is, online round-table group discussions).

In obtaining views beyond London, especially as early conversations in the field highlighted the perception of a north–south divide we engaged with BAME-led organisations across the nine regions of England with a booster reflection from a follow-up work in Wales, where 100 responding organisations were engaged in a survey commissioned by the Ethnic minority Youth Support Team (EYST) into the impact of COVID-19 on BAME-led VSOs in Wales (Murray, 2020c).

Challenges and concerns

In April 2020, at the outset of the pandemic, a considerable number of 'impact' analyses, surveys and consultations were conducted, some of which focused on the implications for the voluntary sector (Women and Equalities Committee, 2020). Perhaps the most telling report was that produced by the Intensive Care National Audit and Research Centre (ICNARC) published in April 2020, which indicated that BAME cases within intensive care units were disproportionately high at 35 per cent compared with their general population rate of 14 per cent (ICNARC, 2020). The underlying concerns raised by the report reflected very much what had been suspected by BAME organisations through on-the-ground personal stories and tragedies that were then rife within BAME communities (Civil Society, 2020; Institute for Jewish Research, 2020).

Even when reports accounted for size and age structure of the population, mortality rates for deaths involving COVID-19, wider health and wellbeing, and economic circumstances, the proportionately higher death rates of those from BAME backgrounds was most pronounced in contrast to the majority White population (ONS, 2020; Platt and Warwick, 2020; PHE, 2020a; PHE, 2020b). Evidence pointed to differences across ethnic groups who were frontline or key workers (ONS, 2020). That is, workers from BAME groups were more likely to be working in at-risk occupations, such as front-facing ones, especially in the health and social care sector as outlined earlier and reinforced in reports produced in the first three months of the pandemic. The Independent SAGE Report (2020), for example, indicated that those from BAME backgrounds appeared to be at greater risk of hospitalisation due to long-standing health inequality concerns, spanning decades of neglect, which now placed BAME communities at greater risk of contracting and dying from COVID-19. Some of these factors, as Becaries and Nazroo (2020) indicated, included socioeconomic disadvantage, which characterised the lived experience of many BAME groups, and the high prevalence of chronic diseases coupled with the impact of long-standing racial inequalities meant that many frontline staff tending to the sick and elderly were BAME workers.

Thus, a challenge that confronted BAME-led VSOs was how to support those within their communities where demand was high and resources limited against a backdrop of precarity brought about by pre-existing socioeconomic inequalities that were worsened by the pandemic. This point was reinforced by Karl Wilding, the then CEO of NCVO, in giving evidence to the Digital, Culture, Media and Sport Committee, when he said BAME-led organisations "came into the crisis already in some trouble" (DCMSC, 2020).

Within the BAME-led VSO sector, it was felt that neither the NCVO nor the major funding bodies at the time truly understood the impact that the pandemic was having on BAME communities generally and, specifically on BAME-led organisations working in those communities. Small community-focused organisations, in particular, felt left behind as they were at even greater risk of losing revenues, as the vast majority are reliant on small contributions, usually derived from organising festivals and events, especially over the summer periods, such as fetes to keep the organisation going. Those who rented small halls or rooms were no longer able to access them and hence programmes had to cease. Existing funding programmes were always difficult to access, and this became even more of a challenge as the only other means through direct fundraising efforts were now impossible due to restrictions in place to curb the transmission of the virus.

Challenged by these wider, structural considerations and concerns, The Ubele Initiative – a catalyst and infrastructure organisation supporting the BAME sector regionally and nationally – conducted a series of 'community conversations' with BAME-led organisations to better understand the concerns and challenges those organisations were facing. Some of those concerns included inability to access funding, an inability to say farewell to loved ones according to tradition, low-paid employment, living in poor and cramped housing conditions, and, of course, psychological anxieties and trauma being experienced as a consequence of the disproportionate impact the virus was having within some communities (that is, African, Asian and Eastern European communities). Ubele commissioned a national survey to better understand the impact the COVID-19 pandemic was having on BAME-led organisations, the result of which was captured in the publication referred to as the 'Ubele Report' (Murray, 2020a). The key findings from the process indicated levels of concern about organisations' ability to meet demands, and sustainability beyond what was then seen as short-term, three-month measures, with a knock-on concern for service delivery in supporting those most at risk. Concerns were also raised about funders not prioritising BAME-led organisations for support, at a time when it seemed that there was an urgent need.

The strain and pressures on organisations echoed Macmillan's (2020) 'three-dimensional' observation more generally. Macmillan, in comparing the impact of the 2008 economic downturn and the accompanying austerity measures with the impact of COVID-19 on the voluntary sector (or third sector), observed that under the pandemic, VSOs were having to face a 'three-dimensional crisis of resourcing, operation and demand'. For BAME-led organisations, the long-standing structural inequalities that exist is a compounding additional factor.

Impact of COVID-19 on BAME-led VSOs

Structural racism

BAME-led organisations operate against and within a racialised environment and their location within the voluntary sector is equally prescribed by the same inequalities that confront BAME communities generally (Byrne et al, 2020), with the implication of ethnic inequalities manifesting themselves arising from the pandemic seen through exposure to infection and health risks, including mortality and exposure to loss of income. The point here overall is that the precarious socioeconomic conditions under which ethnic minority communities live places them at a particular vulnerability of great socioeconomic crisis and upheaval, such as with the COVID-19 pandemic (Byrne et al, 2020; Becaries and Nazroo, 2020). The pandemic merely brought them to the fore.

It wasn't until the early death counts and recorded cases showing the impact and implication for BAME communities (and by default those supporting them) that the concerns were taken seriously. For example, the number of Filipino nurses and BAME doctors contracting and dying from the virus was so pronounced that nationally, it could not be ignored. Kanlungan, a charity supporting the Filipino community, highlighted how workers from that community found themselves having to make choices between the possibility of contracting the virus as frontline workers and needing to feed their families if they did not work (Kanlungan, 2020). The report highlighted, among other things, that the 'hostile immigration environment'[2] deterred precarious migrants from seeking healthcare due to the fear of being reported to immigration authorities, which pushed migrants into temporary, overcrowded housing conditions that made social distancing impossible, and put them at risk of contracting and spreading the virus (p 14). Elsewhere, other research found that relative mortality had been particularly high for Black Africans and higher for all minority groups relative to the White UK majority, once age and location of residence were taken into account (Platt and Warwick, 2020), which had been linked to wider socioeconomic factors (MiNet, 2009).

Some communities faced reactions that were 'racially' directed. An example of this was found in Wales, where we conducted a review on the impact of COVID-19 on BAME communities, where we heard from BAME-led organisations expressing concerns about public reactions that 'targeted' and 'scapegoated' them for the rise and/or incidence of the virus. That is, they were either blamed for it (as in the case of the Chinese community) or they were the cause of the 'spread of the virus' due to multiple housing occupancy and multi-generational living conditions (that is, Asians). As a Chinese community-led organisation told us, 'Many local Chinese are in fear with the outbreak of Covid19, one reason being serious negative impact has been brought to the Chinese in general when it happened in China.' (Murray, 2020c, p 23).

Demand

The proliferation of 'mutual aid' groups that sprung up (Macmillan, 2020; Tierney and Mahtani, 2020; London Community Response, 2021) and 'neighbourhood networks' (Dayson et al, 2020) were expressions of communities coming together in the face of a common crisis, which increased demand for support. For example, in speaking about the impact of the 'volunteer army' that arose to support the NHS, Tierney and Mahtani (2020) proclaimed that 'It may be important to capitalise on the current national enthusiasm for volunteering, as the country has to deal with the social and economic aftermath of COVID-19' (p 4). The effect of the crisis was the creation of a new cadre of 'volunteering' opportunities that both met a national agenda for support of the health service and provided volunteers willing to drop food off and chat to those isolated and shielding ('mutual aid groups' as they became known). The coming together was both promising and encouraging, as many BAME-led organisations started to work more closely across cultures and communities in ways that they had not previously. The new demands created new opportunities, which is perhaps best summarised in the words of one respondent to the EYST report, who stated: 'Most of my work since lockdown has been organising food and other goods deliveries and ensuring that people are not struggling in isolation' (Murray, 2020c, p 23). Demand thus led to new initiatives, though with limited resources.

Respondents to the first survey (Murray, 2020a) found themselves having to consider what they will need against a backdrop of little to no financial income due to loss of their income-generating opportunities from dances, fetes, car boot sales and so on. In line with many other organisations in the voluntary sector, new approaches to service delivery became a challenge for some, while for others it was an opportunity (Murray, 2020d). For example, new demands led to new delivery approaches across a swathe of areas, including accessing digital platforms to conduct traditional business as well as establish new programmes; providing support to those self-isolating or shielding; ensuring medical supplies got through to those who most needed them; support to those struggling under lockdown, especially those suffering from abuse or family estrangement and mental health episodes; and help to those who had lost income due to the lockdown and were now destitute.

Resources

Of those organisations interviewed as part of the follow-up survey and deep dive interviews conducted four months after the first report (Murray, 2020d), many were able to access 'emergency funding opportunities' which enabled those on the cusp of closure to be sustained for up to 12 months. Support from funders was welcomed, especially as many were flexible and open to 'repurposing' possibilities which helped organisations immensely (that is, allowing organisations to use the grant to meet additional challenges brought about by the pandemic that it was not originally intended to deliver).

Despite this flexibility, funders, on the whole, were slow to respond to the specific funding needs of BAME-led organisations more widely (that is, those that were not already in receipt of funding prior to the pandemic lockdown). The amount of funding reaching the BAME sector had been poor, and the pandemic magnified the gap at a time when resources were needed to reach those communities adversely affected. It was not until September 2020 that funders started to focus funding specifically to BAME-led organisations. That is, asking applicants to indicate if they were led by and for BAME communities, LGBT+ communities, deaf and disabled people and/or women – the communities of interest deemed most affected by the pandemic (that is, more than 51 per cent of their leadership with lived experiences related to their beneficiaries). For example, Farah (2021) from City Bridge Trust indicated that they 'learnt that working with and supporting equity groups such as LGBT+ Consortium, Ubele Initiative, Women's Resource Centre, and Inclusion London' helped them to better understand the needs of 'marginalised groups' and their lack of 'access to funding they had historically been excluded from'. Further, the National Emergencies Trust (NET) – which arose partly out of the Grenfell disaster to support major disasters and crises – cited the work of #Charitysowhite

(2020) and the Ubele Report (2020a) as being influential in increasing 'support for those from hard hit BAME communities by setting aside additional, dedicated funds and identifying new distribution partners' (NET, 2020).

This recognition of the under-funding of BAME-led organisations resulted in NET partnering with Comic Relief, the internationally recognised grant and fundraising organisation, as a key distributor partner in providing funding directed to BAME communities through BAME-led VSOs. At the same time, the National Lottery Community Fund partnered with a number of organisations to pilot two targeted funding programmes to BAME-led VSOs, both of which were supported by Ubele, among others. The first was the COVID-19 Community-Led Organisations Recovery Scheme (CCLORS), and the second, the Phoenix Fund. These programmes not only provided financial support to organisations but additional capacity support to the successful applicants.

Implications for BAME-led VSOs going forward

Some of the organisations we engaged with during the course of the research found themselves in a precarious position, with some struggling to stay afloat, whether they adapted or not. The organisations engaged with during this period were either micro or small and not surprisingly, the majority did not have any reserves (68 per cent) and only 19 per cent had reserves covering three months (Murray, 2020a). They will need support in the form of capacity building, especially in recruiting and maintaining volunteers, particularly once the emergency funding comes to an end.

BAME-led VSOs have not fared particularly well over decades with respect to securing sustainable funding, which made the short-term emergency funding programmes that they were able to access all the more 'game changing'. Game changing because, as a result of the crisis and the impact the pandemic was having on BAME communities, this meant that the sector and the communities they serve were seen as genuine 'distributive partners' for the first time. We saw major funders piloting and 'partnering' with BAME-led organisations and supporting infrastructure organisations. We also witnessed the birth of new BAME-led 'funding' bodies such as Resourcing Racial Justice, the Majonzi Fund, Do it Now Now (Common Call) and the BAOBAB Foundation. We have seen a 'quiet' revolution where BAME communities have taken responsibility for their own fortunes with respect to sustainability going forward. Rome was not built in a day and so to rise from the ashes as the Phoenix Way personifies is a testimony to the resilience and compassion of the community and the sector more broadly (Ryan, 2021). Included within this new approach is the need to ensure capacity support development to enable organisations to thrive going forward (for example, the Ubele's Mali Enterprising Leadership (MEL) capacity support programme, Comic Relief and the CCLORS programme).

Small grassroots and BAME-led organisations can (and do) offer a trusted voice, particularly at a time of crisis, and are well placed to reflect community needs and aspirations. We know from the 'rapid review' conducted by Nazroo et al (2020) how crucial it was to hear the voices of those with protected characteristics, especially those feeling they have been neglected during the early phase of the pandemic (Murray and Rolston, 2020). The report echoed some long-held views within the voluntary sector more broadly that VSOs are more likely to know and have the trust of the communities they serve than large or generalist VSOs with no track record of working within those communities (Gardner, Abraham et al, 2021). Micro and small BAME-led organisations have long felt that their voices are not being heard, with large charities – White-led – speaking for them about their lived experiences. The articulation of those voices may not necessarily conform to a prescribed methodology or medium of expression, though able to rightly reflect the lived experiences that are so needed to support and inform knowledge, understanding and practice. Nazroo et al (2020), for example, argued that the voices from the communities through the work of micro and small VSOs are as valuable as are academic studies, which are seen as holding the gold standards in research. He argues that these organisations are closer to the ground than even large charitable organisations, as they are best able to engage and reflect the heartfelt concerns of those who are the subject of investigation. BAME-led organisations must therefore break through the glass ceiling to get their voices heard and in so doing, determine who is best able to capture and present those voices. It is the authenticity and clarity of those voices that will be critical.

Concluding remarks

Given the ebb and flow of the pandemic landscape, we may not be able to look too far ahead, but we can focus on the immediate needs of those affected and those supporting those affected or at greatest risk of being affected. As Macmillan (2020) and Dayson et al (2020) have illustrated, up and down the country communities came together to collaboratively work to the betterment of civil society, which should be continued as we move from crisis to recovery. Prior to the pandemic, many of the BAME-led charitable organisations had been or were in a state of flux, exemplified by lack of funding and lack of strategic direction and leadership (V4CE, 2014). The pandemic threw them into even more turmoil, with some finding themselves pivoting around changes to their operating model and new ways of working, while others struggled with the possibility of having to close. Many have come through partially stronger, some with raised and new vigour. Overall, the sector felt stronger during this phase, largely due to the attention and focus that it received as a result of the pandemic.

This is hopeful, but only if the attention and focus is maintained. The collaborative work over the last two years of the pandemic has demonstrated that there is a strong willingness to cooperate and meet the challenges head on and in a concerted and coordinated way (London Funders, 2021; London Community Response, 2021). We have found that BAME-led VSOs were clearly up to the challenge of having to consider doing things differently – maybe even better. As the Jamaican adage goes, 'as day follows night'; the crisis will pass and so there will be the desire for many to return to the status quo, to what life was like prior to the pandemic, potentially throwing BAME-led organisations back into a precarious position were there to be another crisis. And so, the lessons arising from the pandemic need to be learnt by those directly involved within the BAME sector as well as those external to it. This brings us back to Hall's observation of racism being not just an 'external function' but one that speaks to the 'dominated'. From this, those of us involved in research in the voluntary and community sector (and from a BAME background) should be more involved and engaged in articulating the voices of communities affected not only by the virus but more widely across a swathe of socioeconomic and political endeavours. Within the wider VSO networks, our absence and silence are noticeable with only a few exceptions.

Linked to this, there is a need for an effective BAME-led infrastructure platform or alliance to facilitate and advocate on behalf of the sector, an effective nationally recognised BAME-led infrastructure body that represents BAME-led organisations. There are currently many voices purporting to speak on behalf of the sector which has created a sense of fragmentation and disarray. It is therefore vital that we bolster and/or better coordinate some of those existing localised entities as this fragmentation is breeding mistrust which prevents the voices from being heard (Murray, 2020d).

Finally, the emergence of new BAME-led funders is to be welcomed, especially with regards to established and nationally recognised funders partnering with BAME-led infrastructure organisations. These are hopeful signs of things to come, and ones which offer researchers in the field of voluntary and community sector practice an opportunity to evaluate and assess the differences and effectiveness of these new approaches.

Notes

[1] The widespread use of the acronym BAME as a catch-all term to represent 'Black, Asian and Minority Ethnic communities' became highly contentious during this period, largely because specific ethnic circumstances were being subsumed under a very wide umbrella term which did not speak to particular concerns in relation to the effect the virus was having on particular communities who felt their long-standing socio-political struggles around racial justice lay at the heart of the disproportionate impact seen. For the period

over which we are writing, and to reflect the lens of the time, I will be using the term BAME interchangeably to also reflect some recent reference to 'Black and Minoritised Ethnic' communities. In so doing, the more commonly understood abbreviated form is retained and, hopefully, reflects continuity and alignment with how the term was being used during the period under discussion. For an exposition on this debate, see John, G. (2020) *From BME to BIPOC – Race and Language Hegemony*, c4c7fc_acabdcde2c264 b2fb9e34dc896cc86f8.pdf (filesusr.com)

[2] The 'hostile environment' is a reference to a compliance regime that followed the 2014 and 2016 Immigration Acts, which are a set of policies aimed at disincentivising immigration to the UK by preventing those without leave to remain from accessing housing, healthcare, education, employment, bank accounts and benefits, among others.

References

Becaries, L. and Nazroo, J. (2020) *Racism Is the Root Cause of Ethnic Inequalities in COVID-19*, [online], Available from: //archive.discoversociety.org/2020/04/17/racism-is-the-root-cause-of-ethnic-inequities-in-covid19/ [Accessed 25 February 2022].

Byrne, B., Alexander, C., Khan, O., Nazroo, J. and Shankley, W. (2020) *Ethnicity, Race and Inequality in the UK: State of the Nation*, London: Runnymede Trust.

Civil Society (2020) '#CharitySoWhite demand funding for BAME groups given pandemic impact', 15 May, [online], Available from: www.civilsociety.co.uk/governance/charitysowhite-demands-funding-for-bame-groups.html [Accessed 19 May 2022].

Dayson, C., Bimpson, E., Ellis Paine, A., Gilbertson, J. and Kara, H. (2020) *The Role of the Leeds Neighbourhood Networks during the COVID-19 Pandemic*, [online], Available from: //ageing-better.org.uk/sites/default/files/2020-12/Leeds-neighbourhood-networks-full-report.pdf [Accessed 25 February 2022].

Digital, Culture, Media and Sport Committee (DCMSC) (2021), 'Formal meeting (oral evidence session): Impact of Covid-19 on the charity sector', [online], Available from: https://committees.parliament.uk/event/724/formal-meeting-oral-evidence-session/ [Accessed 19 May 2022].

Farah, A. (2021) 'Embedding an equitable approach to grant-making', [online], Available from: www.citybridgetrust.org.uk/embedding-an-equitable-approach-to-grant-making/ [Accessed 25 February 2022].

Gardner, T., Abraham, S., Clymer, O., Rao, M. and Gnani, S. (2021) 'Racial and ethnic health disparities in healthcare settings: community organisations have a crucial role in involving under-represented population groups', *BMJ*, Mar 8; 372: n605.

Hall, S. (1984) 'Race, articulation and societies structured in dominance', in UNESCO (ed.) *Sociological Theories: Race and Colonialism*, Paris: UNESCO, pp 305–45.

Independent SAGE (2020) *The Independent SAGE Report 6: Disparities in the Impact of COVID-19 in Black and Minority Ethnic Populations: Review of the Evidence and Recommendations for Action*, [online], Available from: www.independentsage.org/wp-content/uploads/2020/07/Independent-SAGE-BME-Report_02July_FINAL.pdf [Accessed 25 February 2022].

Institute for Jewish Research (2020) 'Coronavirus (COVID-19) related deaths by religious group, England and Wales, 2 March to 15 May 2020: considering the implications of the Office for National Statistics report for the Jewish community and population', *JPR*, Available from: archive.jpr.org.uk/object-1185 [Accessed 19 May 2022].

Intensive Care National Audit and Research Centre (2020) *Report on COVID-19 in Critical Care*, [online], Available from: www.icnarc.org [Accessed 25 February 2022].

Kanlungan Filipino Consortium and RAPAR (2020) *A Chance to Feel Safe: Precarious Filipino Migrants amid the UK's Coronavirus Outbreak*, London: Kanlungan Filipino Consortium and RAPAR.

Lingayah, S., Wrixon, K. and Hulbert, M. (2020) *Home Truths: Undoing Racism and Delivering Real Diversity in the Charity Sector*, [online], Available from: www.acevo.org.uk/wp-content/uploads/2020/06/ACEVO_Voice4Change_home_truths_report_v1.pdf [Accessed 25 February 2022].

London Community Response (2021) *Learnings from the London Community Response's Equity-Centred Grantmaking during Covid-19*, [online], Available from: //londoncommunityresponsefund.org.uk/news/london-community-response-learning-reports [Accessed 25 February 2022].

London Funders (2021) *London Community Response: How Civil Society Delivered Differently, and How Funders Need to Support Groups in the Future*, London: London Funders.

Macmillan, R. (2020) 'Somewhere over the rainbow – third sector research in and beyond coronavirus', *Voluntary Sector Review*, 11(2): 129–36.

MiNet (2009) *The Economic Downturn and the Black, Asian and Minority Ethnic (BAME) Third Sector*, [online], Available from: www.rota.org.uk/content/minet-june-2009-economic-downturn-and-black-asian-and-minority-ethnic-bame-third-sector [Accessed 25 February 2022].

Murray, K. (2020a) *Impact of COVID-19 on the BAME Community and Voluntary Sector: Final Report of the Research Conducted between 19 March and 4 April 2020*, [online], Available from: www.ubele.org/publications [Accessed 25 February 2022].

Murray, K. (2020b) *National Mapping of BAME Mental Health Service*, [online], Available from: www.bamestream.org.uk/ [Accessed 25 February 2022].

Murray, K. (2020c) *The Impact of Covid-19 on BAME Community and Voluntary Sector Organisations in Wales: Innovation, Resilience and Sustainability*, [online], Available from: //eyst.org.uk/ [Accessed 25 February 2022].

Murray, K. (2020d) *The Impact of COVID-19 on BAME Led Community and Voluntary Organisations: A Follow Up*, [online], Available from: www.ubele.org/our-research [Accessed 25 February 2022].

Murray, K. and Rolston, Y. (2020) *Rapid Review of the Impact of COVID-19 on the Protected Equalities Characteristics in London: An Analysis of the Lived Experiences and Voices from the Voluntary and Community Social Enterprise Sector*, [online], Available from: www.ubele.org/our-research [Accessed 25 February 2022].

Nazroo, J., Murray, K., Taylor, H., Bécares, L., Field, Y., Kapadia, D. and Rolston, Y. (2020) *Rapid Evidence Review: Inequalities in Relation to COVID-19 and their Effects on* London, [online], Available from: //data.london.gov.uk/dataset/rapid-evidence-review-inequalities-in-relation-to-covid-19-and-their-effects-on-london [Accessed 25 February 2022].

Office for National Statistics (2020) *Coronavirus (COVID-19) Related Deaths by Ethnic Group, England and Wales: 2 March 2020 to 10 April 2020*, [online], Available from: www.ons.gov.uk/peoplepopulationandcommunity/birthsdeathsandmarriages/deaths/articles/coronaviruscovid19relateddeathsbyethnicgroupenglandandwales/2march2020to15may2020 [Accessed 25 February 2022].

Platt, L. and Warwick, R. (2020) *Are Some Ethnic Groups More Vulnerable to COVID-19 than Others?*, [online], Available from: www.ifs.org.uk/inequality/chapter/are-some-ethnic-groups-more-vulnerable-to-covid-19-than-others/ [Accessed 25 February 2022].

Public Health England (PHE) (2020a) *Disparities in the Risk and Outcomes of COVID-19*, London: Public Health England.

Public Health England (PHE) (2020b) *Beyond the Data: Understanding the Impact of COVID-19 on BAME groups*, London: Public Health England.

Ryan, S. (2021) 'The Phoenix way: lessons from the pandemic', [online], Available from: www.alliancemagazine.org/blog/the-phoenix-way-lessons-from-the-pandemic/ [Accessed 25 February 2022].

Tierney, S. and Mahtani, K. (2020) *Volunteering during the COVID-19 Pandemic: What Are the Potential Benefits to People's Well-Being?*, [online], Available from: www.cebm.net/covid-19/volunteering-during-the-covid-19-pandemic-what-are-the-potential-benefits-to-peoples-well-being/ [Accessed 25 February 2022].

Voice4Change England (V4CE) (2014) *Bridge the Gap: What Is Known about the BME Third Sector in England*, London: Voice4Change England.

Women and Equalities Committee (2020) *Unequal Impact: Coronavirus (Covid-19) and the Impact on People with Protected Characteristics*, [online], Available from: //committees.parliament.uk/work/227/unequal-impact-coronavirus-covid19-and-the-impact-on-people-with-protected-characteristics,%20accessed%2019.12.21 [Accessed 25 February 2022].

12

Voluntary sector organisations, older people and healthy ageing during the COVID-19 pandemic

Chris Dayson, Emma Bimpson, Angela Ellis Paine, Joseph Chambers, Jan Gilbertson and Helen Kara

Introduction

Voluntary sector organisations (VSOs) have been at the forefront of local responses to the COVID-19 pandemic in the UK (McCabe et al, 2020). From the coordination of food aid to support for digital inclusion, VSOs have played an important and highly visible role identifying and responding to local needs (Macmillan, 2020). This occurred during various lockdowns, notably March–June 2020 and January–March 2021, when the whole of the UK population was ordered by government to stay at home, but also during the intervening periods of 'unlocking' and when restrictions were eased to enable the reopening of society and the economy (Dayson and Damm, 2020).

Although there is a tendency to discuss VSOs as a homogeneous group, it is important to recognise that their work is diverse, and their role, contribution and experiences vary accordingly (Kendall and Knapp, 1995). For example, many VSOs operate in a specific horizontal or vertical 'field' (Fligstein and McAdam, 2011; Macmillan et al, 2013) supporting defined population groups, providing services aligned with a particular policy area or promoting the interests of specific communities of place or interest. Understanding who different VSOs support and how have become particularly important during the COVID-19 pandemic as they are understood to have played a prominent role in many areas supporting communities who were most likely to be adversely affected by the health, social and economic impacts of the crisis (Bambra et al, 2020; Dayson et al, 2021a), often working in tandem with mutual aid groups, the public sector and local businesses. One such organisational field – VSOs supporting older people – is the focus of this chapter. We present a case study of 'Neighbourhood Networks' in Leeds to explore how their work in support of 'healthy ageing' has been affected by the pandemic.

Each 'Leeds Neighbourhood Network' (LNN) is an independent VSO that aims to support older people (referred to as their 'members') to live independently and to participate in their communities through a range of activities and services that are provided at a neighbourhood level. The LNNs grew from a single initiative established in 1986 as 'Belle Isle Elderly Winter Aid' that was set up to help older people cope with winter weather and the challenges of staying warm and well. Following the success of this initial scheme, the LNN model was gradually adopted across the whole of Leeds, a northern city in England with a socially, economically and ethnically diverse population of approximately 790,000 people. There are now 37 LNNs covering the whole city but they come in different shapes and sizes: some are small local community groups for whom the running of the LNN is their primary activity; others are medium-sized voluntary organisations who run the LNN alongside a wider range of community-based activities and services; and two large national organisations, including a housing and care home provider and a national older person's charity, run LNNs as a complement to their core activities.

Although the form, function, activities and services of LNNs are varied, they also share some key characteristics (Dayson et al, 2020). First, they are all run with the involvement of older people: each LNN has a management committee drawn from the local community with an emphasis on member representation. Second, and although the detail of what is provided varies from network to network, they typically revolve around social opportunities and cover areas such as information and advice, advocacy, activities to improve health and wellbeing, and exercise or physical activity. Finally, the LNNs receive core grant funding from Leeds City Council and the local National Health Service to address four major policy requirements: to reduce social isolation and loneliness; to increase contribution and involvement; to increase choice and control; and to enhance health and wellbeing.

We proceed by outlining our methodology before setting out how the LNNs supported healthy ageing prior to the COVID-19 pandemic, focusing on the functional abilities that enable wellbeing and prevent declining capacity in older age. Next, we discuss the LNN response to the pandemic, highlighting their resilience and how their healthy ageing work initially contracted to focus on meeting basic needs before expanding as they developed new ways to support older people to be socially connected, active and mobile. Finally, we identify some of the key characteristics that the LNNs share and that are associated with their approach to healthy ageing in order to help to explain how and why they responded in the ways they did.

Methodology

The empirical material for our case study comes from a large evaluation of the role LNNs play in Leeds. The evaluation was funded by the Centre for Ageing Better between 2019 and 2022. For this chapter, we draw on two nested studies undertaken as part of this evaluation: a 'Real-Time Evaluation' (RTE) (Herson and Mitchell, 2005) of the LNNs' initial response to the COVID-19 pandemic (see Dayson et al, 2020 and 2021b for more information); and in-depth qualitative research into how the LNNs contribute to healthy ageing. The RTE involved qualitative interviews with five representatives from local social care, public health and VSOs with an overview of the LNN activities in May–June 2020, qualitative interviews with key staff from 22 LNNs in June–July 2020 and follow-up interviews with eight LNNs undertaken in August–September 2020. The healthy ageing study was undertaken between January and August 2021 and involved in-depth qualitative research with six LNNs to explore their work in more detail. In each LNN we interviewed a combination of paid staff, volunteers, members and partner organisations (57 interviews in total). Across the two studies, we sampled purposively to ensure coverage of LNNs operating in a variety of different social, economic and geographic contexts. Our combined data set includes a total of 92 interviews with people involved with the LNNs prior to and during the pandemic. Where necessary, we also draw on documentary evidence collected about the LNNs during the evaluation scoping phase.

How LNNs support healthy ageing

We utilise the World Health Organisation (WHO) definition of healthy ageing as 'the process of developing and maintaining the functional ability that enables wellbeing in older age' (see Rudnicka et al, 2020). Functional ability is described as having the capabilities that enable people to be and do what they have reason to value. This includes their ability to meet their basic needs; to learn, grow and make decisions; to be mobile; to build and maintain relationships; and to contribute to society. Functional ability is linked to an individual's intrinsic capacity (that is, their physical health), which, although likely to deteriorate with age, can be moderated by adapting the environment, including the communities in which older people live and participate, to reduce barriers and mitigate declining capacity.

Each LNN has a unique 'menu' of services and activities for its members to access based on their understanding about the needs of older people and assets in the wider community. Using the WHO definition, in our healthy ageing study we mapped the different ways in which LNNs were working prior to the pandemic and the opportunities they provided for older people at a neighbourhood level (Table 12.1). Although what was on offer varied considerably in terms of breadth, scale and reach, most provision fitted within these categories.

The mapping illustrates how LNN activities prior to the pandemic were comprehensively addressing the capabilities associated with functional ability

Table 12.1: LNN support for health ageing prior to the COVID-19 pandemic

Category	Subcategories	Link to WHO functional abilities
Opportunities for social connection and interaction	Shared hobby or interest groups	Build and maintain relationships; be mobile
	Lunch club or café	
	Games	
	One-off events	
	Day trips and holidays	
Support to engage in physical activity or exercise	Sport or recreation activities	Build and maintain relationships; be mobile
	Fitness classes and activities	
Learning and development opportunities	Hobby or interest	Learn, grow and make decisions
	Fitness	
	IT/digital	
	Religion/faith	
Befriending	Telephone	Build and maintain relationships
	Face-to-face	
Food and nutrition	Shop	Meet basic needs
	Lunch clubs	
	Shopping and food delivery	
	Meals on wheels	
Transport	Car pick-ups	Meet basic needs; build and maintain relationships; be mobile
	Minibuses	
Frailty and long-term conditions clinics	Strength and balance	Build and maintain relationships; be mobile
	Leg clinics	
	Memory loss	
Information, advice and guidance	Newsletters	Meet basic needs
	Websites	
	One-to-one sessions	
	Referral to other agencies	
	Signposting to other agencies	
	Housing	
	Benefits	
Home improvement and adaptation	Handyman services	Meet basic needs; be mobile
	Gardening	
	Fire safety checks	
Volunteering opportunities across a range of services		Contribute to society

outlined by the WHO. They were meeting older people's *basic needs* through shopping and food provision, providing access to transport, offering home improvements and adaptations, and providing information and advice in relation to key issues such as welfare and housing. They were helping older people to *learn, grow and make decisions* by promoting choice and providing developmental opportunities associated with a hobby or interest, fitness, faith or religion, and in emerging areas of need such as information technology and digital and social media. Their support enabled older people to *be mobile* by improving accessibility within the home environment and providing opportunities to take part in physical activity and exercise, including targeted support to build strength and balance among frail members. LNNs also provided transport to activities where this was needed. They provided opportunities for older people to *build and maintain relationships* through a range of activities and events that promoted social connection, participation and interaction in community settings. These included lunch clubs, social events, social groups linked to a hobby or interest and befriending. The LNNs did this in settings in which older people were able to *contribute to society* on their own terms through a wide variety of volunteering roles, many of which overlapped with or provided a pathway to and from being an LNN member.

This menu of LNN provision comprised a combination of *universal* services and activities, which could be accessed by any older person such as a lunch club or craft group, and *targeted* activities focusing on specific health conditions and social issues, such as dementia cafés or strength and balance clinics for frail members. The services and activities were provided through a mix of group, one-to-one, peer-to-peer and clinic-based support. Prior to the COVID-19 pandemic, these typically took place in a range of settings including community buildings, older people's homes (including care homes), public sector buildings and outdoors (in parks and other public spaces). However, and as we discuss in the following sections, online provision and telephone-based support has become more common since the start of the pandemic.

Through this approach, LNNs were able to play a dual role in support of healthy ageing. First, they contributed to primary prevention (that is, preventing ill health before it ever occurs) by helping to combat social isolation and loneliness and improving wellbeing. Second, they contributed to secondary prevention (that is, detecting ill health early and preventing it from getting worse) by helping members better understand health conditions and how best to manage them, thus improving care and avoiding deterioration.

The LNN response to the COVID-19 pandemic

The LNN response to the COVID-19 pandemic has been characterised as evidence of their resilience (Béné et al, 2012;2016; Dayson et al, 2021b).

That is, they demonstrated *absorptive capacity* to moderate and buffer the immediate impact of the pandemic, and then *adaptive capacity* to adjust, on an ongoing basis, their ways of working to identify and respond to needs that emerged in their local communities. The RTE phase of our LNN evaluation explored this process in some detail.

Following the decision to put the whole country into 'lockdown' on 23 March 2020, the initial instinct of LNNs was to focus on the needs of their members and how they could continue to be met in light of the new public health restrictions and the likely impact of these on their members. This meant focusing on sustaining their core mission to support vulnerable older people in the community to stay healthy and socially connected. Most LNNs contacted their members by telephone to understand what their immediate needs were and how they could be met. As one LNN explained, "We have 900 members and we all took lists of members to ring, we spent the first couple of weeks just ringing everyone and talking to them and finding out what they needed" (RTE NN1).

Through this engagement, it became clear to the LNNs that the needs of their members, and the types of support they would have to provide during the pandemic, would be markedly different from what had gone before. As revealed by our mapping of LNN activities (Table 12.1), prior to the pandemic much of their work had involved face-to-face contact with and between older people in community venues, including peer-to-peer support provided through volunteers. The public health restrictions in place during lockdown severely restricted this type of interaction and LNNs had to adapt their operating models in response to new laws and guidance and based on an understanding of how needs had changed.

As with many voluntary organisations around the country (see, for example, Dayson et al, 2021a) a key focus for LNNs became food provision, particularly for members who were shielding (that is, restricting all non-essential contact because they had been identified as clinically vulnerable), socially isolating (if infected with the COVID-19) or recovering. This typically involved doing people's food shopping and preparing and delivering food parcels and hot meals. Many LNNs also ordered, collected and delivered prescription medication. A further focus for the LNNs was to ensure that vulnerable and isolated older people had access to social and emotional support while under lockdown or having to shield. Initially, contact was mostly made by telephone to clarify members' understanding of the pandemic and assuage confusion and anxiety caused by unclear and mixed messages from government. One LNN described their approach during the early days of the pandemic:

> 'I think the biggest kind of thing was first of all making sure everybody understood what was going on. I think for our first two weeks it was literally, you know, telephoning everybody, all of our members, to

explain, you know, what was going on, why it was happening, did they understand what was being asked of them to stay at home and what that meant and you know, a lot of quite in-depth conversations really because a lot of people just didn't get it, they didn't quite understand what they were being asked to do and still to this day some people don't, as much as we've tried doing everything that we possibly can.' (RTE NN3)

A number of LNNs expanded their telephone befriending services so that those in need of more frequent social contact, for reasons such as loneliness or mental ill health, could be attended to. Some LNNs also successfully encouraged their members to keep in touch with each other by sharing contact details to enable them to contact each other and provide an additional layer of peer-to-peer support.

Although face-to-face contact was initially replaced by telephone calls, digital inclusion quickly became an important part of many LNNs' work. They recognised that many people were unable to access essential information, services and support when face-to-face services or groups shut down and moved online because they did not have access to the internet or other mobile technologies. As such, they found ways to loan older people laptops and iPads with a paid-for Wi-Fi facility and helped people access online platforms such as Zoom. One LNN (RTE NN10) moved their chair-based activity sessions on to their Facebook page and showed members how to access it so that they could stay physically active. Some LNNs set up WhatsApp groups so that they could share information, recipes and photos, and to help older people keep in touch and engage with a range of organised social activities.

Staff and volunteers in some LNNs also sought ways to support their members to stay mentally active. A common example was the delivery of 'activity packs' to members which included a variety of options such as craft equipment, crosswords and puzzles, seeds and flowerpots. One LNN described the range of activities on offer:

'We've been looking at ways to try and keep people active, mentally or physically, by delivering activity packs out to people so they've got quizzes or exercise packs in – the latest one we do we've got like a card-making kit, a craft kit or some flower seeds so they can grow little pots and things like that.' (RTE NN9)

The LNNs were engaged in an ongoing process of adaptation, and this continued as the pandemic progressed. As the first lockdown restrictions began to be eased in June and July 2020, some LNNs began to reinstate limited face-to-face contact where appropriate. This involved visiting more vulnerable or shielding members and having conversations with them on doorsteps or in gardens. We identified numerous examples of how the LNNs adapted their services as government guidance evolved and restrictions were lifted. This involved more activities taking place outside. For example, RTE NN10 restarted their allotment project, with small numbers of members visiting the allotment at one time. RTE NN11 organised socially distanced outings, including picking people up and taking them out for picnics. RTE NN3 set up a mobile library and provided assisted shopping trips for members whose physical condition had deteriorated during lockdown or who felt less confident to go out under the new conditions.

When England introduced further lockdowns (in November 2020, for four weeks, and January 2021, for three months) in response to increases in COVID-19 infection rates, the LNNs were much better prepared than they had been in March 2020. Although the limited face-to-face contact that had been possible for a time was once again paused, support for basic needs continued alongside expanded and enhanced digital provision to enable members to retain as much social contact as possible. During this period, the LNNs also played a major role supporting the roll-out of the COVID-19 vaccine through awareness raising and by supporting members to receive the vaccine in appropriate settings. From April 2021 onwards, when COVID-19 restrictions began to be eased once more as part of the government 'roadmap' out of lockdown, most LNNs once again quickly sought to find ways to reintroduce face-to-face contact with and between members where it was safe to do so. This did not mean a return to 'business as usual' from before the pandemic; however, the LNNs were able to carry forward their learning and new ways of working, particularly in relation to digital approaches to support.

The implications of the COVID-19 pandemic for how the LNNs supported healthy ageing

The COVID-19 pandemic clearly had major implications for how the LNNs supported healthy ageing, but our evaluation demonstrated how they were able to draw on their *absorptive* and *adaptive* capacity as VSOs to respond accordingly. Whereas prior to the pandemic they were able to provide a holistic 'menu' of activities (Table 12.1) that covered each of the WHO-defined functional abilities, the public health restrictions severely affected their ability to operate in this way and their provision was forced to 'contract' significantly (Table 12.2).

In response to lockdown in March 2020, LNNs drew on their *absorptive capacity* to focus on meeting their members' *basic needs* for food and medicine through direct practical support and by contacting their most vulnerable members to check in on their welfare and support needs. As the pandemic progressed, the LNNs' *adaptive capacity* came to the fore and they were able

Table 12.2: How the LNNs supported healthy ageing during the COVID-19 pandemic

WHO functional ability	Impact of the pandemic on LNN provision	
	Absorptive capacity Responding to the lockdown by contracting healthy ageing support	**Adaptive capacity** Rethinking healthy ageing support in light of public health guidance
Meet basic needs	Provision of food and medicine; welfare telephone calls	Support for vaccination
Learn, grow and make decisions	Paused to enable focus on meeting needs	Support to access the internet, social media and other digital technology
Be mobile		Socially distant activities in the community; online classes
Build and maintain relationships		Telephone befriending; online social activities; socially distant activities in the community
Contribute to society	Volunteering in support of basic needs (most healthy only)	Expanded range of remote volunteer-led roles; socially distant activities in the community

to expand their healthy ageing provision based on new ways of working. For example, by supporting their members to access the internet, social media and other digital technology, the pandemic became a *learning* opportunity for many older people that also paved the way for them to access a wider range of healthy ageing opportunities. This included online exercise classes that helped them *be mobile*, online social activities that enabled them to *build and maintain relationships* and an expanded range of volunteer roles that could be undertaken remotely and enabled people to *contribute to society*. Where and when possible, LNNs also provided socially distant activities face to face in the community that enabled their members and volunteers to *be mobile, build and maintain relationships* and to continue to *contribute to society* in meaningful ways. For those older people who were unable to access digital technology or socially distant activities, the LNNs sought to provide more straightforward forms of support, such as telephone befriending, which enabled some of the most isolated older people to retain some social contact and the opportunity to build and maintain relationships, even though this didn't involve real or virtual face-to-face contact.

Characteristics of effective and resilient LNNs

The previous two sections have discussed how the LNNs responded to the COVID-19 pandemic, the implications for their ability to support the functional abilities associated with healthy ageing and how their adaptive and absorptive capacity as voluntary organisations enabled them to rethink and adjust their healthy ageing provision. This raises questions about how this was possible and what the characteristics of an effective and resilient VSO are whose role is to support older people age healthily through community-based support. Through the healthy ageing study, we identified five organisational features that are particularly significant in this regard.

Range of activities and services

LNNs provide a wide range of activities and services that members can take part in both in person in community or residential settings and, increasingly, online. This range of activities enables the LNNs to provide a holistic approach and meet different aspects of an individual's needs, and ensures members are able to stay involved and be supported as their needs change over time. Despite the challenges presented by the pandemic, the LNNs found ways to provide as broad a range of activities as possible. However, we also found it is not just what the activities are that is important, but also how they are delivered – in a caring manner which recognises members' differing needs and requirements. The ability to provide services which are both universal and highly personalised is key to how LNNs support healthy ageing.

Relationships

The LNNs provide a highly relational model of welfare (Cottam, 2011), and the trusted relationships that they have built – with members, staff, volunteers and stakeholders – are key to their work supporting healthy ageing. As one participant reflected, good relationships "form the basis for everything". There are several aspects to this, including the relationships LNN staff build with members, the relationships members develop between themselves, relationships with and between volunteers, relationships with other service providers and relationships with families and communities. A desire to retain this relational model was central to how the LNNs responded to the pandemic and many of the adaptations they put in place were done so to create alternative ways for relationships to be developed or sustained.

Responsiveness

Through and within the activities provided and the relationships which underpin them, the LNNs aim to be responsive to members' needs and to the contexts in which they operate. Participants highlighted the in-depth, personal knowledge that LNNs build of their communities and of their members. As one LNN explained, "we know people, their issues, fears, family circumstances". This knowledge was generated by spending time with members and asking them about their background, interests, needs and worries, and then continually reassessing the implications for the care and support provided.

This knowledge, and the care and attention with which it was applied, enabled the LNNs to develop and deliver services and activities that met the changing needs of their members, even during the COVID-19 pandemic. They noticed when people's situations changed, or when they deteriorated, and could respond accordingly by taking steps to adjust their provision or referring members on to other services where appropriate.

Reassurance

We found that LNNs created a deep sense of reassurance for their members. Members talked about the importance of trusting that the LNNs are there and that they will do what they say they are going to do, when they say they are going to do it. This was seen as particularly important during the COVID-19 pandemic when there has been so much uncertainty leading to fear among older people. As one member explained, "I would honestly say that I don't really know how we would have got by without them. I think it was the earliest aspects of what they contributed in one of these things was this hugely reliable structure" (Member, HA NN5). This reassurance extended beyond members to their families and other informal carers, particularly those who could not see their loved ones during the pandemic, who were happy in the knowledge that they were being cared for by people who knew them so well.

Resources

Although we found that in general the LNNs provided a wide range of activities in support of healthy ageing, and that the four features discussed above were important in mediating their effect, it is important to note that there was significant variation across the network. Several factors were found to influence this, the most prominent of which was the level and variety of resource that each LNN has. This included financial resources such as the amount and type of funding received, alongside human resources provided through staff, volunteers and trustees, or committee members. For example, while some LNNs can identify an appropriate befriender from their volunteer pool very quickly, others might take weeks or even months due to a lack of suitable volunteers. This was a particular challenge during the COVID-19 pandemic when many volunteers were unavailable due to having to shield. Similarly, some LNNs are only able to offer a small number of activities because of limited funding or are unable to meet transport needs because they don't have sufficient access to vehicles. During the COVID-19 pandemic, some additional funding has been made available by Leeds City Council and other grant funders to cover the costs of adaptation, development and additional capacity requirements, but this has rarely covered the full costs of the work that has been undertaken.

Conclusion

This chapter has drawn upon a case study of the LNNs to explore the role of VSOs supporting older people in the field of healthy ageing during the COVID-19 pandemic and considered the implications of the crisis for their work. Our study has highlighted the resilience of these organisations during an unprecedented period in their history and development. At their core, VSOs like the LNNs exist to provide opportunities for older people to build and maintain social connections and relationships which help to reduce social isolation and loneliness and sustain or improve health and wellbeing. As such, the COVID-19 public health restrictions that limited everyone's social contact presented a major challenge to the LNNs' established ways of working and their ability to support healthy ageing. However, they demonstrated both *absorptive capacity*, to respond to the immediate impact of the pandemic on the needs of their members and their ability to keep operating as VSOs, and then *adaptive capacity*, to adjust their approach as needs and circumstances evolved (Dayson et al, 2021b). Although this necessitated a contraction of their healthy ageing support in the early days of the crisis to focus on meeting older people's *basic needs*, they were able to adapt and expand their offer quickly to address other functional abilities in new ways, notably through the use of digital technology to reintroduce social contact to enable people to *build and maintain relationships* with key services and their peers. This response was possible in large part due to some key characteristics that the LNNs share and are likely to be present in other similar VSOs.

Although we present a largely positive picture of the LNNs' response to the pandemic, it is important to caveat this with a note of caution. While the features we describe can be thought of as the key 'ingredients' of a healthy and thriving LNN or other type of VSO supporting older people, we have generalised in this chapter, and it is important to recognise that these ingredients are not necessarily present, or distributed evenly, across the LNN or the wider voluntary sector. Moving forward, stakeholders in the voluntary sector and VSOs themselves will need to consider how these ingredients can be fostered and developed further and made more sustainable, particularly if equity of access to community-based healthy ageing opportunities is to be a desirable social policy goal. The role of long-term core grant funding cannot be underestimated in this regard. Arguably, the LNNs were in a unique and enviable position having their core costs covered by Leeds City Council preceding and during the pandemic. This gave them a stable platform from which to build their pandemic response and could provide an exemplar for other areas to follow in the future.

References

Bambra, C., Riordan, R., Ford J. and Matthews, F. (2020) 'The COVID-19 pandemic and health inequalities', *Journal of Epidemiology and Community Health*, 74(11): 964–8.

Béné, C., Godfrey-Wood, R., Newsham, A. and Davies, M. (2012) *Resilience: New Utopia or New Tyranny? – Reflection about the Potentials and Limits of the Concept of Resilience in Relation to Vulnerability Reduction Programmes*, Brighton: Institute of Development Studies.

Béné, C., Headey, D., Haddad, L. and von Grebmer, K. (2016) 'Is resilience a useful concept in the context of food security and nutrition programmes? Some conceptual and practical considerations', *Food Security*, 8: 123–38.

Cottam, H. (2011) 'Relational welfare', *Soundings*, 48: 134–44.

Dayson, C. and Damm, C. (2020) 'Re-making state–civil society relationships during the COVID-19 pandemic? An English perspective', *People, Place and Policy*, 14(3): 282–9.

Dayson, C., Gilbertson, J., Bimpson, E., Ellis Paine, A. and Kara, H. (2020) *Ever More Needed? The Role of the Leeds Neighbourhood Networks during the COVID-19 Pandemic*, London: Centre for Ageing Better.

Dayson, C., Baker, L. and Rees, J. (2021a) *The 'Value of Small' in a Big Crisis: The Distinctive Contribution, Value and Experiences of Smaller Charities in England and Wales during the COVID-19 Pandemic*, Sheffield: Sheffield Hallam University.

Dayson, C., Gilbertson, J., Bimpson, E., Ellis Paine, A. and Kara, H. (2021b) 'The "resilience" of community organisations during the COVID-19 pandemic: absorptive, adaptive and transformational capacity during a crisis response', *Voluntary Sector Review*, 12(2): 295–304.

Fligstein, N. and McAdam, D. (2011) 'Toward a general theory of strategic action fields', *Sociological Theory*, 29(1): 1–26.

Herson, M. and Mitchell, J. (2005) 'Real-time evaluation: where does its value lie?', *Humanitarian Exchange*, 32: 43–5.

Kendall, J. and Knapp, M. (1995) 'A loose and baggy monster: boundaries, definitions and typologies', in R. Hedley, C. Rochester and J. Davis Smith (eds.) *Introduction to the Voluntary Sector*, London: Routledge, pp 66–95.

McCabe, A., Wilson, M. and Macmillan, R. (2020) *Stronger than Anyone Thought: Communities Responding to COVID-19*, London: Local Trust.

Macmillan, R., Taylor, R., Arvidson, M., Soteri-Proctor, A. and Teasdale, S. (2013) *The Third Sector in Unsettled Times: A Field Guide*, Birmingham: University of Birmingham.

Macmillan, R. (2020) 'Somewhere over the rainbow – third sector research in and beyond the coronavirus', *Voluntary Sector Review*, 11(2): 129–36.

Rudnicka, E., Napierała, P., Podfigurna, A., Męczekalski, B., Smolarczyk, R. and Grymowicz, M. (2020) 'The World Health Organization (WHO) approach to healthy ageing', *Maturitas* 139: 6–11.

PART III

Perspectives from practice and policy

13

Emotions in the VCSE sector during the pandemic

Vita Terry, Houda Davis and Marilyn Taylor

Introduction

Voluntary, community and social enterprise organisations (VCSEs) have been at the forefront in responding to the pandemic. They have faced significant challenges, including overwhelmed service provision, having to adapt rapidly to remote working and, for some, temporary or permanent closure. Although we don't know the full extent of the fallout, it is clear that the pandemic has affected individuals' mental health and wellbeing (Abdallah et al, 2021), that there is a risk of emotional burnout and that the workforce could experience post-traumatic stress further down the line.

All this has taken an emotional toll on VCSE leaders, who are having to balance the safety and welfare of their workforce and service users, make tough decisions about staffing and try to plan ahead for an uncertain future, while also managing personal demands, such as home schooling, caring for dependents and, for some, coping with bereavement. Many are feeling stressed, overworked and exhausted.

Dayson et al (2021) have highlighted the particular pressures experienced by small and medium-sized VCSEs. This chapter therefore draws on evidence from a series of structured discussions held throughout the first 15 months of the pandemic, with leaders from 233 such organisations across the UK, to inform thinking about how to ensure these organisations are resilient enough to cope with future shocks and crises.

Emotion in the voluntary sector – what we know

The importance of emotions is understated in voluntary sector literature. Hoggett and Miller (2000) argue that the rational models of management commonly adopted assume a linear process and ignore how 'emotions are often the driving force of motivation and action' (p 338). This chapter thus argues that understanding how emotions shape everyday practices and influence behaviour is essential when trying to understand organisational life. Not only can it help us comprehend the challenges and tensions frontline workers face, but it also explains their commitment, practice and how they make sense of work conditions.

Both positive and negative emotions are experienced by everyone and create meaning in our social interactions. For example, we feel joy and happiness when a child takes its first step, or sadness when we hear about conflict and war. Goodwin and Jasper (2006, p 418) distinguish between:

- *Reactive emotions*: for example, stress, anger or feeling hurt are often impulsive emotional responses to an event or situation;
- *Affective emotions*: for example, love, hate, trust and respect are positive or negative bonds and commitments actors have towards people, places, ideas and things.

Drawing on literature from different disciplines, two key questions arise:

- Why are emotions important in the voluntary sector?
- How are emotions created, played out and harnessed?

Why emotions are important in the voluntary sector

In their study on the management of National Trust volunteers, Greene and Ward (2017) highlight mainstream management theory in which 'emotions are seen as marginal or disruptive to the functioning of the modern organization' (p 36). Personal feelings relate to perceptions of inefficiency and emotions are pushed outside work boundaries. However, Greene and Ward argue that in volunteer-driven organisations, emotions are the foundation for understanding management and organisation.

Emotions help to explain how and why groups form. For example, Doidge and Sandri (2018) describe how positive emotions can convert a bunch of like-minded people into a group with purpose. Emotions fuel movements and 'if harnessed sensitively, provide the basis for creative collective action' (Hoggett and Miller, 2000, p 360). Social movement literature portrays emotions as 'the "glue" of solidarity – and what mobilizes conflict' (Collins, 1990, p 28).

Jasper (1998) describes the motivational power of emotions and the way in which they underpin ideas and ideologies. The literature also describes how people are often driven to act or join a movement by a sense of outrage or moral shock (Thomas et al, 2009). For example, anger at external interventions – such as the closure of a local library or community centre – will often lead to a campaign. Pre-existing emotions such as love and fear (Jasper, 1998) may also be triggered by particularly significant events. A powerful example is the tragic murder in May 2020 of George Floyd in the US which generated collective pain and anger leading to the rise in prominence of the Black Lives Matter movement. Collective action also generates emotions – from the success or failure of a campaign or action, or simply through connecting with the common purpose of other people. Social connection and conviviality build trust and bring people together. Groups and campaigns can therefore become more than a means to an end, but important in their own right.

How do emotions play out and how can they be harnessed?

We see emotions as profoundly social, experienced in and shaped by relationships and interactions with others (Sieben and Wettergren, 2010, p 7). Handling emotions in stressful situations can be very challenging. For example, Robinson (2013a) compares the experiences of social workers in refugee VCSEs in the UK and Australia, demonstrating pressures from work intensification, high demand and the need to keep up to date with complex immigration policies. Additional burdens faced by this workforce include the high emotional demand of supporting clients with traumatic experiences, which can result in physical or mental health issues (Briskman and Cemlyn, 2005). How then can these emotions be harnessed?

Hochschild's (1983) concept of emotional labour refers to the process by which workers are expected to manage their emotions in a paid work setting. She describes how individuals are required to present themselves and interact with others according to the norms of certain professions. She introduces the idea of 'feeling rules' which are created in accordance with organisationally defined guidelines, or socially shared norms, about how people should feel emotions in a social situation. Establishing these is an essential part of managing: 'The act of trying to change in degree or quality an emotion or feeling' (Hochschild, 1979, p 561). Bolton (2003) is critical of these ideas, arguing that actors have agency when navigating a situation and, therefore, are skilful in managing their own emotions. However, Robinson (2013b) demonstrates how supervision is essential to support frontline staff in challenging conditions 'to provide a safe space to reflect on the work, to ensure the long-term wellbeing and motivation of workers and minimise the risk of burnout' (p 6). Of particular concern in her research were the multiple pressures (from policy, politics and public accountability) experienced by the people working with refugees, which could lead to high staff turnover, burnout and sick leave, to the detriment of service users trying to access already oversubscribed and limited service provision.

Hustedde and King (2002) offer a rather different approach to emotion management. For them, rituals provide stability and can promote a sense of solidarity and cohesion amid uncertainty and chaos, providing opportunities for relating, changing, healing, believing, celebrating and building the trust that allows for the expression of differences.

Methodology

In response to the COVID-19 emergency in the UK, the Institute for Voluntary Action Research (IVAR) held a series of structured discussions for VCSE leaders to share experiences and receive peer support throughout the crisis. These peer sessions (which, as of November 2021, were still ongoing) enabled IVAR to build a nuanced understanding of the situation in the sector as it continued to evolve.

From March 2020 to May 2021, IVAR held 119 peer sessions with leaders from 233 predominantly small and medium-sized organisations (with an annual income of less than £1 million) from across the UK, active in a variety of different fields, including arts, migration and homelessness.

The purpose of these sessions was to understand the experiences and responses of VCSE leaders in the UK during the COVID-19 pandemic. We used the following questions as prompts:

1. In what ways have recent events in relation to the rise of COVID-19 impacted on your organisation and the individuals that you support?
2. How has your organisation responded to date? And/or, how do you think you are likely to need to respond/work differently over the coming weeks or months?
3. What are some of the most significant challenges to you being able to do this work/deliver these services under the current conditions?
4. What kind of support does your organisation need to continue doing the work it's doing during this period?

Peer sessions were 90 minutes long, with a researcher taking contemporaneous notes written up into structured templates following the sessions. From the start, peer sessions were designed with sensitivity to the trauma some participants were experiencing. Discussions were conducted in accordance with ethical guidelines set by IVAR. Participants were informed that by engaging in the peer sessions they would be consenting to a process where:

a) Fieldnotes would be taken
b) All responses would remain anonymous and confidential
c) Data would be used to inform published outputs

These peer sessions were not exclusively a research project, nor did the sessions specifically focus on emotions. Rather, leaders (and some trustees) discussed very practical issues like governance, service redesign and staff wellbeing.[1] However, as the sessions progressed, emotions emerged as a prominent theme and facilitators responded by introducing prompts about emotions and wellbeing.

This chapter draws on the session notes and outputs produced by IVAR, including 16 briefings for external stakeholders, such as funders, capturing experiences between March 2020 and May 2021 and a summary report, 'Birds in a hurricane' (Dyson et al, 2021), which mainly focused on experiences between March and December 2020.

These were analysed using two core themes:

1. The emotional impact of the pandemic on the VCSE workforce
2. The response of leaders

Findings

Context

Since March 2020, the COVID-19 pandemic has brought many changes to the voluntary sector, such as increasing demand and more complex needs, moving to remote working, and growing pressure and anxiety around funding and support (Dayson et al, 2021). At the beginning, leaders described a 'manic' sense of adjustment, having to respond rapidly to constantly changing government rules and restrictions, as well as adopting new technologies and appropriate safeguarding policies.

The initial 'moral shock' (Thomas et al, 2009) of the pandemic produced a surge of emotions and mobilised a range of responses by VCSE organisations. It has been widely reported that 'people across the UK and beyond have responded to the pandemic through an outpouring of acts of kindness, mutual aid, volunteering and support within their communities' (Ellis Paine et al, 2021, p 2). In turn, VCSE organisations were recognised for their resilience and flexibility, responding and adapting in a multitude of ways (Dayson et al, 2021).

The emotional impact of the pandemic on the VCSE workforce

Many individuals are drawn towards the voluntary sector because of values and personal experiences, as well as emotions and beliefs connected to injustice or inequality. The peer support sessions confirmed that the conditions created by the pandemic intensified emotional demands on those working in the voluntary sector, especially those supporting vulnerable people, but also those advocating, campaigning and lobbying for change. For example, the workforce has faced increased demand for services and a growth in multiple and complex needs, including mental health and isolation (Dayson et al, 2021). As one leader stated, "The vulnerability of the people that we work with is challenging and distressing". The anger, frustration and anguish felt by service users, as well as grief for the loss of community spaces and services, has been directed at and felt by those delivering services, contributing to the emotional toll experienced by staff: "Our clients are really suffering at the moment which means staff are hearing difficult stories and clients are becoming harder to help – they are starting to take their frustrations out on our staff more, which is very hard".

Overnight, many services were suspended or moved online and staff were expected to work remotely. This involved a rapid shift to digital working, as well as redesigning delivery models or even engaging in completely new activities to meet community needs, such as food deliveries to vulnerable people. Shifting to remote services has brought many benefits; for example, reaching more people, less commuting and more flexibility for home working. However, digital workplaces also negatively affected team dynamics and have disrupted productivity, routine management and leadership tasks: "Our ability to work with each other is beginning to fray, as we haven't seen each other". Engaging with some groups online has also been challenging, given that digital and data exclusion has meant some people do not have the skills or resources to access services. Meanwhile, a lack of in-person delivery has provided little opportunity to build the trusting relationships that are essential for engaging with people who have not previously accessed an organisation's services.

The easing of COVID-19 restrictions in the summer of 2020 brought a new wave of responsibility, anxiety and decisions that had to be made by leaders: "When it seemed this would last a few months, people threw their all into it, but now we're delivering services with PPE and social distancing in place and making decisions about risks. It's getting tougher and harder on everyone".

Staff, as well as service users, had diverging views and appetites for reinstating or returning to usual working spaces and practices: "Some staff really want to get back to frontline work, and, at the other end, we have really nervous staff. COVID has left people in a state of anxiety and it plays out differently for different people".

In some cases, leaders have felt intense pressure to reopen in-person services and have had to make difficult decisions that balance the welfare and safety of staff against the needs of service users: "There's this enormous responsibility I feel towards the families we support, to be there for them, but also to do stuff strategically, as well as responsibility towards my staff and volunteers. The buck stops here".

Staff have often juggled the management of this challenging work environment alongside childcare and other caring responsibilities, coping with bereavement or looking after someone who is seriously ill with COVID-19, all of which has a cumulative impact on health, wellbeing and resilience: "We lost our first volunteer [to COVID-19] last week – this has gone from something distant and scary to something very close".

Leaders voiced concerns about the 'the long-term resilience and mental and physical health' of their paid and voluntary workforce and how far they would be able to sustain current working practices and strains, especially those who were shielding. As the boundaries between work and personal life became increasingly blurred, leaders operated with a high level of sensitivity to individual challenges – vulnerability, caring responsibilities or home circumstances – experienced by their workforce: "We are seeing an incredibly marked rise in mental health issues among our staff at all levels of the organisation". The need to protect staff and volunteers against burnout has also been a major preoccupation for leaders: "That's the thing with charity workers, if they see something that needs to be done, they'll do it even if it's doing something we don't have budget for. We can't ask for this, it's not sustainable … our staff want to do more but we have said no".

How VCSE leaders have responded to the pandemic

The uncertainty created by the pandemic generated negative emotions such as "panic, anxiety, fear and uncertainty" among leaders. As the pandemic continued, repeated lockdowns created a rollercoaster of emotions related to reopening and closing services, and leaders felt increasingly "overwhelmed, exhausted, isolated and stressed": "It is really exhausting and depressing, and we are totally swamped with work". However, they have been sustained and motivated by positive emotions such as "compassion, empathy, and admiration and pride" in their staff and what their organisations and the VCSE sector as a whole have been able to achieve during this period of unprecedented uncertainty.

Supporting staff

Leaders were seriously concerned about the emotional wellbeing of their staff, as well as the long-term effects on poverty and social justice, economic recession, further lockdowns and how public attitudes and long-term public policy might affect their organisations. They struggled to uphold their 'ethical and moral duty' to protect the welfare of their staff in discussions with trustees about furlough, redundancy and reducing wages. They have also constantly faced difficult decisions about allocating resources, and service continuity and redesign: "It's hard making these difficult decisions – what can we keep doing, what we can afford, and what's practically viable? Lots of stresses going on". Decisions have often been 'monumental', and likely to have lasting effects on staff, volunteers and service users, as well as the future size and shape of their organisations.

In the face of these pressures, leaders have adopted new strategies and approaches, including focusing on positives and declining requests that feel unnecessary (in one case, this meant saying 'no' to a proposal for a weekly update to the board). Some have become more open to managing emotions with their workforce, for example, using well-placed humour or sharing more of the emotional burden: "I am managing more with honesty, sharing more about myself, rather than managing from a distance and being cold. I am trying to create a family, to let people be emotional and honest".

Leaders have recognised the need to 'be human'. For example, showing support for and acknowledging individuals' emotional concerns and wellbeing, possibly needing to ask different questions when planning work, accepting some things are not in their control and being more transparent with staff about their own concerns (Terry, 2021): "We're operating in an environment where we're not going to get enough information to make confident, good decisions. We have to allow ourselves the slack to get things wrong and give ourselves permission to say, 'I don't know'". They have had to find new ways to harness the emotions and commitment of their staff and to provide support and reassurance: "I can't give someone a hug ... but we can have a coffee and cake chat on Zoom". Others have used social media platforms like WhatsApp to stay connected and "to lift our spirits" or provide a "trusted space where you can say, 'I'm struggling today'".

They have also provided spaces where staff can work through difficult emotions. Many leaders (and staff) have consciously created new rituals to share emotions, to strengthen the bonds and communication between colleagues in the context of remote working and to actively support staff welfare. Examples include a weekly staff quiz or celebrations of other social occasions, establishing more regular meetings or 'check-ins' and taking time to celebrate successes. These rituals have become opportunities for teams to connect socially, share collective emotions, reinforce affective ties of friendship, solidarity and loyalty. They have helped maintain reciprocal emotions in a remote and highly stressful context.

Other initiatives have included simple routines of self-care, such as encouraging and enabling staff to take a break wherever possible, operating flexible working hours or granting additional annual leave. Some have sent 'care packages' to staff at home to show their appreciation and reinforce ties. Others have invested in more formal spaces, for example, clinical or professional supervision for frontline staff who are supporting people experiencing difficult and, at times, traumatic situations.

The need for self-care

Voluntary sector leaders have taken on huge responsibilities, regularly making tough decisions in the interests of the safety and welfare of their workforce and service users, at the same time as living through the pandemic themselves. As a result, leading their organisations through the COVID-19 crisis has been "exhausting" and "lonely": "As CEO, you straddle the operational and strategic. You are there to be the support to senior managers, and guide trustees. You do stand alone in many ways". In the face of considerable uncertainty, they have felt a burden of personal responsibility for making the right decisions: "I've always been the person that people have looked to for decisions. As a result, everything can seem very personalized". They are also having to regulate their own emotions and anxieties to reassure staff, trustees and service users, to "display positivity" to keep up morale and hope for the future. However, the extended nature of this crisis has led to intense feelings of isolation and "dwindling resilience": "Trying to continue being strong as an individual for everybody else has proved quite challenging at times".

Sharing responsibility/distributed leadership

Some leaders are discovering the power of distributed leadership and decision making (Gronn, 2002), especially in a fast-changing environment, with other staff taking on new roles and responsibilities to support with additional demands and help organisations adapt quickly to new circumstances: "I've been very impressed with the way in which we've been working together". Some staff have not only survived but also thrived during this period, demonstrating commitment, creativity and flexibility by quickly adapting, learning new skills and gaining expertise (Terry, 2021).

These approaches challenge traditional hierarchical styles of leadership and can help build new internal relationships, an appreciation of others' work and help managers recognise the value of the workforce. Staff can achieve greater autonomy, an increase in core motivation, purpose and job satisfaction. Greater autonomy has also encouraged people to take ownership over their working day and workload, for example, staff being able to say 'no' to back-to-back remote meetings and stepping away from the computer to go on a daily walk. More open and regular communication, and devolving and sharing decision making across teams, has led to more spaces for reflection, reaffirmed organisations' missions and values, ensured individuals feel listened to and built supportive relationships.

Supporting themselves

Robinson argues that having a safe space to reflect can 'ensure the long-term wellbeing and motivation of workers and minimise the risk of burnout' (2013a, p 6). Leaders have sought out their own, confidential spaces where they can offload, often in peer spaces with other leaders (such as the IVAR sessions): "It's good to talk"; "I think it's invaluable – and it helps my mental health – to hear about other ways people are responding". These spaces have allowed them to take a break from the emotional labour involved in 'putting on a brave face' and speak in confidence about things they did not feel they could share with staff or trustees. They have been able to discuss anxieties and stresses, hear different perspectives, broaden thinking and sense check ideas. As well as attending the IVAR peer sessions, many leaders use other spaces and forums to share challenges and reflect on practice. Some are drawing on external coaches who understand the CEO role and can provide a mixture of challenge and support: "Someone I can download to, who understands my role and the pressures, and helps me organise my thinking". Technical and emotional support from trustees has also been appreciated, although many leaders have also reported how detached or distracted their board members have been during the crisis.

Discussion and conclusion

The pandemic has touched everyone's lives. In many ways, it has brought people together, reinforced collective action, generated a collective purpose and a sense of mutual responsibility. While there have been mounting negative emotions during this period, IVAR's peer support sessions suggest that sharing these emotions has been essential in fuelling positive action towards a common purpose – ensuring the most vulnerable people can access basic needs like shelter, accommodation, food and general support in an otherwise challenging time.

For many VCSE organisations, equal rights and social justice are a driving ethos underpinning organisational approach and service delivery. During the pandemic, we have seen pre-existing social inequalities – relating to age, class, gender and ethnicity (Ellis Paine et al, 2021) – exacerbated, and this 'moral shock' (Thomas et al, 2009) has been a further driver for many organisations to respond quickly to meet needs. Anger, fear and compassion have all fuelled organisations' adaptation and resilience. In turn, shared emotions have left many leaders feeling proud that their organisations have survived these difficult times, confident both about the invaluable work undertaken by staff and volunteers and that the value of the sector appears to have been more broadly recognised.

That said, unmanaged negative emotions can intensify if not addressed, affecting individual and team dynamics. This can impact on an organisation's ability to respond to emergencies and external shocks, including future lockdowns, funding cuts/austerity, refugee crises or climate-related disasters. During the pandemic, leaders recognised the importance of adopting new approaches to supporting their staff and themselves, including encouraging self-care and new rituals. They have tried to focus on the positives, shift towards distributed leadership and recognise the value of being 'human' with their workforce. Creating spaces which allow people to work with heightened emotions has undoubtedly made a significant contribution to organisational commitment, drive and effectiveness during the pandemic. Different forms of engagement have also promoted a culture in which people can express difficult emotions. This has helped staff to act together and thrive, not just survive. Meeting people's needs in this way can bring out the best in them and enable them to continue their work, even in difficult circumstances (Uhnoo and Persson, 2020). Peer support beyond their organisation has also been an important resource for leaders themselves.

This chapter has illustrated that emotions (both positive and negative) are not static but shift and change over time. Providing emotional support should not therefore be viewed as a one-off or tick-box exercise, but rather be fully embraced into organisational culture and spaces maintained for people to work through difficult emotions. There is no one-size-fits-all approach to supporting the emotional wellbeing of a workforce and what is required for one organisation might be different for another. Some of the rituals, practices and spaces developed at the beginning of the pandemic may no longer be relevant, whereas others may be appropriate long into the future. This illustrates the importance of bringing leaders together to have an ongoing dialogue about what does and does not work for them and to keep learning together about how to support staff wellbeing into the future.

These findings also have implications for funders and policy makers – and not just in crisis situations. We argue for a heightened acknowledgement of emotions in the voluntary sector – recognising the strength, value and resilience this brings and the potential to create a stronger collective response to any national crises in the future. However, more formal or informal support and capacity to manage emotions has resource implications. For example, this might involve funders considering how they could cover wellbeing costs, as well as support for staff dealing with complex and distressing issues. For leaders themselves, IVAR's peer support sessions have demonstrated the need to recognise the role of emotions and the importance of creating an organisational culture that supports and maintains spaces and rituals for people to work through their difficult emotions. By creating such a culture, the workforce will be encouraged to take ownership of their own emotions and become adept in skilfully navigating them in the future.

Note

[1] We did not collect any demographic data, for example on age, gender or ethnicity.

References

Abdallah, S., Wren-Lewis, S. and Maguire, R. (2021) *The Impact of the Pandemic on Subjective Wellbeing Inequalities*, London: What Works Centre for Wellbeing.

Bolton, S. (2003) *Introducing a Typology of Workplace Emotion*, Lancaster: The Department of Organisation, Work and Technology, Lancaster University.

Briskman, L. and Cemlyn, S. (2005) 'Reclaiming humanity for asylum-seekers: a social work response', *International Social Work*, 48(6): 714–24.

Collins, R. (1990) 'Stratification, emotional energy, and the transient emotions', in T. Kemper (ed.) *Research Agendas in the Sociology of Emotions*, Albany: SUNY Press, pp 27–57.

Dayson, C., Baker, L. and Rees, J. (2021) *The Value of Small Charities in a Big Crisis*, Commissioned by Lloyds Bank Foundation England and Wales.

Doidge, M. and Sandri, E. (2018) '"Friends that last a lifetime": the importance of emotions among volunteers working with refugees in Calais', *The British Journal of Sociology*, 70(2): 463–80.

Dyson, E., Firth, L. and Taylor, M. (2021) *Birds in a Hurricane: Voluntary Sector Adaptation and Resilience through and beyond Covid-19*, London: Institute for Voluntary Action Research.

Ellis Paine, A., McCabe, A., Wilson, M. and Afridi, A. (2021) *Community Responses to COVID 19: Power and Communities*, London: Local Trust.

Goodwin, J. and Jasper J.M. (2006) 'Emotions and social movements', in J.E. Stets and J.H. Turner (eds.) *Handbook of the Sociology of Emotions*, Boston: Springer, pp 611–35.

Greene, A. and Ward, J. (2017) *The Management of Volunteers in the National Trust*, Leicester: DeMontfort University.

Gronn, P. (2002) 'Distributed leadership as a unit of analysis', *The Leadership Quarterly*, 13(4): 423–51.

Hochschild, A. (1979) 'Emotion work, feeling rules, and social structure', *American Journal of Sociology*, 85(3): 551–75.

Hochschild, A. (1983) *The Managed Heart: Commercialization of Human Feeling*, Berkeley: University of California Press.

Hoggett, P. and Miller, C. (2000) 'Working with emotions in community', *Community Development Journal*, 35(4): 352–64.

Hustedde, R. and King, B. (2002) 'Rituals: emotions, community faith in soul and the messiness of life', *Community Development Journal*, 37(4): 338–48.

Jasper, J. (1998) 'The emotions of protest: affective and reactive emotions in and around social movements', *Sociology Forum*, 13(3): 397–424.

Robinson, K. (2013a) 'Voices from the front line: social work with refugees and asylum seekers in Australia and the UK', *British Journal of Social Work*, 44(6): 1602–20.

Robinson, K. (2013b) 'Supervision found wanting: experiences of health and social workers in non-government organisations working with refugees and asylum seekers', *Practice*, 25(2): 87–103.

Sieben, B. and Wettergren, A. (2010) 'Emotionalizing organizations and organizing emotions – our research agenda', in B. Sieben and A. Wettergren (eds.) *Emotionalizing Organizations and Organizing Emotions*, London: Palgrave Macmillan.

Terry, V. (2021) 'Experimenting and learning during a crisis: a voluntary sector perspective', in *Human Learning Systems: Public Service for the Real World*, pp 289–301, [online], Available from: //realworld.report/assets/documents/hls-real-world.pdf [Accessed 8 October 2021].

Thomas, E.F., McGarty, C. and Mavor, K.I. (2009) 'Transforming "apathy into movement": the role of prosocial emotions in motivating action for social change', *Personality and Social Psychology Review*, 13: 310–33.

Uhnoo, S. and Persson, S. (2020) 'Emotion management of disaster volunteers: the delicate balance between control and recognition', *Emotions and Society*, 2(2): 197–213.

14

The experience of community-led businesses during the COVID-19 pandemic

Sophie Reid

Introduction

This chapter outlines the experiences and responses of community-led businesses during the first six months of the COVID-19 pandemic in England, drawing on findings from five studies funded by Power to Change – the charitable trust championing community businesses in England. It argues that while their 'hybrid' business models, which typically balance grants with higher levels of trading income than the wider voluntary sector, meant community businesses were uniquely affected by the pandemic, they were also well placed to respond to the needs of their communities.

The chapter covers four themes. The first explores how community businesses demonstrated resilience by adapting their operations during the first lockdown between March and June 2020, and subsequent reopening. The second covers changing workforce demands as staff were furloughed or redeployed, and volunteer numbers fluctuated. The third looks at the support community businesses needed, and how they made use of support provided. Finally, the fourth theme looks at collaboration, which was a defining characteristic of community businesses' pandemic response. The chapter concludes by looking ahead. Drawing on findings from Power to Change's Community Business Market Survey in 2021, it explores the short- and long-term implications for the sector, what issues the pandemic highlighted for community businesses and how they now understand their stability, and the role they might play in the future.

What are community businesses?

Community-led businesses are voluntary sector organisations, defined by Power to Change according to four factors: they are locally rooted, accountable to the local community, have a broad community impact and are trading (or working towards trading) for the benefit of the local community.[1] In 2020, there were estimated to be around 11,300 community businesses in England (Higton et al, 2021a). These include venues like community hubs and village halls, public-facing support services, retail enterprises like community shops and pubs, and community-led arts and sports facilities. Their main areas of impact include improving community cohesion, community pride and empowerment, reducing social isolation and improving the health and wellbeing of local people.[2] The definition is agnostic as to size, legal structure or sector. This makes community businesses a very diverse group and – as would be expected – their experiences of the pandemic have been equally diverse.

Despite this variation, community businesses' position as 'hybrid' organisations makes their experiences during the pandemic worthy of further exploration in the context of the wider voluntary sector. Billis (2010) theorises hybrid organisations as those adhering to a mixture of the principles of management and operation of private, public and/or third sector organisations – but which have their 'roots' in just one of those sectors, according to their accountability structures (Billis, 2010, p 55). Voluntary sector organisations may move into 'entrenched' hybridity through the introduction of paid staff roles and sources of income from public or private sources (such as grants or sales) (Billis, 2010).

This echoes the formation of community businesses, many of which have developed from communities coming together in various forms of association around a social purpose – to tackle a local issue or save a community asset like a pub (Kleinhans et al, 2020).[3] Over time, these organisations may become formalised through offering paid work, or by seeking trading income. Community businesses' income generation strategies may fluctuate over time (Stumbitz et al, 2018, p 5), and Ellis Paine et al (2021) argue that combining community goals with business practices can create a fluid and sometimes contested interplay between the 'community' and 'business' aspect of the model. During the pandemic, these tensions resulted in pressure on many community businesses, which suffered from loss of trading income yet experienced greater demand for their services (including from vulnerable populations).[4]

Methodology

The chapter draws on five pieces of primary research funded by Power to Change during the first six months of the COVID-19 pandemic in England, alongside findings from a more recent survey of community businesses to give some indication of future outlook. Table 14.1 summarises the studies, their methodology and the chronology of fieldwork. The studies were analysed using NVivo qualitative data analysis software to identify common themes. Bringing together findings from multiple data sets provided the opportunity to identify areas of convergence or divergence.

Table 14.1: Overview of studies included

Study	Author/s	Main methodology	Fieldwork timeframe
Community business peer networking before and during COVID-19	Dobson, J., Harris, C. and Macmillan, R. (Sheffield Hallam University)	Interviews (n=16 people)	April–May 2020
The Bevy in lockdown	Reid, S. (Power to Change Research Associate) James, C. and Newitt, S. (Self/Other)	Ethnography (n=9 people)	April–June 2020
Community Business Market in 2020	Higton, J., Archer, R., Merrett, D., Hansel, M. and Howe, P. (CFE Research)	Survey (n=449 respondents)	May–June 2020
Digitally enhanced advanced services in community businesses	Gardner, M. and Bradley, P. (University of the West of England) Parry, G. (University of Surrey) Webber, D. (University of Sheffield)	Interviews (n=29 people)	First wave: May 2020 Second wave: October–November 2020
Navigating uncertainty and remaining resilient	Avdoulos, E., Wilkins, Z. and Boelman, V. (The Young Foundation)	Online ethnography (n=27 community businesses)	June–August 2020
Community Business Market in 2021	Higton, J. et al (CFE Research)	Survey (n=571 respondents)	June–July 2021

Findings

Theme 1: resilience

The impact of the first six months of the pandemic on community business activities was considerable but varied. Two thirds of community businesses surveyed in May and June 2020 had decreased their business activity, while a quarter had seen their business activity *increase* (Higton et al, 2021a). This increase was mostly led by community shops, especially in rural areas, who found demand surging as people stayed closer to home. Community businesses such as community energy projects found their activities less affected by the pandemic restrictions, with work taking place mainly outdoors. Others were drastically affected, including community pubs, who along with the rest of the hospitality sector were forced by law to close their doors.

Community businesses adapted their existing services, started new ones and repurposed their resources to respond to community need. Of those community businesses who were still able to operate at least in part (about two thirds of those surveyed), the vast majority (89 per cent) had changed or adapted their activities in response to the pandemic (Higton et al, 2021a). The main adaptations were offering a new or existing service remotely, providing a community service to meet a new need and delivering their products to people's homes. At the Bevy, a community pub in Brighton, they adapted their existing hot food takeaway service to become 'Bevy Meals on Wheels', offering free meals to members of the community (and pub regulars) who were vulnerable and/or shielding (Reid, 2020).

One aspect of the locally rooted nature of community businesses is the way they use assets, including buildings, for social and commercial purposes. However, this posed issues for community businesses during the strictest COVID-19 restrictions. As one community hub put it in Avdoulos et al's (2020) study, 'the main problem is that our [building] is a multi-use space where there are lots of chance encounters leading to collaboration. Bumping into each other is part of our business model, and that suddenly seems undesirable' (p 30). Similarly, in an assessment of the impact of the pandemic on community hubs, researchers commissioned by Local Trust found that their role as 'spaces for connection that anyone can access' was threatened (Langdale et al, 2021, p 5). While assets like buildings are usually seen as a strength, community businesses with assets were particularly hit by loss of income from people using the building (through hiring out the space, having tenants, running events and so on). Many community buildings found ways to improve and use outside spaces, made creative use of their forecourts and windows/hatches for serving, created social distancing inside, offered their closed spaces for community members to organise food donations or used the closure as an opportunity for refurbishment.

These adaptations often prompted community businesses to consider how they might operate differently in the future. For example, at the Bevy the process of refurbishment was a symbolic crossroads between what the pub had been and what it would be (Reid, 2020). Some community businesses felt a sense of accountability connected to managing a community asset, to use it in the best interests of the community – even if that meant not being able to prioritise income during the pandemic. Community accountability is a key aspect of community business and their ownership of assets, which are managed through a cooperative approach, seeks to provide benefits to a wide community of people, often those facing disadvantage (Buckley et al, 2017). Community businesses also had to consider what their purpose was and what role they could play, without their physical building. For some, this meant finding meaning and identity in intangible aspects of the community business like the people, activities or networks it created. Almost three quarters of Community Business Market Survey respondents identified opportunities from the pandemic (Higton et al, 2020), while almost half of community business leaders interviewed in Avdoulos et al's study (2020) reported feeling innovative, embracing the opportunity to do something new.

Alongside adaptations to the physical fabric of buildings, adaptations and forays into digital technology characterised community business responses to the pandemic. Almost half (46 per cent) of community businesses who adapted their services had offered some of these remotely. This has been successful and provided new opportunities but has also highlighted issues of digital exclusion and the need to supplement online services with face-to-face forms of support, such as food deliveries with doorstep chats (Avdoulos et al, 2020). The shift to digital included rapidly setting up or strengthening existing ways of communicating and engaging with local communities through digital channels. Services and groups that had previously met in person moved on to virtual video conferencing platforms (in one instance, a community choir was set up digitally overnight), while some retail also moved online. Avdoulos et al (2020) found that participants were reaping the benefits of using digital tools to communicate internally between staff members and with trustees, or to strengthen connections with local mutual aid groups and local authorities by having more regular contact. These digital adaptations were sometimes accelerations of community businesses' existing plans, such as efforts to upgrade digital infrastructure like online booking or membership, contactless payments and Wi-Fi connectivity. In some cases, provision of digital services led to greater uptake, including counselling sessions offered by one community hub, which they attributed to people feeling more secure to take part from the familiarity of their own homes (Gardner et al, 2021). Greater digitalisation of services also opened up new business opportunities, by increasing the geographic reach of their offer, for example through digital gym memberships and online fitness classes at community sports facilities or online cookery sessions connected to community farms.

However, some community businesses struggled to provide the same level of social impact through digital delivery, including where services involved connecting people to tackle social isolation and loneliness, or where people were supported as a by-product of doing another activity like gardening or crafts. This echoes findings from other research with VCSE leaders during the pandemic, which found that organisations struggled to build rapport online with new users, or to offer therapeutic benefits when services were delivered virtually (Moran et al, 2020). Low levels of digital literacy in some communities were a limiting factor and there was often a drop-off in attendance of virtual sessions over time (Gardner et al, 2021).

The challenges wrought by the COVID-19 pandemic for for-profit businesses have been widely discussed, with numerous media reports of business failures.[5] The Community Business Market Survey in 2020 found that while a minority (15 per cent) of community businesses were fully operational in May/June 2020, only 1 per cent had ceased operating and did not anticipate reopening (Higton et al, 2021a).[6] Overall, these findings suggest that community businesses demonstrated high levels of resilience – the ability to bounce back from adversity – during the pandemic. In their work on the experiences and contributions of smaller charities during the first wave of the COVID-19 pandemic, Dayson et al (2021) apply three aspects of resilience to the pandemic context: absorptive capacity, adaptive capacity and transformational capacity.[7] The studies of community businesses also show them demonstrating absorptive and adaptive capacity to continue to serve their communities and fulfil their missions. As for transformational capacity, many community business leaders and their teams demonstrated this not only through changes to ensure the survival of the business, but also by thinking about how they could improve and learn from their experiences to contribute to longer-term change too. Survival and longer-term change were often linked: as the pandemic continued some community businesses allowed themselves more time to reopen or make decisions. At the Bevy, research participants spoke about the need to "pace [them]selves" in order to maintain their financial sustainability and energy, to meet anticipated demand in the longer term (Reid, 2020). Avdoulos et al (2020) also argue that social capital contributed to the resilience of community businesses, which is further discussed in Theme 4.

Theme 2: changing workforce demands

Although the average (mean) total number of community business employees remained relatively stable during the pandemic, there was variability by sector. Community businesses who reported an increase in staff were more likely to be in rural areas, driven by the increased activity of rural community shops (Higton et al, 2020). However, 80 per cent of community pubs in rural areas reported furloughing staff (Plunkett Foundation, 2020). Over a quarter of Community Business Market Survey respondents reported a decrease in their staff between February 2020 and May/June 2020 (Higton et al, 2020) and over two thirds (69 per cent) took action to reduce their staff costs, including furloughing staff (57 per cent of respondents), asking staff to reduce their hours (16 per cent) and asking staff to take a pay cut (9 per cent) (Higton et al, 2020).

In the early stages of the lockdown, some community businesses reported tensions and feelings of guilt between those staff furloughed (or shielding) and those who weren't, coupled with staff having to balance competing priorities across work and family. At the Bevy, one research participant voiced this as a sense that "everything is laced with 'I should be doing something else'" (Reid, 2020, p 19). For those who were involved in multiple projects (for example as trustees) the pandemic meant that many different areas of their lives demanded a crisis response at the same time (Reid, 2020). Some participants described the impact this had on their wellbeing, including feeling overwhelmed, disrupting their sleep patterns and a sense that "days started to blur" (Reid, 2020, p 12).

Although many community businesses have been able to reopen following periods of lockdown, changing COVID-19 restrictions resulted in higher staff-to-customer ratios (Avdoulos et al, 2020). In some cases, the loss of trading income left community businesses unable to afford staffing costs. At the same time, some community businesses required more staff in order to reach vulnerable groups in their communities. As one community shop reported, "to specifically support vulnerable members of our community we would need additional staffing to reach out to them specifically. As a business we rely on sales income so need to focus on this but know we could do more to support vulnerable community members" (Avdoulos et al, 2020, p 32).

As well as mobilising physical assets in a community, community businesses also mobilise volunteers, both as a resource within their business model and for social reasons. Before the pandemic, community businesses had on average four volunteers for every member of staff and some had no paid staff at all (Higton et al, 2019). Volunteering during the pandemic has been a tale of two halves. On the one hand, with an older volunteer base compared to the wider population, many community businesses saw a drop in volunteering hours as some of those older people needed to shield (Higton et al, 2021b). Yet, there was also an increase in volunteering from working age people who found themselves with more time temporarily as a result of furlough. Ultimately, though, with community businesses often reducing activities and therefore having fewer opportunities for volunteers, overall volunteering hours dropped during the pandemic. This reflected the picture of volunteering nationally, where the number of people in the UK who volunteered through a voluntary organisation fell by a fifth in 2020/21 compared with the previous year (NCVO, 2021).

The ability of community businesses to respond to the pandemic and maintain support and services for their communities has been testament to the hard work of staff and volunteers. Gardner et al (2021) identify the skills, flexibility and dedication of staff as crucial to the successful digitalisation of services during the pandemic. At the Bevy, acknowledgement of the important role staff and volunteers played resulted in the business committing to greater staff involvement in decision making in future (Reid, 2020).

Theme 3: support for community-led businesses

When it came to the support community businesses needed, respondents to the Community Business Market Survey prioritised flexible grants, financial support to pay salaries and advice on adapting product or service delivery (Higton et al, 2020). Most community businesses received support from local authorities (61 per cent), followed by central government agencies

(30 per cent), other community businesses (25 per cent) and industry or sector membership bodies (22 per cent) (Higton et al, 2020). Support from central and local government was predominantly financial, such as business rate relief grants (Higton et al, 2021a). As for grants, almost three quarters (74 per cent) of community business respondents reported receiving a grant, with a median grant amount of £11,763 (Higton et al, 2020).

Community business participants in Avdoulos et al's study (2020) were asked at the beginning and end of the research (May and August 2020) about how supported they felt by a range of different actors. These changed throughout this period, with feelings of support from central and local government falling over time: 42 per cent of respondents felt supported by their local council 'often/always' in May, falling to 31 per cent by August (Avdoulos et al, 2020). This pattern was echoed in terms of support from their communities, which reduced from 81 per cent in May 2020 to 64 per cent in August (Avdoulos et al, 2020). Conversely, community businesses felt slightly more supported by external organisations or support groups over time. The study also found that although financial support from both local councils and central government were particularly helpful, general support from local residents and virtual peer support from other businesses were also highly valued (Avdoulos et al, 2020).

During the pandemic, there was a notable flexibility in funding practices, including unrestricted grants and minimised application processes. This flexibility by funders was key to allowing community businesses to test out new digital methods of delivery (Gardner et al, 2021). As funders responded to the pandemic, community businesses reported that the amount of information about what funding was available was sometimes overwhelming (Avdoulos et al, 2020). Unfortunately for some community businesses, due to their hybrid business models, they were not always eligible for funding, as it tended to be tailored to *either* charities or businesses. Some community businesses with assets reported being ineligible for business support grants because the asset was counted towards the rateable value of the business (Avdoulos et al, 2020). In the longer term, the diversion of funds from major funders to the pandemic response may mean community businesses will have to put their fundraising strategies or longer-term growth plans on hold (Avdoulos et al, 2020). Many community businesses are instead looking towards consolidating the digital services and skills they have built during the pandemic and may benefit from further digital and technological advice to help them make effective investments in new systems and training (Gardner et al, 2021).

Theme 4: collaboration, trust and reputation

Financial support has been essential to the survival of many community businesses during the pandemic. However, Avdoulos et al (2020) argue that rather than just financial capital, it is *social* capital which has allowed community businesses to get through challenging times and remain accountable to and supportive of their communities. This includes the professional networks they have developed (with other community businesses and organisations), support from their communities and cooperative ways of working. For example, community businesses pooled resources, including diverting volunteers to other organisations or donating space for food banks (Avdoulos et al, 2020). At the Bevy, they used their delivery infrastructure in partnership with Brighton Aldridge Community Academy to produce pre-prepared meals for families with children who usually received free school meals (Reid, 2020).

Working in partnership with others was a common response to the pandemic. Over a quarter (28 per cent) of Community Business Market Survey respondents contributed to the efforts of mutual aid groups in their area, including a minority who were leading these efforts (Higton et al, 2020). Respondents also anticipated partnership working contributing to their recovery from the pandemic, with nearly two thirds (64 per cent) expecting to develop new partnerships or collaborations with other organisations. For many, it was important that these activities were developed in a spirit of mutuality, rather than delivering a service to users. Research participants at the Bevy, for example, were conscious of resisting the desire to "serve everybody and save everybody" and instead created genuinely mutual relationships within their communities (Reid, 2020, p 20).

Existing peer networks for community businesses came into their own during the pandemic, such as the Health and Social Care Community of Practice, funded by Power to Change since 2018. Members found it invaluable during the pandemic, both for information sharing and as a space to 'offload' given the stresses and challenges of staying afloat (Dobson et al, 2020). This was based on trusting relationships built up between members over time and with expert facilitation. Newer peer networks also proved valuable, including the Community Business Patchwork, a mutual aid network for community businesses, which brought community businesses together through a series of forums, events, meetings and resources, and was described as "the most genuine peer-to-peer experience" one community hub CEO had ever had (Avdoulos et al, 2020, p 25). This suggests the value of continued funding and facilitation for peer networks, to strengthen them for future crises.

Some community businesses have found the pandemic has acted as a 'testing ground' for their value through which they have been able to build networks and social capital. Community businesses reported that their response throughout the pandemic has enhanced their reputation with their local authorities, who now have a better understanding of their role, leading to some new partnerships (Avdoulos et al, 2020). This was not the case everywhere, however, and some community businesses have felt undervalued (Avdoulos et al, 2020). In addition, some community businesses reported increased trust from their communities as a result of the 'boundary spanning' role they played to help understand complex information and provide a conduit between the community and local authorities and health services – to signpost members of the community to the most relevant support (Gardner et al, 2021). They were well placed to do so given their local rootedness and accountability to their communities which enabled them to overcome the communication and trust barriers which are often faced by statutory services in their engagement with marginalised communities (Gardner et al, 2021).

Conclusion: the future outlook for community businesses

The studies referred to in this chapter took place within the first six months of the pandemic (March–September 2020). At that time, it was unclear to what extent COVID-19 restrictions would remain and for how long, so the studies looked to the immediate future and how community businesses could be supported to become 'COVID-friendly'. It was also unclear whether the changes wrought by the pandemic would be temporary interruptions or lead to longer-term shifts in how people accessed goods and services, supported each other and carried out their work. To some extent, this uncertainty remained at the time of writing. Nevertheless, some aspects of change have become clearer and data collected through Power to Change's 2021 Community Business Market Survey indicates how things have changed for community businesses since the early days of the pandemic.

Business activity has increased for most community businesses (62 per cent), in comparison with April 2021, following the easing of COVID-19 restrictions (Higton et al, 2022). Furthermore, almost half (49 per cent) of community businesses believed that they would restore full operations to pre-COVID-19 levels over the next year (Higton et al, 2022). This represents a more positive picture than the previous year, in which only a third of community businesses expected to restore full operations at their pre-pandemic level (Higton et al, 2021a). The anticipated increase in demand has also materialised, especially for services like mental health support and financial advice, with 88 per cent of community businesses offering mental health support and 80 per cent offering financial advice reporting increases in demand (Higton et al, 2022). In addition, more than three quarters (78 per cent) of community businesses offering health and social care services reported increased demand (Higton et al, 2022).

Looking ahead, two thirds of community businesses are aiming for partnerships with others to support their development over the next year, as well as shorter-term changes to their staffing structure (Higton et al, 2022). Delivering services and products remotely is also set to continue and in some cases, community businesses are exploring ways to monetise digital services offered during the pandemic to aid income generation (Garner et al, 2021). These digital services have allowed a minority of community businesses to increase their geographic 'reach' during the pandemic. For example, almost a fifth (18 per cent) of community businesses expanded their geographical area of operations during the pandemic, and the majority of those (83 per cent) planned to continue serving a wider area in the future (Higton et al, 2022). Although extended reach may help to increase trading income, community businesses are also defined by their local rootedness, and it will be interesting to observe the implications of serving a wider audience for other aspects of their ethos, such as local community accountability.

Avdoulos et al (2020) reported that some community businesses based on asset ownership and development feared reduced income from tenancies either as a result of greater home working, or reduced income on the part of tenants themselves. Others have experienced reduced income from venue hire, although it is hoped that this will recover once COVID-19 restrictions have been eased (Avdoulos et al, 2020). Thus, Dobson (2021) argues that while asset ownership is generally considered a boon to financial stability, COVID-19 has highlighted the risks of dependency on assets, suggesting that community businesses with more diverse income streams could be best placed to tackle future crises. Understanding the viability of different business models will be important if, as Dobson (2021) argues, changes wrought to towns and cities during the pandemic create further opportunities for community ownership and repurposing of assets.

This chapter has argued that community businesses, as a subset of the wider voluntary sector, were uniquely affected by the pandemic as a result of their 'hybrid' business models. Yet, the findings show how community businesses were also well placed to respond rapidly and meaningfully due to their local rootedness and accountability to their communities. The pandemic has also exposed and exacerbated inequalities in society according to gender, age, ethnicity and income. Community businesses can play an important role in creating more inclusive economies, mobilising social capital, building community wealth and making communities more resilient to future crises and shocks (CLES, 2019). This will not be straightforward, however, and maximising the potential of community businesses to play this role in the future will require ongoing support tailored to their 'hybrid' business models to build skills, diversify income streams and maintain peer networks.

Notes

[1] For more on this definition, see the Power to Change website: www.powertochange.org.uk/community-business/what-is-community-business/.

2   At least 95 per cent of community businesses surveyed in the Community Business Market Survey in 2021 (of a sample of 548) stated they had at least some impact on these areas (Higton et al, 2022).
3   Legislation including the Localism Act 2011 and Community Right to Bid have supported these actions.
4   The proportion of community businesses drawing most of their income from trading fell by a third to 42 per cent between February 2020 and June 2021 (Higton et al, 2022).
5   According to an LSE blog, confidence among UK businesses about their survival over the next three months reached an all-time low between 29 December 2020 and 10 January 2021. 15 per cent of businesses surveyed in the ONS Business Impacts of Coronavirus Survey reported low or no confidence in their survival (of 8,764 UK businesses surveyed), representing 390,000 businesses at risk of failure before April 2021 (Lambert and van Reenan, 2021).
6   This low figure was repeated in the 2021 iteration of the survey, although it is likely that non-response from community businesses that have ceased trading will be high.
7   Where absorptive capacity is the 'ability to moderate or buffer the impacts of the COVID-19 pandemic', adaptive capacity is 'incremental changes and adaptations … in order to continue functioning' and transformational capacity is larger-scale change to ensure survival and 'ultimately to use the crisis as an opportunity to contribute to lasting change' (Dayson et al, 2021, p 17).

References

Avdoulos, E., Wilkins, Z. and Boelman, V. (2020) *Navigating Uncertainty and Remaining Resilient: The Experience of Community Businesses during Covid-19, Research Institute Report No. 28*, London: Power to Change.

Billis, D. (2010) 'Towards a theory of hybrid organisations', in D. Billis (ed.) *Hybrid Organisations and the Third Sector: Challenges for Practice, Theory and Policy*, Basingstoke: Palgrave Macmillan, pp 46–69.

Buckley, E., Aiken, M., Baker, L., Davis, H. and Usher, R. (2017) *Community Accountability in Community Businesses, Research Institute Report No. 10*, London: Power to Change.

Centre for Local Economic Strategies (CLES) (2019) *Building an Inclusive Economy through Community Business: The Role of Social Capital and Agency in Community Business Formation in Deprived Communities*, Manchester: CLES.

Dayson, C., Baker, L. and Rees, J. (2021) *The Value of Small in a Big Crisis: The Distinctive Contribution, Value and Experiences of Smaller Charities in England and Wales during the First Wave of the COVID-19 Pandemic*, London: Lloyds Bank Foundation.

Dobson, J., Harris, C. and Macmillan, R. (2020) *Community Business Peer Networking before and during Coronavirus*, London: Power to Change.

Dobson, J. (2021) *Place-Based Approaches and Power to Change: A Short Review*, Unpublished.

Ellis Paine, A., Damm, C., Dean, J., Harris, C. and Macmillan, R. (2021) *Volunteering in Community Business: Meaning, Practice and Management*, Sheffield: CRESR and Birmingham: TSRC.

Gardner, M., Bradley, P., Parry, G. and Webber, D. (2021) *Helping Ensure Survival: Digitally Enhanced Advanced Services in Community Businesses*, London: Power to Change.

Higton, J., Archer, R., Steer, R., Mulla, I. and Hicklin, A. (2019) *The Community Business Market in 2019, Research Institute Report No. 24*, London: Power to Change.

Higton, J., Archer, R., Howe, P. and Choudhoury, A. (2020) *The Community Business Market in 2020: Impact of the COVID-19 pandemic*, London: Power to Change.

Higton, J., Archer, R., Merrett, D., Hansel, M. and Howe, P. (2021a) *The Community Business Market in 2020, Research Institute Report No. 29*, London: Power to Change.

Higton, J., Archer, R., Merrett, D., Hansel, M. and Spong, S. (2021b) *The Role of Volunteers in Community Businesses*, Leicester: CFE Research.

Higton, J., Archer, R., Francis, N., Merrett, D., Milner, C. and Choudhoury, A. (2022) *The Community Business Market in 2021*, London: Power to Change.

Kleinhans, R., Clare, S., van Meerkerk, I. and Warsen, R. (2020) *Exploring the Durability of Community Businesses in England: A Comparative Analysis*, London: Power to Change.

Lambert, P. and van Reenan, J. (2021) 'A wave of COVID-related bankruptcies is coming to the UK. What can we do about it?', [online], Available from: //blogs.lse.ac.uk/businessreview/2021/02/02/a-wave-of-covid-related-bankruptcies-is- coming-to-the-uk-what-can-we-do-about-it/ [Accessed 18 November 2021].

Langdale, E., Macmillan, R., O'Flynn, L., Oxborrow, L. and Wilson, M. (2021) *Community Responses to COVID-19: Community Hubs as Social Infrastructure*, London: Local Trust.

Moran, R., Cairns, B., Firth, L. and Dyson, E. (2020) *Taking Some Control: Briefing 6 on the Challenges Faced by VCSE Leaders during the Covid-19 Crisis*, London: IVAR.

National Council for Voluntary Organisations (NCVO) (2021) *UK Civil Society Almanac 2021*, [online], Available from: //beta.ncvo.org.uk/ncvo-publications/uk-civil-society-almanac-2021/volunteering/ [Accessed 18 November 2021].

Plunkett Foundation (2020) *State of Rural Community Business: A Snapshot View in June 2020*, Woodstock: Plunkett Foundation.

Reid, S. (2020) *We Can't Actually Be a Pub, We Can Only Be 'more than' a Pub: The Bevy in Lockdown*, Brighton: The Bevy.

Stumbitz, B., Vickers, I., Lyon, F., Butler, J., Gregory, D. and Mansfield, C. (2018) *The Role of Community Businesses in Providing Health and Wellbeing Services: Challenges, Opportunities and Support Needs*, London: Power to Change.

15

The response of voluntary community sports clubs to COVID-19

Geoff Nichols, Lindsay Findlay-King and Fiona Reid

Introduction

This chapter describes how community sports clubs (CSCs) have adapted to the restrictions imposed during the COVID-19 pandemic. Exploring the role of CSCs in depth is important because of their role in promoting physical and mental health, especially important during a pandemic and enforced lockdowns, and the context they provide for a large amount of volunteering in both the UK and other countries. The chapter makes the case that CSCs are mutual aid organisations in the sense used by Beveridge (1948), with the welfare of members central to their mission. They contrast, therefore, with more professionalised, philanthropic-focused organisations. Understanding CSCs as a particular type of small, local mutual aid organisation explains how they have been able to respond quickly to changed circumstances to meet the needs of members. However, we argue that they have not changed to meet the needs of broader society beyond their membership. We also highlight a significant adaptation to restrictions due to the use of digital technology, which has both included and excluded members.

CSCs are the context in which a large amount of sports participation and volunteering takes place. In England, there are approximately 72,117 CSCs, with an average of 100 adult participants, 77 junior participants, 44 non-playing members and 24 volunteers in each (Barrett et al, 2018; Sport and Recreation Alliance, 2018). The only national survey of sports volunteering to estimate the amount of time contributed, in 2002, found that volunteers in sports clubs account for a large majority of sport-related volunteering, which is itself a large proportion of volunteer activity (Taylor et al, 2003). The same national population survey (Taylor et al, 2003) showed that 14.8 per cent of adults aged over 16 in England volunteered for sport in 2002, each contributing an average of just under 208 hours over the year (approximately four hours each week). More recently, a national survey for Sport England found that 4.9 per cent of the population over 16 volunteered weekly in sport in 2019/20 (Sport England, 2021). The structure and scale of volunteer-led sports clubs is similar across most European countries (Nagel et al, 2020), Australia and New Zealand (Cuskelly et al, 2006).

Methods

The main sources for this chapter are three research projects into how CSCs have adapted to the pandemic: a set of interviews with 13 CSCs, in England and Scotland, in July 2020 (Findlay-King et al, 2020); repeated with 12 of the sample in January/February 2021 (Nichols et al, 2021); and a larger research project conducted between March and August 2021 (Reid et al, 2022). The first two sets of interviews were self-funded and aimed to understand how CSCs had responded in general to pandemic-related restrictions. The sample was chosen to contrast clubs which delivered indoor and outdoor sports, team sports and individual sports, and clubs with and without their own facility. The last project was England-specific and included 13 telephone interviews with national sports organisations, including ten national governing bodies (NGBs) of sports to which CSCs would normally affiliate; a snapshot survey completed by 74 CSCs; and in-depth interviews with 8 CSCs, selected to illustrate successful innovations in response to the restrictions of the pandemic. This project was contracted by Sport England with the aim of finding out innovations made by CSCs in response to the pandemic, and which might be continued as good practice. Further details of the methods are in the referenced reports. These sources are supplemented, where appropriate, with results from other national surveys.

CSCs as mutual aid organisations

Understanding CSCs as particular types of mutual aid organisation helps explain their response to the pandemic. For Lyons et al (1998), it is 'the product of people's ability to work together to meet shared needs and address common problems' (Lyons et al, 1998, p 52). Recently, in studying 20 organisations which have emerged to respond to the pandemic, mutual aid has been defined as 'a volunteer led initiative where groups of people in a particular area join together to support one another, meeting vital community needs without relying on official bodies. They do so in a way that prioritises those who are most vulnerable or otherwise unable to access help through regular channels' (Benton and Power, 2021).

Our CSCs match this definition in that they are 'volunteer-led initiatives' of people 'in a particular area', joining together to support each other to meet 'community needs' and they do not rely on official bodies. It is, of course, debatable whether community sports qualify as 'vital community needs', in the spirit of the 'five giants' set out by the 1948 report by Beveridge on voluntary action and mutual aid – want, disease, ignorance, squalor and idleness. We argue, however, that this conceptualisation is too narrow, and that sports clubs do contribute very significantly to community needs. A recent estimate is that in England, sport creates societal benefits in terms of improved health, reduced crime, improved education and enhanced subjective wellbeing. Sport England's social return on investment model estimated that for every £1 invested in sport, £1.91 worth of social benefit is generated (Davies et al, 2019).

A second difference from Benton and Power's (2021) definition is that CSCs do not necessarily prioritise those who are most vulnerable. In line with Beveridge (1948), however, we argue that in contrast to philanthropy, mutual aid arises from individuals' sense of their own needs rather than from philanthropists' view of what society needs. So mutual aid organisations need not necessarily prioritise those who are most vulnerable but are to promote the mutual interests of members as they see fit. Examples include the two remaining mutual building societies in the UK, which are wholly owned by members. Arguably, newer organisations set up explicitly to respond to the pandemic may in fact be more philanthropic than mutual aid, if their main aim is to help others who are more vulnerable.

There are three further, inter-related characteristics of CSCs as mutual aid organisations worth highlighting, which help us to understand their response to the pandemic. Firstly, CSCs are small organisations in which the same volunteers take on roles of governance and delivery. A committee normally includes named posts, such as chair, secretary, treasurer and so on, but these officers will also do whatever needs doing to run the club, such as maintenance jobs. This overlap of governance and delivery enables CSCs to be very sensitive to the needs of members, especially the need for social support, and to act very quickly to respond to changed circumstances. In contrast, in much larger organisations, paid staff govern and volunteers are used for delivery. For example, the National Trust in England employs over 14,000 staff and is supported by over 53,000 volunteers.

The second characteristic is that the rewards of club membership are experienced at least as much by the volunteers running the clubs as the members, and for the volunteers can be conceptualised as a form of 'serious leisure' (Stebbins, 1996), conferring a sense of purpose, identity and status (Nichols et al, 2016). The social rewards of 'conviviality' (Rochester, 2013, p 31) are extremely important. Thus, the key volunteers identify with the club and their volunteering confers significant rewards. Furthermore, the complete overlap of governance and delivery in CSCs, combined with the volunteers' commitment and sensitivity to members' needs, means the volunteers are extremely strongly motivated to maintain the club in the face of the challenges of COVID, contributing to its resilience.

A third important characteristic is that the aims of the CSC may be stated in a constitution but in this type of small group, a consensus of the members is more important in determining what the club does. This again contrasts with large organisations with clearly defined objectives, in which governance and delivery are often split. In these larger organisations, it is possible to use the aims as a reference point for a rational systems approach to management, in which the resources available, including volunteers, can be deployed most effectively to meet the organisation's aims (see McCurley and Lynch, 2006). Again, the National Trust in England is an example of this type of organisation.

Volunteer resilience

Volunteers, within the CSCs, had to deal with changed financial circumstances and membership packages, adapting their sports to allow as much participation as possible, and react quickly to changed guidance on what activity could take place.

Income was reduced through loss of membership fees, if these were not renewed (or regular payments paused), reduced numbers in coaching sessions, cancelled competitions, closure of catering facilities, hiring of facilities and sponsorship. Increased costs included sanitising premises, equipment and travel, while facility maintenance costs remained the same. Despite this, our sample was in a better financial position in February 2021 due to grants, rate relief, the Job Retention Scheme and careful cost management, combined with healthy reserves. Most of the CSCs had not suffered a significant fall in members. The national decline in sports participation (Sport England, 2020) was not reflected in a fall in the clubs' memberships because members remained loyal, despite not being able to play as much. Some CSCs offered adapted membership packages, especially to account for the impact of lockdowns on seasonal sports.

A major challenge was reacting quickly to changes in government guidance on what sports participation was allowed. Sport England and the national governing bodies of the sports to which CSCs are affiliated had no advance notice of these changes so had to provide guidance to CSCs after central government had announced them. Only then could CSCs make the required changes, but the implications of regulations were difficult to interpret for different sports. One sailing club illustrated this:

> 'we could start doing organised dinghy sailing from July the 13th as long as on any one boat, it was either one person, so a single hander or it was people from the same household. This allowed members to compete, if they met these conditions. It's not clear how the club could ensure that any two people in a boat were from the same household. A difficulty was that clubs were restricted to five households per

session, but for any formal activity there would be people on the shore, launching and retrieving the boats.'

CSCs had to adapt quickly to changes. For example, a tennis club had four days to react to the announcement they could open the courts on 29 May:

'This presented volunteers with a lot of work in a short period of time; we had to un-padlock the gates; a few of us had to make notices; we had to set up a booking system because we had to follow LTA / Tennis Scotland guidelines ... each time there's a change. And ... some of them are a bit contradictory because they've got bits for venues, bits for players, bits for coaches ... you've got to really go through them and find what will work.'

CSCs adapted the way the sports were played to achieve 'social distancing' (for example, by restricting the numbers of bowls rinks used to allow a gap between them), limiting the size of groups (for example, for mountaineering and gymnastics) or reducing physical contact (for example, no scrums in rugby).

The adaptations illustrate the considerable extra work required by volunteers running the CSCs. However, their willingness to do this reflected their strong commitment to the club and the rewards they experienced from volunteering. A volunteer from a group that facilitates riding for disabled people explained: "I have to be honest and say [our group] is a lifesaver, because I think I to the club and the rewards they experienced from volunteering mean I love it; I've done 28 years with them now and it's my passion".

Stoical commitment and a mutual aid ethos was illustrated by a sailing volunteer: "To be honest, it's just all been a bit frustrating ... it's just been really difficult. But that's just the way it is ... almost a volunteering deal, which is you volunteer to do something, and you get your reward in terms of seeing people are benefiting from what you're doing".

Loyalty to the club and members meant volunteers would do whatever it took to keep the club going, as this golf volunteer showed: "you know, you're the temporary custodians of an institution and that's it and you have to accept that".

Meeting the social needs

A survey of CSC members in England in 2015 found that for 62 per cent 'the club was one of the most important social groups I belong to' (Nichols and James, 2020). Members placed a higher value on companionship and conviviality than on sporting success and competition. Volunteers recognised the importance of trying as far as possible to meet the social rewards of the club members which could not be met in the usual ways. For example, pre-pandemic, a bowls club, which had an older membership, would offer a social evening once a month in the club house. Members would also normally be able to have refreshments after a game and the club ran a 'president's tour' for a week in the summer, when members took a coach to a resort and stayed in a hotel for a week, playing bowls during the day and with social events in the evening. This was extremely popular and for some members was their main annual holiday. Similarly, a mountaineering club reported:

> 'The big thing we are missing is the ability to meet together in larger numbers ... the social thing is really important to members. We would normally have five weekend trips where we'd share accommodation and a meal, including a Christmas meet. Other social activities would generally be based at the club building, and they tend to be more so in the winter so that we keep people together so with our AGM in the winter will have a little party afterwards sort of tea and buns sort of affair.'

As members could not meet physically, virtual substitutes were required. Some replicated pre-pandemic activities as far as possible, such as talks, competitions, quizzes, virtual Christmas parties and general social exchanges, using WhatsApp groups and Zoom events. In some clubs, it allowed members who had moved away from the area to meet others who they would normally only see two or three times a year. Clubs set up group fitness training events; these might involve a challenge, such as club members running a sufficient distance to collectively reach New Zealand.

Sometimes these activities actually increased social interaction; for example, a golf club member reported the amount of "stuff that was going around you know just supporting each other and sending fun stuff to each other throughout the time we were locked down, checking on the older ones and making sure that they were all right. I think it's brought out a little bit more community spirit". In some clubs, this extended to doing shopping for older members and delivering newsletters by hand when they did not have internet access, for others, checking on members' mental health. This illustrates a positive outcome of the club's social networks being used to provide other support to members and social solidarity being enhanced. As one archery club illustrated, being able to "share ailments, illnesses, situations" among themselves as volunteers was invaluable. However, these mainly virtual communications were not a complete substitute, and the novelty could wear off. For example, in a group that facilitates riding for disabled people, volunteers were "missing the social interaction, they're missing the connectivity of people and to a degree you need your 'horse fix', volunteers do get very fond of equines".

Meeting the needs of existing members, or the rest of society?

Haldane speculated that 'The Covid crisis is the latest in a long historical line, with social capital gluing together communities otherwise at risk of coming unstuck; the ... policies put in place globally to contain the spread of the disease ... reinforced the sense of community purpose and social solidarity ... causing social capital to flourish' (Haldane, 2020, p 1).

That the voluntary sector could 'offer ... new ideas, approaches and visions' to meeting society's needs has been posed as a pragmatic solution and research question (Macmillan, 2020, p 134). However, the glue of social capital does not necessarily emerge from change. In some circumstances, change has been associated with diminishing trust, as individual groups 'hunker down' to meet the needs of pre-existing members (Putnam, 2007).

While CSCs showed a heightened concern to meet the needs of their existing members, there was little evidence of them changing what they did to meet society's broader needs. This was not because they were oblivious to them but because this was beyond their purpose, as defined by the collective interests of members within a mutual aid organisation. A hockey club summed up this response:

> 'While we want to be like that, I think first and foremost, we are just going to remain a sports club, of course, we want to offer support [to members], but we don't want to do that in ... a formalised manner. Because we're not counsellors at the end of the day, ... obviously, it's really great to see clubs engaging like that, and rugby clubs, delivering meals, and that, but it's not something that we really thought about or approached. I think, you know, our main focus is delivering sport as best we can.'

Some clubs broadened the sport they offered to attract new and different members, but this was consistent with their collective aims. For example, developing women's sections in rugby, or providing different versions of their sport such as field archery courses and recreational sailing, as opposed to competitions. The latter, however, didn't see itself "becoming [anything] other than a sailing club".

However, while CSCs were not offering new ideas and visions to meet society's needs, the support they gave members reflects the depth of social capital within the clubs, which in some cases was deepened by the concern for members' welfare. Bonding social capital predominates, between club members who share a passion for the sport and their social relationships with each other, rather than bridging social capital outside these relationships (Nichols et al, 2013). The 'hunker down' effect (Putnam, 2007) was seen as clubs coalesced around carrying on and meeting the needs of their members, despite the pandemic. A football club showed this deepening of social relationships: "it wasn't something we were expecting to have to deal with. But actually, I think it's helped us to come together more as a group of trustees because we've had to get on together and get this done. So yes, I think it's had its benefits definitely".

A catalyst for digital innovation: skills, technology and exclusion

The pandemic has accentuated a trend towards the use of digital technology (GSMA, 2020).

The major change for CSCs was the increased use of digital communication to substitute as far as possible for face-to-face contact and to develop services. We have noted how this was used to try and retain the social rewards of membership. At the club level, it was also used for meetings, training sessions and online sessions such as gymnastics for juniors. Digital communication was embraced by national governing bodies of sport, where it saved much time travelling to meetings, which could be run digitally, and could be used to deliver training. It included volunteer awards, Annual General Meetings, even online national championships. One national organisation ran online championships, where participants would send in a video which would be judged virtually.

A common innovation for CSCs was the use of online booking systems to restrict numbers at sessions and keep records of attendance to comply with COVID-19 regulations. There were mixed views on whether these were a positive innovation. Interviews with NGB representatives reported that they had been encouraging these innovations for some time and that the pandemic had been the catalyst for clubs to adopt them. They had a mixed reception. For example, a golf club respondent noted that "It was fastest finger first, when you tried to book a time, when the system opened up". This caused "endless emails about why they couldn't get a booking". In general, while systems could improve services for the member, there were still some frustrations with using digital systems, as one table tennis club showed: "Mainly me as Club Secretary learning how [X booking system] worked, with much support from Table Tennis England, and occasionally another volunteer. Most players learnt to use online booking, but a minority haven't, and just text me to book them in".

The pros and cons of 'going digital' reflected those noted in a NCVO review in August 2021 (NCVO, 2021). Advantages included the ability to make contact with a wider range of people or groups, some services could be expanded and meetings were made more efficient through cutting travel time and costs. The main barriers, in order of significance, were the skills of staff and volunteers, the cost of equipment and software, the skills of service users and the access of users to equipment. The NCVO noted that this could lead to 'digital exclusion' especially of older people, and this was reflected in CSCs. The use of digital communication required both volunteers and members to have the technology to do it, either know-how to use it or being prepared to invest time and energy into learning how to use it, have support if required and approach it with a positive mindset. These conditions were not always in place. Some interviews with NGBs showed an assumption that volunteers and members could use it if they made the effort.

> 'I'm trying to be diplomatic … when people have done something for so long in a certain way, to ask them to change so radically … it's difficult, so that's when we're asking them. But COVID wasn't an option, so people didn't have the choice but to change and some have embraced it and have kind of, you know, pulled into the 21st century and some haven't. And we're now seeing them struggle.'

However, as the NCVO review indicated, some older people will not have the technology, or the know-how, to use it. This was illustrated by a bowls club where most of the Green Stewards left their role when they were asked to use a digital booking system to check that bowlers' fees had been paid. Some members may not have Wi-Fi access at home, including some young people in disadvantaged circumstances. The criticism that volunteers and members should make the effort to learn to use the technology also fails to recognise that they are freely engaged in a leisure activity where they might not want to. Volunteers who had digital skills described how it took time to adapt and make systems work for their needs, particularly with online registration and payment systems. For some CSCs, adoption of what may seem a minor digital innovation represents a big change, so support from national sport organisations would need to recognise this. There were a few examples of digital technology increasing 'inclusion' in terms of new CSC members. The strongest example was of members from a wider geographical dispersion being able to attend meetings.

Conclusions

This chapter has shown how CSCs, as an example of mutual aid organisations, have adapted to the pandemic. A strength of these organisations is the very strong commitment of key volunteers who are bound to the organisation by social ties and as a form of serious leisure. The close link between volunteers and members, with little distinction between governance and delivery roles, has allowed rapid and innovative responses. This may have been more rapid and innovative than in a more formal organisation where governance and delivery are split. The nature of a mutual aid organisation as an expression of shared enthusiasms, in this case for the sport and for the club as a social institution, has meant that adaptations have focused on supporting existing members, although social bonds may have grown in the face of adversity. This has built on existing bonding social capital but has created very limited extension to bridging social capital with new individuals and groups. This reflects this type of mutual aid organisation, where the purpose is defined by the enthusiasms of members. It may not apply equally to mutual aid organisations who have a wider social purpose. For example, a food bank with a general aim of community support may have responded to the pandemic by broadening the range of support services it offers. For CSCs, the major innovation in response to the pandemic has been the accelerated use of digital technology, which for some has been a major innovation, and for others has led to exclusion.

References

Barrett, D., Edmondson, L., Millar, R. and Storey, R. (2018) *Sport Club Volunteering*, [online], Available from: //sportengland-production-files.s3.eu-west-2.amazonaws.com/s3fs-public/sirc-se-sports-club-volunteers-report.pdf?VersionId=JlTZP10e0j_9kzTQYOF3InPLGuAvMEVn [Accessed 30 September 2021].

Benton, E. and Power, A. (2021) 'Where next for Britain's 4300 mutual aid groups?', [online], Available from: //blogs.lse.ac.uk/careers/2021/06/30/where-next-for-britains-4300-mutual-aid-groups/ [Accessed 10 December 2021].

Beveridge, W.H.B. (1948) *Voluntary Action: A Report on Methods of Social Advance*, London: Allen & Unwin.

Cuskelly, G., Auld, C. and Hoye, R. (2006) *Working with Volunteers in Sport: Theory and Practice*, London: Routledge.

Davies, L.E., Taylor, P., Ramchandani, G. and Christy, E. (2019) 'Social return on investment (SROI) in sport: a model for measuring the value of participation in England', *International Journal of Sport Policy and Politics*, 11(4): 585–605.

Findlay-King, L., Reid, F. and Nichols, G. (2020) *Community Sports Clubs Response to Covid-19*, [online], Available from: //sway.office.com/7vwbaHlJwaF3OTlE [Accessed 29 September 2021].

GSMA (2020) *The Mobile Economy 2020*, [online], Available from: www.gsma.com/mobileeconomy/ [Accessed 30 September 2021].

Haldane, A. (2020) 'Social capital, the economy's rocket fuel', in *Civil Society Unleashed*, pp 1–4, [online], Available from: www.probonoeconomics.com/essay-collection-civil-society-unleashed [Accessed 29 September 2021].

Lyons, M., Wijkstrom, P. and Clary, G. (1998) 'Comparative studies of volunteering: What is being studied?', *Voluntary Action*, 1(1): 45–54.

Macmillan, R. (2020) 'Somewhere over the rainbow – third sector research in and beyond coronavirus', *Voluntary Sector Review*, 11(2): 129–36.

McCurley, S. and Lynch, R. (2006) *Volunteer Management: Mobilizing all the Resources of the Community*, Kemptville, ON: Johnstone Training and Consultation, Inc.

Nagel, S., Elmose-Østerlund, K., Ibsen, B. and Scheerder, J. (eds.) (2020) *Functions of Sports Clubs in European Societies, A Cross-National Comparative Study*, Switzerland: Springer.

NCVO (2021) *Respond, Recover, Reset: The Voluntary Sector and COVID-19*, [online], Available from: //cpwop.org.uk/wp-content/uploads/sites/3/2021/02/NTU-Covid-voluntary-sector-report-Feb-2021_DIGITAL.pdf [Accessed 29 September 2021].

Nichols, G., Tacon, R. and Muir, A. (2013) 'Sports clubs' volunteers: bonding in or bridging out?', *Sociology*, 47: 350–67.

Nichols, G. and James, M. (2020) 'England, a long tradition, adapting to changing circumstances', in S. Nagel, K. Elmose-Østerlund, B. Ibsen and B.J. Scheerder (eds.) *Functions of Sports Clubs in European Societies*, Switzerland: Springer, pp 93–120.

Nichols, G., Findlay-King, L. and Reid, F. (2021) *Community Sports Clubs' Response to Covid-19, July 2020 to February 2021: Resilience and Innovation*, [online], Available from: //sports-volunteer-research-network.org.uk/2021/04/26/community-sports-clubs-response-to-covid-19/ [Accessed 29 September 2021].

Nichols, G., Hogg, E., Knight, C., Mirfin-Boukouris, H., Storr, R. and Uri, C. (2016) *Understanding Motivations of Sport Volunteers in England: A Review for Sport England*, [online], Available from: //sports-volunteer-research-network.org.uk/wp-content/uploads/2013/02/Motivations-of-sport-volunteers-29-1-16.pdf [Accessed 1 October 2021].

Putnam, R.D. (2007) 'E pluribus unum: diversity and community in the twenty-first century', *Scandinavian Political Studies*, 30(2): 137–74.

Reid, F., Findlay-King, L., Nichols, G. and Mills, C. (2022) *Innovation during the Covid-19 Pandemic: Volunteers and Voluntary Sports Organisations in England: Summary Report*, [online], Available from: //sportengland-production-files.s3.eu-west-2.amazonaws.com/s3fs-public/2022-01/Volunteer%20innovation%20during%20the%20pandemic%20-%20summary%20report.pdf?VersionId=wOqQFtsIbHXEyCrjhPXIJCwYsxtqKHkL [Accessed 25 February 2022].

Rochester, C. (2013) *Rediscovering Voluntary Action: The Beat of a Different Drum*, Basingstoke: Palgrave Macmillan.

Sport and Recreation Alliance (2018) *Sports Club Survey Report 2017/ 18*, [online], Available from: //sramedia.s3.amazonaws.com/media/ documents/b8ddaf87-e6f2-45c5-9c59-11ae4dff67ef.pdf [Accessed 30 September 2021].

Sport England (2020) *Active Lives Adult Survey Mid-March to Mid-May 2020. Coronavirus Covid-19 Report*, [online], Available from: //sportengland-production-files.s3.eu-west-2.amazonaws.com/s3fs-public/2020-10/ Active%20Lives%20Adult%20May%2019-20%20Coronavirus%20 Report.pdf?2L6TBVV5UvCGXb_VxZcWHcfFX0_wRal7 [Accessed 30 September 2021].

Sport England (2021) *Active Lives Adult Survey November 2019/20 Report*, [online], Available from: //sportengland-production-files.s3.eu-west-2.amazonaws.com/s3fs-public/2021-04/Active%20Lives%20Adult%20 November%202019-20%20Report.pdf?VersionId=OjWdwCLnI3dNgD wp3X4ukcODJIDVG7Kd [Accessed 1 October 2021].

Stebbins, R. (1996) 'Volunteering: a serious leisure perspective', *Non-Profit and Voluntary Sector Quarterly*, 25: 211–24.

Taylor, P., Nichols, G., Holmes, K., James, M., Gratton, C., Garrett, R., Kokolakakis, T., Mulder, C. and King, L. (2003) *Sports Volunteering in England*, London: Sport England.

16

The latent strength of community ties: how voluntary sector infrastructure organisations utilised their local networks in response to COVID-19

Lucy Smith

Introduction

While the COVID-19 pandemic has had an unprecedented effect on many aspects of social life, the impact upon the voluntary sector is arguably yet to be fully realised (Macmillan, 2021). Prima facie, COVID-19 appeared to usher in a new era of public and community engagement – with an estimated 10 million people volunteering during the initial lockdown period in the spring and summer of 2020 (Legal & General, 2020). Because of this, many local authorities formed 'community response hubs' – interim local spaces where the statutory sector, voluntary sector (VS) and residents came together to coordinate and provide support to the surrounding community. These hubs delivered multiple aid provisions, from the distribution of food parcels, household goods and medication, to specialised services such as befriending, bereavement support and later, providing stewards to vaccination sites.

What has been less acknowledged was the contribution made to these initiatives by voluntary sector infrastructure organisations during this period, such as councils for voluntary service (CVSs), voluntary actions (VAs) and volunteer centres (VCs). While it has recently been argued that the pandemic brought about a period of re-enchantment and renaissance in policy making for voluntary sector infrastructure (Macmillan, 2021), there has not yet been a thorough examination of how these organisations operated throughout the pandemic – in particular, their contribution to key services (Macmillan 2021) such as community hubs and other similar approaches to coordinating aid and support.

This chapter utilises social network analysis and the theoretical work of Granovetter (1973) to illustrate how voluntary sector infrastructure organisations were able to mobilise their cross-sector relationships to make a significant contribution to community-level support. Drawing on two London-based case studies of CVSs in operation during lockdown, the aim of this chapter is to demonstrate how the 'embedded' position of these organisations (Dayson et al, 2017) paid unlikely dividends – enabling information, resources and aid to flow between otherwise unconnected parties at both a local and a regional level. Finally, this chapter concludes by considering the latent strength of voluntary sector infrastructure and makes a case for the societal value (Putnam, 1993) added by these organisations to the local VS and wider community.

The role of voluntary sector infrastructure

The primary ambition of voluntary infrastructure organisations is to improve communities through 'voluntary action', a process whereby individuals 'spend unpaid time doing something that aims to benefit the environment or [other] individuals or groups' (Ellis Paine, Hill and Rochester, 2010, p 9). This ambition is part of the wider view that volunteers and charitable organisations are fundamental to the health of society, providing 'specialised services on a national scale ... to needs which might otherwise be neglected' (The Seebohm Report, 1968).

While the influential Aves (1969) report and advisory work of the Seebohm Committee (1968) represented initial attempts to bring voluntary action into the realm of public policy and post-war recovery efforts, the history of English voluntary sector infrastructure predates this period. As Rochester (2012, p 103) observes, 'today's Councils for Voluntary Service (CVSs) are descendants of the Councils for Social Service (CSSs) that existed at local level for much of the 20th century'. Early CSSs, such as the Hampstead Council for Social Welfare (which later became Voluntary Action Camden[1]), were founded as the direct result of philanthropist efforts to improve the delivery of charitable services. The purpose of the CSS was to coordinate the activities of 'all the churches, all the municipal bodies and all the voluntary associations in a given local area' under a broadly based body which would address the social needs of its residents and by 1931, 122 CSSs existed nationally (Nunn in Rochester, 2012, p 103).

Later publications such as the Wolfenden Report (1978) defined the role of CVSs further, referring to the latter as 'local generalist intermediary bodies' which served to coordinate and reconcile 'the inherent tension' between the interests of autonomous individual charitable organisations and 'the pursuit of common purposes' at the local level (Wolfenden in Rochester, 2013, p 104). The report identified five key functions performed by CVSs which included 'development' work, 'services to other organisations', 'liaison', 'representation' and 'direct services to individuals' (Wolfenden in Rochester, 2013, p 104). More significantly, the report established the CVS model which we know today. New elements were brought into practice such as membership schemes for local voluntary organisations which included direct support to members and representation of their interests to statutory bodies including local authorities and their subsidiaries (Wolfenden in Rochester, 2013). Crucially, this enabled CVSs to begin to foster relationships on behalf of the VS with other sectors – a point we shall return to later in this chapter.

In the early 2000s, the practice of 'development' became a core source of funding for CVSs. The emphasis on 'local capacity building' saw many CVSs receive core funding from local authorities and was also a key tenet of New Labour's wider strategy for the voluntary sector. This included the ChangeUp (Home Office, 2005) programme which emphasised the role of CVSs in developing understanding of, and improving through direct services, the needs of local frontline organisations (Home Office, 2005). Tasked with local capacity building, many CVSs began to establish myriad connections with local voluntary organisations and groups through the provision of support services, including secretariat and the provision of training resources to generate revenue (Macmillan, 2013).

Although the election of the coalition government in 2010 saw the dismantlement of the ChangeUp initiative and similar 'capacity building' schemes, many CVSs still continue to work with local authorities and other statutory bodies in the pursuit of core funding (Dayson et al, 2017). These political developments have led most English CVSs to establish direct partnerships with statutory bodies and to also deliver some public services on their behalf (Rochester, 2012). In addition, there has been a gradual shift over the past decade towards an experimental managed market approach through 'demand-led' capacity building, which has been shaped by funders at both the local and national level (Dayson et al, 2017). The availability of this type of funding has led many 'umbrella organisations', such as CVSs, to prioritise the provision of development services over other core duties such as networking[2] and advocacy work (Macmillan, 2021). This has led some CVSs to adopt the wider role of community 'service provider' and diversify their offering beyond the needs of the traditional membership base, extending provisions to other organisations such as community interest companies (CiCs), grassroots groups and, in some cases, individual residents.[3]

As a result of these developments, most CVSs now rely upon multiple funding sources and work also to generate revenue by delivering various services (Rochester, 2012). This places them in a unique position in so far as they 'straddle' the statutory *and* voluntary sectors, while attempting to satisfy the interests of both in the services they deliver. In this way, CVSs operate at 'the crossroads' between local authorities and the voluntary sector (Rochester, 2012, p 108) – a position which, while often challenging, also grants voluntary sector infrastructure organisations an array of contacts both within the statutory sector, such as local authorities and clinical commissioning groups, and also within the local voluntary sector, including small grassroots organisations.

Over time, this has led to particular ways of working whereby the CVSs have become the central point of contact for multiple organisations operating across multiple sectors and with different interest groups. Voluntary sector infrastructure organisations can therefore be said to have become 'embedded'[4] (Granovetter, 1985) within the sector through funding relationships with key strategic actors at both the local and national level (Dayson et al, 2017). These relationships, built over time and mediated through the awarding of funds in exchange for the delivery of multiple services, had led to many infrastructure organisations, such as CVSs, establishing both a spatial and reputational presence within local authority areas (see 'Territorial Embeddedness' in Dayson et al, 2017). Most significantly, a greater degree of embeddedness has been argued to have strengthened the hand of some voluntary sector infrastructure organisations – enabling them not only to achieve continued funding but also to develop diverse networks of multifaceted contacts across different sectors and fields (Rumbul, 2013 in Dayson et al, 2017). When the pandemic occurred, it follows thus that embedded infrastructure organisations – such as CVSs – were in an opportune position to directly respond to the many unanticipated challenges which occurred within their 'territory'. By virtue of their embedded position, they were able to respond not only to local challenges within the surrounding neighbourhood but also to wider dilemmas which affected other organisational actors within their professional, cross-sector networks.

The next section of this chapter examines how the embeddedness of these organisations paid unexpected dividends during the first national lockdown (March–June 2020). It illustrates the function of spatial, reputational and institutional relationships in the case of two London-based CVSs who were responsible for delivering community aid. The chosen case studies demonstrate how two CVSs mobilised their networks to resolve both simplistic and advanced challenges at local and regional levels.

Research methodology

The data discussed in this chapter is qualitative in nature and was obtained through a series of focus groups and one-to-one interviews with senior management staff from London-based infrastructure organisations. The participants were recruited through London Plus, an umbrella organisation for voluntary sector infrastructure which aims to champion voluntary action across the capital (London Plus, 2020). The initial purpose of the research was to gather qualitative insights about the activity and needs of its membership. Participants attended a series of three focus groups where they were encouraged to share their experiences of working through the pandemic linked to the following themes: successes, challenges and reflections on the COVID-19 recovery period and the role of their organisation in the post-pandemic world. Many participants also discussed organisational partnerships, funding needs and staff wellbeing. By the end of the initial research period in July 2020, 14 voluntary sector infrastructure organisations from various boroughs within London had taken part. Colleagues from London Plus and participants from the chosen CVSs were then approached in September 2021 for one-to-one interviews to clarify and validate the case studies discussed in the following section.

Findings

Case study 1: Voluntary Action Camden

Voluntary Action Camden (VAC) is an embedded organisation, spatially, institutionally and historically. It is one of the oldest voluntary infrastructure organisations in London and began life as part of the Hampstead Council for Social Welfare (CSS) (Rochester, 2012). Predating the establishment of the NHS in 1948, the Hampstead CSS offered a variety of social welfare provisions for the surrounding community including health, social care and legal support services (Voluntary Action Camden, 2021). Its subsidiary bodies, known as 'committees' and 'subcommittees', were also the first voluntary organisations in the borough of Camden.

The legacy of Hampstead CSS is an important aspect of VAC's identity and continues to shape its work to date. Interviewees from VAC cited the 'health component' of the organisation's history as continuing to influence their relationship with both medical practitioners and voluntary organisations providing health and wellbeing services. Because of this, VAC became an early adoptee of social prescribing – a programme whereby GPs make referrals to local voluntary organisations with the aim of improving the wellbeing of patients with particular conditions.[5] VAC's social prescribing scheme is borough-wide and enables the CVS to work in direct partnership with both the local VS and other statutory bodies, such as the NHS North Central London Commissioning Group (NCL CCG). Through the scheme, VAC had therefore already established cross-sector relationships and a local reputation for delivering wellbeing services prior to lockdown.

Most significantly, the CVS had also developed relationships with other intermediary actors, such as GP surgeries and pharmacies across the borough. When a national lockdown was initiated on 23 March 2020, VAC found itself inundated with requests for support from local organisations and residents in need. Some of these requests came directly from GP surgery staff and members of the NCL CCG, who raised concerns with VAC about the effects of lockdown upon vulnerable patients, particularly those who were self-isolating and could not access their regular medication. Local pharmacies had become overwhelmed with delivery requests and were unable to respond to unprecedented levels of demand for the service.

VAC had to innovate to respond to this request. Unlike some CVSs, it does not have an in-house volunteer centre or engage in volunteer brokerage. Supplying volunteers directly to resolve the distribution issue was not possible for an organisation like VAC – instead, it had to draw upon its network of VS contacts to source appropriate support. VAC enlisted the support of GoodGym, a charity which collaborates in the social prescribing programme and whose volunteers combine exercise (such as jogging) with acts of community service (GoodGym, 2021). Its volunteers are registered, and fully DBS checked – which made them suitable to courier medication for vulnerable people. Because the volunteers also travel predominantly by foot, they did not require any additional resources (that is, vehicles and fuel) to establish the interim delivery service. This enabled VAC to set up the delivery service rapidly and forward requests received directly from local surgeries and pharmacies to GoodGym volunteers operating across the borough.

While it may appear to be a relatively simple solution, the prescription delivery service illustrates how voluntary sector infrastructure organisations played an essential role in coordinating these types of interim services (see Macmillan, 2021). As previously discussed, these organisations occupy a unique position in between the statutory sector and the VS (Zammer in Rochester, 2012). VAC's long-standing historical presence, its local reputation and institutional relationships with the NHS NCL CCG and wider VS are key indicators of its territorial embeddedness (Dayson et al, 2017) and subsequently, it's latent strength. In this scenario, the direct relationships formed between VAC and its partners came to function as 'bridges' – pathways through which information and resources could flow. In *The Strength of Weak Ties* (1973), Granovetter describes this phenomenon as network 'diffusion', a process through which information spreads, by virtue of existing relationships between two parties ('bridges'), to an array of indirect contacts. If a relationship exists between A and B, but C is not a known contact of A, then the most efficient way of C to reach A is via contact B (Granovetter, 1973, p 1364). In this example, VAC acted as part B of the A-B-C network – effectively creating an indirect connection from local GP surgeries and pharmacies (A) to GoodGym (C). Through this lens, VAC's role as a central point of contact for medical practitioners, charitable partners and isolated residents is a by-product of dense and rich local networks developed over many years and through long-term investment in VAC as the local CVS.

Figure 16.1: Diffusion model between the NCL CCG, Voluntary Action Camden and GoodGym

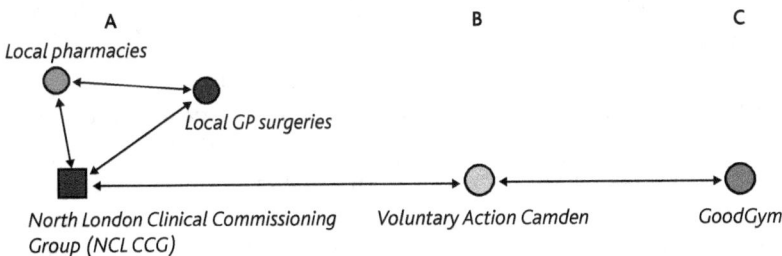

VAC's embeddedness is therefore demonstrated by the organisation's network centrality (it's 'B' position); that is, if many local actors are aware of B, then by virtue of its relationship with A, anybody who seeks the contact of B has a form of indirect contact to A (Granovetter, 1973). This meant that anyone requesting the CVS's support directly was also *indirectly* positioned to receive assistance from its wider network of VS contacts too (that is, partner charities, local businesses, grassroots groups and so on). These indirect relationships, known as 'weak ties', are crucial to the process of 'network diffusion' in so far as 'whatever is to be *diffused* [that is, information, resources] can reach a larger number of people, and traverse a greater social distance, when passed through weak ties rather than strong' (1973, p 1336). From a network analysis perspective, the creation of an interim prescription delivery service coordinated by VAC between the NHS NCL CCG and GoodGym is an example of diffusion at work. Prior relationships formed between the CVS and its statutory and VS contacts meant that resources (in this case, specialist volunteers) were able to reach locations across the borough, enabling many vulnerable people – unconnected directly to the CVS – to access their medication. Figure 16.1 shows the relationship between NCL CCG, Voluntary Action Camden and GoodGym.

Case Study 2: Croydon Voluntary Action

Croydon Voluntary Action (CVA) is a CVS with its own volunteer centre. Like Voluntary Action Camden, CVA had spent many years prior to the pandemic working at 'the crossroads' (Zammer in Rochester, 2012, p 108) between the statutory sector and the local VS. Most significantly, it has spent the past decade delivering a borough-based Asset Based Community Development (ABCD) scheme in collaboration with the local authority to the surrounding community, including local organisations and groups outside of the VS (Croydon Voluntary Action, 2021). The purpose of the ABCD scheme is to create and deliver community initiatives 'from the ground up', with residents appointed as 'community connectors' who are supported by the CVS to lead their own projects (Croydon Voluntary Action, 2021). Since its inception in 2011, the project has been largely successful – enabling over three hundred community-based projects to be led and delivered by residents (Croydon Voluntary Action, 2021).

The scheme is relevant to this chapter because, arguably, it has enabled CVA to become deeply embedded within the local area (or 'territory', see Dayson et al, 2017). Through delivering the scheme, the CVS has not only established myriad statutory and VS partnerships but has also developed a local presence and reputation through engagement and co-production with residents over the past decade. As such, CVA also became a central point of contact for statutory agencies, charities and residents during the pandemic. Much like VAC, CVA had initially began by responding to requests for help on a case-by-case basis. However, because CVA has an in-house volunteer centre, it also found itself inundated with applications for volunteering roles and offers of support from local residents. As a result of this, the CVA began to incorporate its efforts within the wider work of the fledgling 'community hub' established within the borough. The hub incorporated volunteers from CVA, who worked in direct collaboration with local charities, faith groups and food banks, alongside input from some local businesses, mutual aid groups and individuals who had contacted the CVS to offer their support. During this period, CVA played a key role in coordinating the work of the hub by overseeing the management of its volunteers, distribution of resources, delivery of borough-wide aid and the administration of requests for support, for example, responding to food bank shortages across London.

CVA was an active member of the London Plus CVS network – a professional network for CVS staff. The purpose of this network, and more generally of London Plus as an organisation, is to advocate for the interests of VS infrastructure at the city region level. As such, London Plus had been invited by the Greater London Authority to join the Emergency Response Committee (ERC), a group formed in response to the COVID-19 pandemic. In April 2020, London Plus was asked to gather evidence of the resources needed to support the voluntary effort across London (London Plus, 2020). As coordinator of the community hub, CVA was able to report directly to London Plus about shortages affecting Croydon. When this information reached the ERC, it acted quickly to provide resources through large organisations such as the British Red Cross, Team Rubicon and Tesco. However, the logistical staff required to enable the implementation of a successful supply chain were scarce and in high demand (Voluntary Action Camden, 2022). Furthermore, while the committee had its own supply of volunteers through the British Red Cross and Team Rubicon, it lacked local connections, making it a challenge to plan the effective distribution of goods within each borough. To resolve this problem, the ERC's volunteers collaborated directly with members of the London Plus network, including CVA in Croydon, to set up delivery points in each borough for food aid distribution. This strategic partnership was highly effective, enabling perishable goods to be delivered quickly and effectively across London (London Plus, 2020). Figure 16.2 shows the relationship between Croyden Voluntary Action, London Plus, the ERC and its donors.

The example above illustrates precisely why weak ties are so valuable to social networks. When discussing the diffusion of information and resources among different groups, Granovetter argued that A and C require the presence of B, the central node, to connect with one another (1973). Most significantly, the role of 'B' is heightened in instances where one party is close-knit and distanced from the other. According to Granovetter, 'self-insulation' occurs when a group lack the 'indirect contacts ... through which ideas, influences or information socially distant from [the individuals] may reach them' (Granovetter, 1973, p 1370). Self-insulation is therefore likely to have affected the ERC when it tried to deliver aid. While its membership had strategic power, it was operating under exceptional circumstances whereby the resources to generate a supply chain were scarce. Because of this, indirect contacts such as CVSs were pivotal because they were able to provide the committee with a route into each borough – working directly with the committee's volunteers to enable central aid drops to take place, then mobilising their own local networks to facilitate distribution.

Hence, as Granovetter observes, 'as with bridges in a highway system, a local bridge in a social network will be more significant as a connection between two sectors to the extent that it is the only alternative for many people – that is, as it's degree increases' (1973, p 1365). In the midst of a pandemic, the 'B' position (that is, the degree of centrality) of these organisations was therefore heightened by their ability to function as local bridges through which aid and other forms of support could be diffused from the regional level directly to the frontline within the borough.

Nevertheless, there is also an argument to be made about embeddedness within this context. As discussed previously in this chapter, CVSs often work at the crossroads between the statutory sector and the wider VS (Zammer in Rochester, 2012). By virtue of their work, voluntary sector infrastructure organisations become 'embedded' in the local community through funding relationships and the delivery of services (Dayson et al, 2017) which, in turn, can be generative of dense local networks. It is because of this that CVSs were able to function as 'local bridges' into the community during the April 2020 food crisis. This is clearly evident in the case of CVA and its ABCD scheme, which had enabled the organisation to build up relationships not only with the VS, but also local groups and residents. Critically, this reach into the wider community enabled the supply chain in Croydon to become

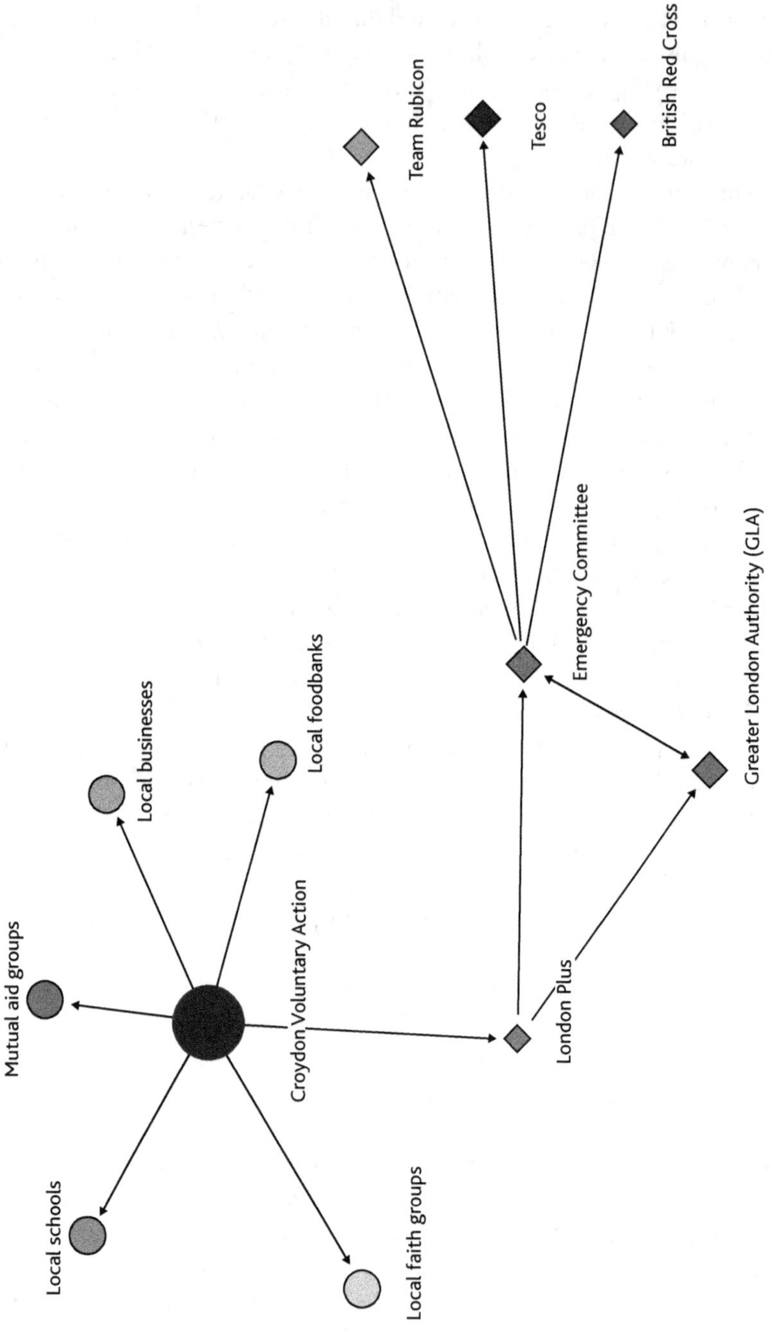

Figure 16.2: Diffusion model between Croydon Voluntary Action, London Plus, the Emergency Committee and its donors

particularly effective. When news of the incoming supplies reached CVA, the organisation acted quickly to mobilise both the community hub and the borough's wider voluntary network to distribute aid across the area. Within a short period of time, it had established a borough-wide supply chain encompassing sorters, packers and a fleet of 85 drivers. This included additional support from organisations outside of the 'community hub' such as schools and businesses who had available drivers and vehicles that were not being used.

While the goodwill of Croydon's residents shouldn't be understated within this case study, the CVS played a pivotal role in coordinating these spontaneous expressions of altruism into tangible activities, avoiding the duplication of efforts and potential waste of resources. Instead, it was able to direct these efforts to generate additional manpower to directly support the work of the community response hub – replenishing the hub with volunteers and mobilising vital resources, such as delivery vehicles and fuel. The scale and success of the community response in Croydon can therefore be attributed, at least in part, to the embeddedness of the CVS. Because the organisation had spent the past decade co-producing projects within the community, it had developed a dense network of contacts and, alongside this, a reputational presence within the wider community. This meant that when the time came, CVA was able to extend its reach beyond the parameters of the community hub into other spaces, such as schools, businesses and even further afield to enlist the help of individual residents.

In this sense, much of the groundwork required for the distribution of regional food aid in London had already been laid years prior to the pandemic by infrastructure organisations such as CVA through the delivery of myriad community development schemes. That is to say, their embedded position within the borough of Croydon (Dayson et al, 2017) provided a ready-made route into spaces where equivalent relationships would have otherwise been difficult to create at the same speed and on the same scale. These organisations played a pivotal role in the distribution of aid *because* they were able to repurpose their established local networks in response to the crisis. Their contribution to the food crisis can therefore be considered as twofold: first, by providing an invaluable 'way in' to local spaces for interim ensembles such as the ERC, and second, by also acting as the coordinator of the local aid response, bringing together the efforts of charities, businesses, mutual aid groups and individuals into coordinated, tangible action.

Conclusion: the latent strength of community ties

The purpose of this chapter has been to highlight how voluntary sector infrastructure organisations played an important role in community support and aid provision during the first COVID-19 lockdown. Particular attention has been given to the position of CVSs and similar organisations prior to the pandemic, exploring how their role in delivering community projects such as social prescribing programmes (see Voluntary Action Camden, 2021) and ABCD schemes (see Croydon Voluntary Action) laid the foundations upon which the aid response was later built. The concept of 'territorial embeddedness' (Granovetter, 1985; Dayson et al, 2017) was utilised to illustrate how institutional relationships formed with contacts in the statutory sector, the VS and local residents enabled the CVSs in both case studies to function as central 'B' nodes in wider A-B-C aid networks. As the diagrams in this chapter illustrate, the presence of these networks enabled the diffusion of information and resources to take place during a time where alternative solutions were unavailable (Granovetter, 1973). Furthermore, these local networks also supported wider regional projects, enabling supplies to reach food banks across London when stocks ran critically low.

The impact of these networks should not be underestimated. As Putnam (1993) observes, the generation of social capital required to form community networks happens over time – something that is not readily available during a crisis, where speed of response is a key requirement. In this sense, the unique position occupied by CVSs at 'the crossroads' between the statutory sector and VS (Zammer in Rochester, 2012, p 108) enables the formation of dense local networks which provides them with latent strength which can be drawn upon during a crisis such as the COVID-19 pandemic. Under exceptional circumstances, the 'networks, norms and trust' (Putnam, 1993, p 1) generated through the work of these embedded organisations are not simply 'nice to have' – they are inherently valuable to society precisely *because* they can be mobilised to respond to unanticipated challenges.

Although this chapter has provided a novel insight into the work of VS infrastructure organisations during the pandemic, the scope of this analysis is limited by the number of case studies included and we do not yet fully understand how important these organisations were in supporting communities through the crisis, how this varied across the UK, and what they may be capable of in the future. To gain greater understanding of the impact made by VS infrastructure during the pandemic and beyond, further research is required to ensure that the work of these organisations is neither underestimated nor overlooked.

Notes

[1] The work of Voluntary Action Camden will be discussed later in this chapter.
[2] Refers to formal networking services, that is, membership-based networks.
[3] See *Asset-Based Community Development (ABCD): Looking Back to Look Forward. In Conversation with John McKnight about the Heritage of ABCD and its Place in the World Today* (Russell, 2022). For a discussion of this in practice refer to pages 9–10.
[4] See Granovetter, M. (1985) 'Economic action and social structure: the problem of embeddedness', *American Journal of Sociology*, 91(3): 481–510.

⁵ Conditions may be chronic/long term, relate to mental health, loneliness, isolation or complex social needs (NHS, 2021, n.p.).

References

Aves, G. (1969) *The Voluntary Worker in the Social Services*, London: Allen & Unwin.

Croydon Voluntary Action (2021) *Asset Based Community Development*, [online], Available from: www.cvalive.org.uk/abcd/ [Accessed 9 September 2021].

Dayson, C., Macmillan, R., Paine A.E. and Sanderson, E. (2017) 'Third sector capacity building: the institutional embeddedness of supply', *Voluntary Sector Review*, 8(2): 149–68.

Ellis Paine, A., Hill, M. and Rochester, C. (2010) '"A rose by any other name …" Revisiting the question: "what exactly is volunteering?"', Working paper series: 1, London: Institute for Volunteering Research.

GoodGym (2021) *About GoodGym*, [online], Available from: www.goodgym.org/about [Accessed 9 September 2021].

Granovetter, M. (1973) 'The strength of weak ties', *American Journal of Sociology*, 78(6): 1360–80.

Granovetter, M. (1985) 'Economic action and social structure: the problem of embeddedness', *American Journal of Sociology*, 91(3): 481–510.

Home Office (2005) *Developing Capacity: Next Steps for ChangeUp*, London: Home Office Active Communities Directorate.

Legal & General (2020) '10 million Brits volunteering as the nation unites in the Isolation Economy', [online], Available from: www.legalandgeneralgroup.com/media-centre/press-releases/10-million-brits-volunteering-as-the-nation-unites-in-the-isolation-economy-says-legal-general/ [Accessed 9 September 2021].

London Plus (2020) 'Supporting the sector during COVID-19', [online], Available from: //londonplus.org/news/london-plus-supporting-the-sector-covid-19 [Accessed 6 January 2022].

Macmillan, R. (2013) 'Demand-led capacity building, the Big Lottery Fund and market making in third sector support services', *Voluntary Sector Review*, 9(4): 385–94.

Macmillan, R. (2021) 'A surprising turn of events – episodes towards a renaissance of civil society infrastructure in England', *People, Place and Policy*, 15(2): 57–71.

NHS (2021) 'Social prescribing', NHS [online],. Available from: www.england.nhs.uk/personalisedcare/social-prescribing/ [Accessed 20 May 2022].

Putnam, R.D. (1993) 'The prosperous community', *The American Prospect*, 4(13): 35–42.

Rochester, C. (2012) 'Councils for voluntary service: the end of a long road?', *Voluntary Sector Review*, 3(1): 103–10.

Rochester, C. (2013) *Rediscovering Voluntary Action: The Beat of a Different Drum*, Basingstoke: Palgrave MacMillan.

Rumbul, R. (2013) 'Structurally excluded? Structural embeddedness and civil society competition for funding', *Journal of Civil Society*, (9)3: 341–60.

Russell, C. (2022) *Asset-Based Community Development (ABCD): Looking Back to Look Forward: In Conversation with John McKnight about the Heritage of ABCD and its Place in the World Today*. Published Independently.

Seebohm Committee (1968) *Report of the Committee on Local Authority and Allied Personal Social Services, Cmnd 3703*, London: HMSO.

Voluntary Action Camden (2022) *Social Prescribing: A Guide for Residents*, [online], Available from: //vac.org.uk/our-services/social-prescribing/ [Accessed 9 September 2021].

Wolfenden, J. (1978) *The Future of Voluntary Organisations: Report of the Wolfenden Committee*, London: Croom Helm.

17

How many of us had pandemic in our risk register? A snapshot of experiences of community buildings during the first lockdown of 2020

Ann Hindley and John Wilson

Introduction

This chapter summarises two pieces of research conducted during the COVID-19 pandemic in 2020–21 (Community Matters, 2021a; Community Matters, 2021b). The aim was to discover the different ways in which community buildings responded to the immediate situation of lockdown in March 2020 and the impact of their closure on both their short- and longer-term future. The question quoted in the title was a semi-flippant remark made by an interviewee which summarised the situation in which community buildings found themselves as infection rates increased in the UK. It became the title of the first report produced by Community Matters in January 2021. It was followed by a second report in summer 2021 entitled 'A Significant Place in the Local Landscape', which documented the results of a bigger piece of research using both quantitative and qualitative methods. The aim this time was to follow through the response and situation of community buildings after two further lockdowns in November 2020 and from January to July of 2021 and to develop a picture of their contribution to their local community.

This is a start to gathering intelligence about urban-based community spaces to complement the annual survey of village halls by Action for Communities in Rural England (ACRE) (Archer et al, 2020) which could be used to influence national thinking about community buildings generally. The first report (Community Matters, 2021a) was being written as the second lockdown was announced in November 2020, which made the common comment made by respondents that "we shall survive provided there are no further lockdowns" all the more poignant. Many participants felt the survival of their organisation was dependent upon the avoidance of further lockdowns, which made this research more pressing in light of the second lockdown. However, as interviews took place during the third lockdown, it became clear that a number of centres were developing sound financial surpluses and attracting new and different volunteers.

What does the wider literature say about the impact of COVID-19 on community buildings?

The Community Matters research was taking place concurrently with work by ACRE and Sheffield Hallam University (Archer et al, 2020), which documents the position of village halls in rural settlements on a regular basis. The ACRE research, concentrating on rural areas, estimates a population of 10,000 village and community halls in England alone, containing a capital value of between £5.2 and 8.9 million and generating the equivalent of £131,926,000 in wellbeing benefits. This gives some indication of the value of the sector if also replicated across urban areas but, currently, a wider picture of community space across all settings is not available.

Research by Carnegie (Coutts et al, 2020) demonstrated the importance of community buildings even during the time of enforced closure as many were used as community hubs by public sector bodies working with voluntary organisations and local groups to respond quickly and sensitively, developing new partnerships and different methods of service delivery both during the pandemic and on the recovery period. At least two of our respondents were host to a community hub.

The pandemic has had implications for both financial and human resources of community buildings. They were faced with potentially reduced future usage, and therefore income, with a concern that long-standing volunteers would not return. Research carried out by GMCVO in 2020 (Bell, 2020) included an account by the manager of the Manchester Settlement, describing income in March 2020 reducing by £4,000 per week as they lost childcare provision and room rental revenue. They struggled with shifting and contradictory guidance as they applied for funding and explored government schemes, and had a sense that partner organisations were reviewing their use of community buildings and considering permanent home working. There was little evidence of these organisations rushing to resume service delivery from community spaces, such as the Settlement. Organisations the size and nature of the Settlement have been encouraged for some years by government bodies to move away from dependence on grant income and develop a business-based model of raising funds through trading to fund their other activities. This is a policy the organisation is in the process of rethinking in light of the pandemic.

These experiences are consistent with the findings of the regular barometer of voluntary organisations maintained by Nottingham Trent University, Sheffield Hallam University and the National Council for Voluntary Organisations (NTU Centre for People, Work and Organisational Practice 2020; 2021), the first of which reported 14 per cent of respondents anticipating closure in November 2020, 39 per cent seeing a deteriorating situation and 57 per cent experiencing an increased demand in services. At the time of our second report being written in March 2021, the barometer still reported increased demand, accompanied by reduced overall income and rising costs but, in line with our findings, also revealed a more nuanced position with some organisations experiencing a financial uplift as they banked government grants but spent less on utilities and furloughed staff.

This finding confirmed what our research participants had discussed during interviews, but with a note of caution. Some organisations are experiencing dwindling reserves as they face an uncertain future, certainly in the case of community buildings, with many unsure of how soon they can return to full functioning and what distancing requirements will be in place. This feeling of caution is underpinned by a view coming from the Charity Commission chief executive, Helen Stephenson (Weakley, 2021), that charities were financially less resilient in 2021 than they were in 2020. Evidence provided by the Charity Commission to the Public Accounts Committee found no sign of significant numbers of charities generally closing yet, but a concern about the percentage of charities with incomes of under £500,000 per annum, with negative or no free reserves, increasing from 9 per cent in April 2020 to 28 per cent in March 2021. This is being exacerbated by a 'capacity crunch' being predicted across the sector due to rising levels of demand combined with falling incomes (Martin and Henley, 2021).

A number of reports produced during the pandemic predict many voluntary sector bodies whose organisational lives will never be the same again (BVSC, 2021). Further research from ACRE and Sheffield Hallam (Archer and Skropke, 2021, and Chapter 10 in this volume) reported on signs that at least 1.4 per cent of their village halls will not reopen which, if scaled up, could mean the closure of 140 halls across England. Their findings echo those of our research, with three types of response to the pandemic from community spaces – those playing either a formal or informal role in the response to the pandemic (but receiving no additional resource), those closing completely during lockdown and those who took the opportunity to improve and invest in their premises during this time. ACRE also found a polarisation of financial health with the same proportions seeing their finances improve as worsen. Those serving bigger communities saw a worsening in their financial position, relying more heavily on reserves. The long-term outlook is uncertain, with a concern about former users returning.

Methodology

The initial study took place during summer 2020, as restrictions were lifting in some places, but tier restrictions imposed in others.[1] The aim was to make visible the work of those managing community buildings during the first lockdown of spring 2020, both paid and unpaid, and to discover what constraints were being imposed on their reopening. The Community Matters database of community buildings across England, Scotland and Wales was developing as managers recognised the need for support and advice. An invitation to take part in the research was distributed to the membership and 15 agreed to be interviewed; seven more were sought to ensure a more representative sample geographically and in terms of size and activity.

Over half were large centres, often with sports halls and nursery facilities with paid staff, but some were very small, run entirely by volunteers. The geographical spread covered all areas of England and two interviews were also carried out with individuals from centres in Wales.

A semi-structured phone or video interview was conducted, based on a set of key lines of enquiry to elicit a description of the building and its history and provision, actions during lockdown, plans for reopening, potential financial position and the return of volunteers and trustees. This information was supplemented by an examination of each organisation's accounts on the Charity Commission website. A review was carried out of websites, where they existed, to explore how they had communicated with the public during this time.

The first report, 'How Many of Us Had Pandemic in our Risk Registers?', was produced in January 2021 and was circulated to Community Matters members, voluntary sector infrastructure bodies and government ministers. The second stage of the research started during the lockdown of early 2021. It aimed to include a larger number of community organisations and to find out more about the position of community buildings as they coped with a further prolonged period of closure and restrictions. We invited members to respond to an online survey, asking for some practical information about support received, levels of turnover, the position of trustees and volunteers in terms of retention and recruitment, potential issues for reopening and support needs. 122 responses were received.

Respondents were asked to volunteer for a video interview and 23 were chosen. A discussion guide asked about both the organisation's financial position and their volunteer position in relation to reopening and how their potential closure might impact the wider community, although this is not covered in this chapter. The sample was chosen to reflect geography, turnover size, level of current reserves, those who chose to reopen during summer of 2020 and those who had remained closed, the level of problems experienced and what issues were anticipated on reopening in 2021.

Findings

Our findings document the provision made by community buildings pre-pandemic and how they adapted to lockdown and the easing of restrictions. Interviews produced a long list of the activities normally carried out within these community spaces, ranging from nursery services to bars and social clubs to French conversation classes, to name but three, demonstrating the provision made across the range of community buildings. Some described themselves as being instrumental in addressing the issues of loneliness, "catching people before they get to a point of needing support", often simply providing a safe space for people to meet within their locality.

An example of a community centre that provided this type of support was Abbotsdale Community Centre. They described an older resident who had previously come in each day for coffee and a chat with volunteers, but, despite efforts of the centre to work with the local COVID team to organise phone and email networks, had died. It appeared that the community centre was her only social contact, which was denied her once lockdown took place. "Once lockdown was announced, she simply shut down and stopped eating. In effect, she died of loneliness."

Community buildings were often in a good position to react once the first lockdown was announced suddenly and with strict enforcements. Some opened again very quickly during the summer of 2020 and some barely at all. The second piece of research documented the position in which the buildings were left in respect of finances and human resources, particularly volunteers, as buildings managers coped with the impact of further and generally unanticipated closure. We also explored some of the practical issues facing them as restrictions started to lift in 2021.

Response to lockdown

Our findings from the first piece of research echoed those of ACRE (Archer and Skropke, 2021) in that there were generally three types of response to lockdown. The first was simple closure. The reasons given varied from the need to protect vulnerable volunteers to a perceived absence of local need. A second group took the opportunity of a prolonged closure to carry out long planned maintenance or improvement work. A third group made their premises available for responses to need arising from the lockdown. Many who closed closed early as they predicted developments. Some paid managers continued to work and furloughed staff. The first issue for all of them was loss of income from room hire and fundraising – "income dropped off a cliff". Paid managers and unpaid trustees spent time applying for government assistance to support their income and to charitable bodies for grants.

The second issue was how to support their users and local community members through an "unprecedented event" which isolated people from each other and imposed restrictions on movement never previously seen. Descriptions were given of a range of activities undertaken by paid staff and volunteer trustees to meet predicted needs. They built on their local knowledge of neighbourhoods and the people who lived in them. Examples given included activity packs delivered to houses, moving sessions online, weekly postings on Facebook, opening up for people providing support for specific needs such as autism and developing telephone and email networks between centre users. One community centre café was described as 'agile' as they adjusted their service to provide deliveries, having used their contacts in the local community to find people who needed them. This enabled them to find new ways of making money, by "working flat out for six months".

Another centre was used as a Scrub Hub, providing materials to people sewing from home and collecting and distributing the finished articles. As there was a constant physical presence at the centre, people who felt vulnerable often just turned up and the manager was able to identify a service to refer them on to.

A community centre that was so small in size it had to close early because of the need for physical distancing teamed up with a local COVID-19 support group and set up book, jigsaw and toy swaps, turning over 3,000 books between March and June outside the building. Staff there were also involved in telephone and email support to regular users and food distribution and, as restrictions started to lift, supporting the local library with story time in the park.

An example in a small community with no local shop brought together the village hall with a local restaurateur with access to wholesale food provision. It was provided primarily for shielding older residents who were unable to book grocery slots as many others doubled up on orders. It was restricted to residents in the village and run on a not-for-profit basis. A corollary of this provision was "that people had a purpose of leaving their houses and opportunity to see and communicate with each other, thus alerting others if someone failed to appear for a few days". The same village hall started a range of activities quickly in summer 2020, with a produce show, apple day and a scarecrow competition, all observing guidelines but providing social activity and contact for people deprived of it for some months.

The sample for the first survey was very small and it is not possible to discern any pattern that would explain why some centres simply closed and others adapted very quickly. In some cases, there was concern about the vulnerability of volunteers; in some, there were others locally meeting the immediate need; in others, there was no discernible need but it would be unwise to draw conclusions from such a small sample. The second survey was more concerned with reopening and included a considerably larger number of respondents but, again, there was no discernable pattern that would enable us to draw any conclusions about what would determine successful reopening. Community buildings are so diverse and so individual; some further in-depth research would be needed to determine what were the common factors, if they exist, that affected the way in which committees and staff operated and how local communities responded.

Reopening in summer 2020

As restrictions eased in some parts of the country, so there were moves towards reopening community buildings. Respondents complained of "woolly guidelines" which appeared not to be written for their situation and open to interpretation. One example of this was the "rule of six" which prevented people meeting in groups bigger than six, both indoors and out, but involved some complexities in terms of ages of the group and how group members related to each other. The four nations of the UK were subject to differing restrictions and different counties in England were subject to local restrictions that then became enshrined in law, thus preventing some centres reopening. Some centres reported room bookings returning as normal, while others reported their income "not returning to anticipated levels". Those groups who did reopen reported smaller numbers returning, which had the potential for rendering the group unviable. Some groups made the decision not to return. Others were restricted by space if their lettable rooms were too small for safe distancing.

One dilemma was faced of receiving enquiries from groups who had used other centres not yet open and for use of premises for delivery of lateral flow testing, thus blocking the bookings for regular users, should they decide to return. An issue predicted for the winter was the need for ventilation while also maintaining a warm building. One centre described themselves as "pretty well down in the bank" as they started to draw on financial resources to pay regular weekly and monthly outgoings. Human resources were also scarce in some instances as some older volunteers decided not to return. This was not a universal experience though and is discussed further below.

The second study took place in spring 2021, as the third lockdown was ending and restrictions were starting to ease. Interviews and responses to the online survey produced evidence of a number of issues, which had also started to emerge after the first research. These included space issues, including the viability of operating with small numbers, and small buildings with small rooms. Government guidance continued to be unclear, leaving the onus on the managers of the building to interpret. Financial support finally ceased in September 2021 as the furlough scheme ended but costs of cleaning and protective equipment were increasing. Problems were identified with enforcing compliance with distancing requirements and face coverings. Alongside these, there was a continual requirement for updating of risk assessments and passing that requirement on to centre users.

Information was sought on financial status. The position in terms of reserves is shown in Table 17.1.

On a positive note, there was no indication of mass closures at this stage, with many interviewees admitting that they had greater annual financial surpluses than at the same time the previous year, as a result of government

Table 17.1: Levels of reserves at the two periods

Reserve position	At start of first lockdown	By spring 2021
No reserves	0	8
Under three months running costs in reserve	20	20
Between three and six months running costs in reserve	30	36
Over six months running costs in reserve	68	55
Non-responses	3	2
Total	121	121

support and lower spending. Despite this, they felt that they were facing an uncertain future. Those taking part in the research were aware of the need to maintain the financial viability of their buildings, along with ensuring the safety of users, maintaining a sound volunteer base and keeping abreast of shifting guidelines. There were concerns that a further lockdown or restrictions might be introduced in 2021, with no indication of further government support. Finances would have been further depleted as income falls, but utility and maintenance bills still incurred. To summarise, there was a general cautious optimism on the part of both paid staff and management committee members about the future of their buildings, accompanied by a nervousness about an uncertain future with events beyond their control, whether that be further restrictions or lockdowns or users simply exercising caution about returning to activities where they feel unsafe.

Issues affecting volunteer numbers

The buildings included in this research were many and varied in terms of size, geography and structure. Some were managed by paid staff with support from volunteers and some totally by volunteers; all had volunteer trustee boards. Most had some sort of volunteer involvement and depended on volunteer support to continue. We asked them about the volunteer situation in the second phase and found a varied picture of involvement both during the lockdowns and as the centres emerged into reopening.

Experiences ranged from a complete closure of the building and all volunteer activity ceasing, in some cases with no indication of volunteers returning, to others experiencing considerable increases in the numbers of volunteers. A pattern developed of increasing numbers of volunteers during the first lockdown, with some numbers dropping as people returned to work. At the time of the research, the furlough scheme had not ended and there were still people with time available. There was a trend for some new volunteers to remain involved during lockdown three and beyond. Reports were made of: "an increase in volunteer numbers from seven to 42 to deliver food parcels … and now gone down again" and "all but one volunteer isolated who were replaced by new people who then went back to work". In the last example, isolating volunteers carried out telephone volunteering but some had still not returned to face-to-face work at the time of the research.

In common with other studies carried out during the first lockdown (Thierry et al, 2020; Macmillan, 2020; Harris, 2021), most reports of volunteering activity during this time were positive with instances of numbers increasing from 20 to 100, café volunteers changing their method of working to delivery, 38 volunteers all moving to providing external support and recruitment of an additional four volunteers. Another claimed not to have used volunteers at all until prompted by the interviewer and then mentioned 50 people involved in delivering the village COVID-19 service. One outreach programme was supported by volunteers with them all being willing to continue. Where concerns were expressed about volunteering, they were about lost contact with people who had benefitted from being a volunteer and worries about ensuing feelings of loneliness and isolation.

The general view of people interviewed was of a positive future, although one expected a decline in numbers and another appreciated a need to re-engage with people who had withdrawn from volunteering as a result of temporary closure. Another expressed concern that safety issues would prevent return as well as a feeling that people will have moved on into other responsibilities. More, however, talked about gaining some committed volunteers and a hope to recruit more, and confirmed a commitment to working with volunteers. There was a general expectation of volunteers returning where they had stepped back. There was also one report of people moving into the neighbourhood and enthusiastic for activities to start again and willing to commit.

Some groups had adapted their provision completely away from being building-based and were committed to this as a future method of working. One example is of a community centre which had elected a new chair of trustees as lockdown happened. The trustees decided that community activities should not focus in its entirety on the village hall and started keeping in touch with residents and developing activities away from the building. They circulated a regular newsletter with offers of help, organised Christmas carol services and Easter egg hunts, and started to work more closely with the Parish Council. They have COVID-19 relief money and Re-start grants,[2] so left their reserves untouched. No reticence has been observed from users returning.

Summary and conclusions: what this means for the position of community buildings in England, Scotland and Wales

The research described here was of a rapid and relatively small-scale response to the challenge of COVID-19. We aimed to carry out some real-time research that would produce a picture of the community building sector's response to the first lockdown and the likely impact of that lockdown on their future, followed by a further picture of how they fared during the reopening, which was followed by two further lockdowns. It should be restated that not all were able to reopen during summer 2020 if they were in areas subject to the tier restrictions imposed by government during that time, and also some chose not to even if they were legally enabled. We are conscious that the pandemic is by no means at an end and that uncertainty still hangs over many aspects of life. Any further restrictions without accompanying government support will have implications for the viability of community spaces, and this is a key risk.

The two studies provide a variable picture of community buildings contributing to the welfare of the people living in their local communities, often in imaginative ways, at the start of the first lockdown. The lengthy list of the normal activities taking place in community buildings demonstrates the diversity of provision made, often dependent on the size and location of the building and on the people involved in managing it. The variation in response to the first lockdown reflects this diversity as some saw no role for themselves while others responded with imagination and energy, and others took advantage of the time closed to invest in preparing the building for the future. In some cases, other agencies locally were seen to be filling emerging needs; in others, there was no perceived need to be met and there were those who decided that it was not their role.

There is a gentle trend towards financial reserves being expended but not disastrously so as yet, and examples of annual surpluses increasing in some cases, at least for this year. Some of these surpluses may have to be carried forward into a future year without government support and reduced hall usage. Some were starting to adapt by reconsidering their offer and developing promotional exercises; others by developing new ways of working with the local community and moving away from a focus on the building, although this was by no means universal. For some, it may be possible to invest that money into the building and develop a reserve to cope with future events. Reports of human resources in the shape of volunteers are positive but again, this is a moment in time, and the ending of furlough in September 2021 may have had an impact on volunteer numbers.

Most have survived and emerged into a world where some are able to take advantage of a 'new normal' and work in different ways with new user groups and hirers but, at the same time, having to cope with a proliferation of requirements around social distancing, cleaning schedules, risk assessments and protective equipment. What started as an opportunity for innovation and imagination has developed for many into a round of sanitising, ventilation and policing one-way systems, while keeping abreast of changing guidance, making the prospect of running a community building on a volunteer basis somewhat less attractive.

There are two opportunities for further research. A strong national body (ACRE) exists providing support for village hall networks in rural settings often supported by rural community councils. There is a regular English Village and Community Hall Survey but there has been no similar study of urban-based facilities. This is probably because of the sheer diversity of urban community buildings available, which are hard to document and record. Community Matters is now starting to rebuild a database and recognises the need to develop a clearer picture of the scale and nature of the sector. Our research has made a very small start on raising its profile which can be built on, both in terms of assessing its size and measuring its impact, in normal times and throughout the pandemic.

Secondly, we have been able to draw only some very tentative conclusions about the position of community buildings following the pandemic, partly because we are still not yet in a post-pandemic world and there is no clear idea of what that will look like. Longitudinal studies of the community centres and halls involved in both these studies would provide a clearer picture of long-term survival and provision and of the measures taken to ensure survival as they grapple with trying to reassure potential users of their safety and finding new ways of making provision and new hirers and tenants. Following a sample through the process would provide some indication of the future for community buildings of all types, sizes and geographies, given the situation in which they find themselves, and give an opportunity to document what continued impact, if any, they have on their local communities.

Notes
[1] The tier restrictions refer to how different parts of the country were designated to a particular level of restriction according to infection rates, following the first lockdown.
[2] Restart grants provided support for 'businesses' in the hospitality sector among others with a one-off payment to enable them to reopen safely as COVID-19 restrictions lifted.

References
Archer, T., Parkes, S. and Speake, B. (2020) *The English Village and Community Hall Survey*, Cirencester: Action for Communities in Rural England.

Archer, T. and Skropke, C. (2021) *The Impact of Covid-19 on Village and Community Halls in England: Findings Report*, Sheffield: CRESR, Sheffield Hallam University and Action for Communities in Rural England.

Bell, A. (2020) 'When the funds dry up', in *Macc, No Going Back*, [online], Available from: manchestercommunitycentral.org/sites/manchestercommunitycentral.co.uk/files/No%20Going%20Back%20Report_Final.pdf [Accessed 19 May 2022].

Birmingham Voluntary Sector Council (BVSC) (2021) *Reflections One Year On. Covid-19 and the Birmingham Voluntary, Community and Faith Sector*, Birmingham: BVSC.

Community Matters (2021a) *How Many of Us Had Pandemic in Our Risk Register? A Snapshot of Experiences of Community Buildings during the Lockdown of 2020*, Leeds: Community Matters.

Community Matters (2021b) *A Significant Place in the Local Landscape*, Leeds: Community Matters.

Coutts, P., Ormston, H., Pennycook, L. and Thurman, B. (2020) *Pooling Together: How Community Hubs Have Responded to the COVID-19 Emergency*, Dunfermline: Carnegie UK.

Harris, M. (2021) 'Familiar patterns and new initiatives: UK civil society and government initial responses to the Covid-19 crisis', *Nonprofit Policy Forum*, 12(1): 25–44.

Macmillan, R. (2020) *Rapid and Spontaneous Response by Mutual Aid Groups Operating at Street, Neighbourhood and Community Level – Briefing 3*, Sheffield: Third Sector Research Centre, Sheffield Hallam University and Local Trust.

Martin, A. and Henley, A. (2021) *PBE Covid Charity Tracker*, London: Pro Bono Economics in partnership with Charity Finance Group and Chartered Institute of Fundraisers.

NCVO (2021) *Respond, Recover, Reset: The Voluntary Sector and COVID-19*, [online], Available from: //cpwop.org.uk/what-we-do/projects-and-publications/covid-19-vcse-organisation-responses/ [Accessed 25 February 2022].

Thierry, H., Ballantyne, E., Cook, J., Burchell, J., Walkley, F. and McNeil, J. (2020) *Building Local Responses to Identify and Meet Community Needs during Covid-19*, [online], Available from: //doit.life/esa/channels/11997/move-findings/experiences/142043/report-3-building-local-responses-to-idea [Accessed 25 February 2022].

Weakley, K. (2021) 'Charity Commission sees evidence of "worsening financial resilience in the sector"', [online], Available from: www.civilsociety.co.uk/news/charity-commission-sees-evidence-of-worsening-financial-resilience-in-the-sector.html#sthash.YAGsZ3jN.dpuf [Accessed 25 February 2022].

18

Leading through a pandemic

Patricia Armstrong with Jayne Stuart

Introduction

A study early in the pandemic showed that 50 per cent of charities in Scotland feared running out of cash within six months and closure, 70 per cent believed there would be cuts to services and budgets after COVID-19, and most anticipated a surge in demand for services (SCVO, 2020). This chapter explores how third sector leaders have coped with these perceived challenges and brings together relevant research and lived experiences of those on the frontline. As a leadership support organisation, the Association of Chief Officers of Scottish Voluntary Organisations (ACOSVO) has been following the impact on the leaders it supports and looking at what has helped them maintain their resilience throughout this period. This has been done through tracking key themes emerging from online engagements as well as through gathering case studies from early in the pandemic which explored the impact on individual leaders as a baseline, and then followed up after the immediate crisis period. The research also involved my own real-time personal reflections as a CEO (of ACOSVO) operating during the pandemic. The chapter concludes with what has been learnt from leaders' experiences of the pandemic and how these lessons offer insights for future leader support and development in challenging times.

At the time of writing, some two years since the pandemic started, third sector leaders are exhausted. They talk of 'sprinting a marathon', as what was thought would be a few months of emergency response continued while adrenalin and energy dissipated. 'Putting on your own oxygen mask before helping others' has become more difficult in practice. Leaders have been either ramping up their delivery of services or closing them, losing staff and being unable to operate. With the focus on staff and beneficiary wellbeing, who looks after the leader? Is it a responsibility of the board or does the leader have to find their own solutions? Never has good leadership been more important but never has it been so stretched.

Setting the context

A study by Ecclesiastical (Ecclesiastical, 2020) found nearly half of senior leaders of 252 surveyed charities are considering walking away from their roles due to burnout. Almost half (44 per cent) admitted they were considering their futures because of the increased demands due to COVID-19 – a major cause for concern for a sector under pressure from staff and volunteer exhaustion. As a sector with such significance both economically and socially for the wellbeing of citizens, the resilience of its leaders is crucially important. Challenges at home such as childcare or home schooling (33 per cent), concerns about the health of family or friends (30 per cent) and the fatigue of home working (30 per cent) were all cited as main concerns for colleagues as the effects of the pandemic impacted on their mental wellbeing.

The sector's lack of capacity and resource can also exacerbate the 'normal' challenges of leadership, with a 2019 study finding that third sector leaders work three months of the year for free, doing an average of ten hours per week over and above their paid role (ACEVO, 2019).

This style of working is clearly unsustainable, with previous research demonstrating that overloading the brain can have negative impacts, including causing anxiety (Gruszka and Nęcka, 2017; Kirsh, 2000). Allcock Tyler (2017) suggests that third sector leadership is a vocation, not a profession. The widely held perception that the third sector should be the more 'caring' sector makes leadership even more complex to navigate as it needs to encompass passion and empathy to a cause, a drive for excellence, growth and high performance, and value for money and evidence of impact. That they have line managers who are volunteers (that is, board members, often the chair), who may not have experience in this area, and where the CEO is expected to support the board, also adds to the complexity.

Studies have demonstrated that individuals experiencing burnout reduce their job involvement and organisational commitment (Lee and Ashforth, 1996; Maslach et al, 2000). Consequently, burnout is not only detrimental to the CEO's wellbeing but can also adversely affect the performance of the organisation; as an interviewee in one study described it, "if the CEO of an organisation is in a bad place, then the organisation is bound to suffer too" (Jones, 2019, p 7).

Research to date has shown that much of the spotlight has been placed on workforce wellbeing and there is generally a lack of focus on CEO wellbeing (Barling and Cloutier, 2017). There is increased pressure on leaders to perform well in an increasingly complex and unpredictable context (Jones, 2019) and there is also an increased need for sustainable leadership to cope with increased demand for services and support (Gerard et al, 2017).

Early COVID-19, 2020: real-time reflections and lived experiences

The shock of COVID-19 hit sector leaders hard. The phrase 'redesigning the plane while in flight' was used as their organisations' operations were moved online. This had a huge range of impacts, from providing emergency support to service users in some cases, to closing doors in others as lockdown restrictions on numbers meant organisations were no longer able to operate.

An extract from a blog I wrote in the first few weeks of the pandemic tried to capture the mood, stating:

> I know from speaking to other leaders through the ACOSVO network that the feeling of loneliness in the role can feel even more enhanced when we need to default to 'game face' and pretend all of that isn't in our minds. We of course will put every ounce of energy into keeping our organisations alive and our beneficiaries supported, but we shouldn't have to pretend we aren't human and that we don't have all these other thoughts racing through our heads at the same time. We are all leaders, but we are more than our role and to ensure our wellbeing and resilience we need to recognise this and find support that encompasses a more holistic understanding. (Armstrong, 2020)

Several guest blogs from leaders ran alongside weekly 'check-ins' set up by ACOSVO to address the issues of leader isolation as the pandemic hit.[1]

The blogs and check-ins highlighted that CEOs were sharing how to 'encourage conversations around mental health ... (making) it easier to talk about feeling overwhelmed, and the concept that "bringing your whole self to work" (had) never felt more real. There's no such thing as work–life balance now: there's only life'. This situation was 'not the same as "working from home" – rather, people are at home during a crisis and are trying to work'.

These reflections from the early days of the pandemic in spring 2020 also show how little idea there was of what the length and breadth of impact of the pandemic would be.

With the number and participation in these check-ins increasing, ACOSVO started to track the key issues for leaders over the first year of the pandemic, recording themes at each online engagement, and reviewing them alongside event evaluation quotes and comments.

Tracking the change

ACOSVO (2021) developed and used a tracking system from April 2020 to March 2021 to capture key insights and themes from the discussions. During this period, 2,197 participants engaged in 179 online group events and 46 one-to-one discussions with staff.[2]

The most frequent themes emerging over this entire period were future planning, health and wellbeing of staff, managing staff, support for CEOs, and board leadership and engagement.

The data also identified changing themes over each quarter of the year, with the most frequently discussed themes in April–June 2020 being future planning, followed by CEO support; board leadership and engagement; strategic planning; and new ways of working. By the final quarter of the period (January–March 2021) the order of top themes had shifted slightly with health and wellbeing of CEOs becoming the most common concern, followed by board leadership and engagement, health and wellbeing of staff, leadership qualities and working digitally.

The biggest increase in discussions between October–December 2020 and January–March 2021 were around health and wellbeing of CEOs, financial challenges, working digitally, succession (of CEOs), and health and wellbeing of beneficiaries. Themes relating to managing staff, leading others, strategic planning and sustainability were less frequently discussed.

The changing priorities suggest that leaders were dealing with challenges as they emerged throughout the pandemic, often discussing the most pressing issues at any given time. Coming together to share and "engage regularly with other leaders from across the sector … helped (leaders) both personally and professionally", as one participant put it.

The tracking evidence supports the case that at the outset the immediate and primary focus for leaders was other people (with the health and wellbeing of staff and beneficiaries, managing staff and continuing support for beneficiaries at the forefront), but as the year continued, focus shifted towards themselves in their roles as CEO.

Some challenges were interlinked and expressed in slightly different ways under broad themes throughout the entire period. For example, in the early stages of lockdown, leaders often raised their own need for support alongside concerns about their health and wellbeing. Over the year, the prevalence of concerns raised about leaders' health and wellbeing increased, emerging as the most frequently identified challenge by the final quarter of the year. This coincides with an overall health and wellbeing theme that emerged (mainly in relation to staff and less often beneficiaries and board members) across all other challenges and issues raised.

Board leadership and engagement was an issue consistently raised in relation to governance, but from different perspectives. Some participants reported low levels of board engagement "with Trustees often absent as they dealt with their own lives and day jobs", while others reported overly high levels of engagement, with Trustees checking in "too much" and "too often". Striking a balance was difficult to achieve in relation to governance and board support.

Working digitally, and the rapid change consequently of how people work together, were the biggest operational shifts that emerged over the first year of the pandemic. The disruptive nature of lockdown has revolutionised charities, with the new context accelerating change to flexible working, service provision and stakeholder engagement.

Sharing and learning together supported leaders' ability to respond rapidly to challenges and opportunities, and, as one participant observed, "discussions with peers and other sector leaders (were) helpful during what (was) a fast changing and traumatic experience for many". Another noted that the very act of coming together proved to be "an invaluable source of emotional support from peers during the highly demanding and stressful responses needed in the wake of coronavirus". This suggests that while leaders may come together to focus on helping others and safeguarding their organisations, connecting with peers is important to their own wellbeing.

Finding "safe spaces to talk" was an important factor in how leaders coped with the pandemic. According to one CEO, opportunities to engage with "a network of professionals who understand both the challenges of (the) organisation but also for (the leader) as an individual" was key. Often leaders "came away (from CEO check-ins) with reassurance, ideas and energy". Participants told us it was important to connect and "talk through things with people who are in the same boat", and that this was "absolutely crucial in helping (people) lead and support (their) team and gain insights into how to solve common challenges".

With these key themes emerging and changing during the pandemic, ACOSVO asked members to contribute their stories as case studies to provide a more in-depth and richer qualitative picture of experience.

Case studies from 2020 and 2021

ACOSVO members shared their stories, supported each other and showed amazing innovation, resilience and endurance. Case studies (ACOSVO, 2020) were completed in May 2020, with follow-up stories being collected 12 months later – 32 responses from 25 sector leaders were received over 2020 and 2021.[3] As lockdown hit in 2020, three of the leaders sharing their stories were new in post. The case studies capture and share leaders' stories as a snapshot of how the sector continued to be an essential part of the response to the pandemic and how people have responded to each new challenge. CEOs were asked to reflect on questions about the impact of the pandemic (on leaders, staff, beneficiaries and organisation) and future fears and hopes.

Impact on leaders

The case studies helped identify key impacts of the pandemic on leaders, drawing out how the impact on others and their organisations also impacted on them as leaders.

Leadership throughout the pandemic was 'extremely lonely and (added) to feelings of isolation'. This was heightened by 'not having that face-to-face contact with peers and other people that provide moral and other types of support'. In being alone, leaders now felt 'responsible for absolutely everything'. The positive side of this was 'enjoying being able to 'get on with things' at home with no interruptions, where in the office environment ... this time is unfortunately very scarce'. Leaders talked about their worry, anxiety and stress, and identified the need for resilience, as illustrated here: 'An emotional mixture of complete loss, fear (for my team/ members/community), quiet and calm, panic, grieving (for recent international partnership potential lost and years of work on the edge), guilt (as can't do more), anxiety (of what is to come), gratitude (for our organisations agility) and the list goes on'. The mix of being in 'a constant rotation of ... excited, exhausted and worried' along with the 'concern for staff and the future of the charity' suggests the state of heightened alert many leaders found themselves in, with some describing their own feelings of burnout and exhaustion. While most identified worry and stress as being negative, one participant commented they were 'definitely more able to put aside minor stresses and problems as not worth worrying about'.

Being a leader during this time brought new challenges, with decision making, motivation and drive, and refocusing priorities and 'energy ... from working ON the organisation to working IN the organisation' being key. A different style of leadership was required during the height of the pandemic when 'centralised decision-making' was needed 'to effect a crisis response'. As the crisis started to abate there was a struggle for the leader and team in resetting these behaviours.

Motivation and drive lifted for some with 'the need to respond to the COVID-19 emergency actually (giving) some focus and drive that was missing previously'. This led to people identifying their need to rethink the future, move jobs and take time 'to review personal plans and begin to focus on retirement at the end of the current planning cycle', reflecting the life-changing perspective the pandemic has brought for many.

Changing approaches to leading and managing others proved challenging as 'at first, (leaders) went into command-and-control mode'. This was for many not their 'normal style' of leading and left them feeling 'anxious and unsettled', and ultimately 'exhausted'. As time moved on, leaders found ways of 'finding a bit of equilibrium'. Communication proved more challenging in the early part of the pandemic as people struggled with working digitally. These challenges had an impact on staff and leaders, with loss of connections having an impact for beneficiaries. Relationship and communications with the board, partners and funders had an impact more strategically on the organisation and leader.

Increased workloads and responsibilities, coinciding with a loss of staff due to redundancies, furlough or sickness, led to a sense of increased pressure and over-reliance on leaders. The pace of work was challenging, and increased workload came in part 'through the additional challenges of moving the team to online working', 'adapting services to provide immediate support' for beneficiaries and 'coordinating and supporting the sector's response'.

The challenges of working from home, digitally, and finding new ways of operating had both positive and negative impacts. While service disruption and adaptation had an impact on leaders, but less so than its impact on the organisation, staff and beneficiaries, the serious disruption to services were addressed with increased agility and creativity, and in some cases a total realignment of work. This demonstrates that faced with operational disruption, people found ways through and in some cases reconfigured their whole approach. The need for future thinking throughout the pandemic had an impact on leaders and 'while there (were) very short-term needs to address' it was important to 'keep focused on the medium to long term'. This was viewed as 'necessary to stand the best chance of charting a course through the crisis'.

The worries and anxiety the leader has for staff, beneficiaries and organisations can lead to further stress and wellbeing concerns for the leader themselves. Exhaustion, burnout, loneliness and isolation were experienced by all, but for leaders this was coupled with sudden additional responsibilities. The broader economic impact of the pandemic, and any impact on beneficiaries resulting in increased poverty and financial hardship, were concerns for leaders. Increased fears and worries in turn could exacerbate health and wellbeing challenges for the leader.

Similarly, challenges for the people and communities served by the charity cannot be separated from the leader's sense of responsibility. Responding to increased need and demand and providing beneficiary support while overseeing reduced services and potential charity closures, furloughing staff (reducing the workforce) and managing volunteer contributions highlights some of the many tensions and challenges faced by leaders. Child welfare and protection, increased risk to vulnerable people and potential increased social exclusion for some were among the concerns keeping leaders awake at night.

Achieving strategic change and maintaining future thinking, while managing in a crisis, became an ask leaders made of themselves in the early stages of the pandemic. Leading towards the emerging future became a way for leaders to focus beyond the immediate crisis and move beyond their fears.

Future fears

The impact the pandemic would have on people and communities, particularly if there were charity closures and/or an inability to engage with beneficiaries, was a cause for concern, with fear that this could result in intense poverty/increase in crime and complete 'community hopelessness'. Not being able to meet beneficiary demand or support increasing needs was a fear for some, with circumstances potentially deteriorating:

> There has been lots of talk about building back better, building forward but as things start to settle again, I am not seeing this translated into differences just yet - in fact in many ways things have got worse. People who didn't require support before lockdown now require support and several local services have stopped or are operating at reduced capacity.

A significant concern was income loss and funding reductions for charities, along with the longer-term economic impact of the pandemic. Some charities were 'experiencing such a dramatic loss of income' that their 'very future is at threat' with fears that if the situation continued, their 'centres will close permanently'. Concerns about the 'financial recovery and in turn the future of the organisation' left some feeling helpless and at the 'mercy of external forces we can't control'. Service disruption and the need to adapt were causing concern particularly in relation to people and communities served. Online working resulting in beneficiaries being 'unable to participate because of digital exclusion' would compound exclusion further.

The impact of the 'huge amount of uncertainty around what the new normal will look like' was a concern. As one leader put it, 'Knowing whether (we) will be able to adapt to the next phase effectively and continue to support (beneficiaries) to the quality to which we aspire was cause for a sleepless night'. Leaders tended to revert to focusing their priorities on other people and issues, both at micro and macro levels. Consideration went mainly to how the pandemic would impact on people, communities and strategic issues such as the finance and economy, with any concern for more personal issues such as their own health and wellbeing being mainly related to whether they would keep things going forward for the sake of others. Similarly, fears relating to their organisations and any disruption of services were mainly orientated towards how this would impact on the people and communities they serve. This reflects a sense of caring deeply for who charities are there to serve, and a sense of leader as servant to the greater good (Greenleaf, 1970). This suggests that when times are hard, leaders in the third sector cope by refocusing on their dedication to the mission, who they are there to support, and why they are there to support them, and therefore genuinely leading with purpose. A sense of purpose and passion helped leaders look to hope and opportunity to create new visions for the future.

Future hopes

As well as being a cause of anxiety, most future hopes related to service disruption and adaptation, with 'finding new ways of working' coming at the top of a list of hopes. This also linked to, but was broader than, digital ways of working. Increased creativity was also a key hope among respondents, as was maintaining ongoing agility and adapting. Achieving aspects of strategic change also featured heavily in hopes for the future. This included achieving a positive environmental impact alongside reduced travel, with one participant saying: 'Wouldn't it be marvellous if one of the outcomes of the deeply worrying and traumatic time we find ourselves in due to the climate emergency and now the COVID-19 pandemic is a step-change that gives much greater priority to our individual and collective health and wellbeing and that of our planet?' Realising societal change with different social norms and values was well expressed by one participant when they said: 'I believe we need a step-change, a paradigm shift in our social norms, our values and the way we all live'.

Participants discussed hopes relating to people and communities and to 'building back better'. These focused on positive economic impact, with wellbeing and inclusive growth at the heart; changed future thinking and building on what we learn through the pandemic; and overall political and system change being expressed by participants. One participant expressed this well in imagining a future where:

> 'We listen to people to understand what works and to ensure values of dignity and fairness are reflected in systems and processes. That new learning and perspectives show that we can work differently and be more effective. We cut out red tape and we resign inequality and poverty to history. We've been able to rapidly house people, distribute food and provide financial safety nets and foster a huge team effort. We can't go back on this.'

Some hoped for greater third sector recognition, with one respondent commenting that they 'hope that the leadership and contribution of the third sector is valued, supported and collaborative working is embraced as a positive force for change'. The key hope for improved relationships and partnerships was in further building on the 'incredible networking and collaborative working that has built up across organisations and sectors' and that the good work started through the pandemic would 'continue and go from strength to strength'. Leaders hoped they would be able to build their leadership further, be able to 'prove that we can make it work' and emerge stronger to survive and thrive.

Turning fear into hope and looking beyond the immediate challenge suggests a level of optimism, positivity and belief in a better future, reflecting a sense of leading with purpose, passion and dedication to the mission. For some, being optimistic was crucial at this time of great upheaval and uncertainty, providing an important coping mechanism. In the context of COVID-19, Conway (2021) argued that leaders can choose to be optimistic about the future, and in doing so, their organisations are more like to be successful and innovative.

Conclusions: lessons learnt and implications

While both challenging and concerning (especially for beneficiaries), service disruption is reported to have brought about some positive change and innovation, resulting in increased reach and engagement in some cases, and some creative and rapid development of services. It could be argued that the pandemic was a catalyst for change that was needed prior to lockdown. This is arguably shown by the fact that service disruption and adaptation was the area most identified by leaders as both a future fear and a future hope. Digital working, flexible and hybrid working, entirely new ways of engaging and delivering services all shifted rapidly, and in many ways, the pandemic has triggered disruptive innovation, accelerating the pace of change for charities.

Health and wellbeing emerge as a cross-cutting theme in these engagements with charity leaders. It is sometimes explicitly expressed as an issue, and sometimes implicitly through other challenges, tensions and pressures. Being able to talk openly and to share concerns safely (whether health and wellbeing-related or more broadly) helped leaders cope. Concern about the health and wellbeing of leaders and staff, related partly to the increased pressures experienced throughout the pandemic, was and remains a key issue. The pandemic left little time for self-care. The heightened importance of wellbeing (for self and others) became an additional burden for leaders. Balancing the needs of the employees, beneficiaries and organisation became the biggest tension for leaders.

Charity leaders' immediate response to crisis is often to focus on others first. It took some time (almost six months) before attention came back to them and challenges relating to 'being a CEO'. In finding a balance of self and others, leaders can lead without detriment to themselves and ultimately others. Leading well meant not leading at the expense of themselves. Strong connections and good relationships are key in reducing isolation and loneliness. This in turn affects health and wellbeing, feeling supported and being able to communicate effectively. Connections with the people affected by organisational decisions are crucial. Finding balance in giving and receiving the right amount of support and challenge, without going overboard or adding to the chaos, was important. This was the case with regards to board and CEO relationships. For some, there was too little connection with their board; for others, too much.

Leaders take care of their own needs for support and development in ways that feel safe. Peer support is critical, and in particular 'knowing you are not alone and that others understand and are going through the same experiences is more valuable and empowering than ever before'. Coming together to learn and share offers 'invaluable connection, networking, insight and discussion'.

Leading with purpose and passion, leaders get through tough times by constantly coming back to who they are there to serve and why. At the height of the first wave of the pandemic, in spring 2020, leaders were looking ahead and calling for strategic change. They held on to their vision and future thinking to get them beyond the immediate crisis. Dealing with the immediate, while looking outwards and forwards with realistic optimism, is reflected in the fact that almost every area identified as having potentially negative impacts was countered with positive impacts, and many future fears also held future hopes within them.

Notes

[1] Rather than reference each extract, the blogs can be found on the ACOSVO and SCVO websites: //acosvo.org.uk/news-blog and //tfn.scot/opinion/we-shouldnt-pretend-we-arent-human.

[2] At each online session, participants were asked to consent to the data being collected. Participants were all leaders (CEOs, senior managers or chairs) of Scottish voluntary organisations. The organisations they lead range in size and turnover, with 43.7 per cent of members leading organisations with a turnover under £500k, 14 per cent between £500k and £1m, 34.1 per cent over £1m and 8.3 per cent with no recorded turnover or being retired or out of post leaders. Themes were identified by 'tagging' the occurrences of keywords that emerged across our member engagements taken from contemporaneous notes of meetings. Each keyword was assigned a 'theme', and each theme assigned a 'family'. Due to the number of potential keywords, we chose to analyse the discussions at the thematic and family level only. While every effort has been made to ensure that the data recorded was as accurate as possible, and there was consistency in a full team effort to collect data, we were very much in a position of establishing methods and processes as new ways of working emerged. As such, there may be some discrepancies regarding how much data has been collected at different times, and how the data has been categorised.

[3] Only seven responses were received in the second tranche of case studies, after numerous prompts and requests to the original respondents. This could be indicative of the increase in demand on CEO time and partly because, at the time of the follow-up, two of the original respondents were no longer in post, another has since left their post and one charity has closed.

References

ACEVO (2019) *Pay and Equalities Survey 2019*, [online], Available from: www.acevo.org.uk/2019/03/pay-and-equalities-survey-2019-this-year-the-average-charity-ceo-will-spend-three-months-working-for-no-pay/ [Accessed 3 March 2022].

ACOSVO (2020) *COVID19 Impact on Voluntary Sector Organisations: Case Studies*, [online], Available from: //acosvo.org.uk/resources/wellbeing-succession-ssn32 [Accessed 3 March 2022].

ACOSVO (2021) *Knowledge & Insights Report 2021*, [online], Available from: //acosvo.org.uk/resources/insights-apr-mar [Accessed 3 March 2022].

Allcock Tyler, D. (2017) *It's Tough at the Top: The No Fibbing Guide to Leadership*, London: Directory of Social Change.

Armstrong, P. (2020) *Leadership and Being Human: ACOSVO*, [online], Available from: //tfn.scot/opinion/we-shouldnt-pretend-we-arent-human [Accessed 3 March 2022].

Barling, J. and Cloutier, A. (2017) 'Leaders' mental health at work: empirical, methodological, and policy directions', *Journal of Occupational Health Psychology*, 22(3): 394–406.

Conway, J. (2021) 'The power of the optimistic leader', [online], Available from: //waldencroft.com/the-power-of-the-optimistic-leader/ [Accessed 3 March 2022].

Ecclesiastical (2020) *Charity Risk Barometer 2020*, Gloucester: Ecclesiastical Insurance Office.

Gerard, L., McMillan, J. and D'Annunzio-Green, N. (2017) 'Conceptualising sustainable leadership', *Industrial and Commercial Training*, 49(3), 116–26.

Greenleaf, R. (1970) *The Servant as Leader*, Cambridge, Mass.: Center for Applied Studies.

Gruszka, A. and Nęcka, E. (2017) 'Limitations of working memory capacity: the cognitive and social consequences', *European Management Journal*, 35(6): 776–84.

Jones, V. (2019) *The Wellbeing of Chief Executives in the Charity Sector*, [online], Available from: //manchestercommunitycentral.org/sites/manchestercommunitycentral.co.uk/files/The%20wellbeing%20of%20Chief%20Executives%20in%20the%20charity%20sector%20-%20Victoria%20Jones.pdf [Accessed 25 February 2022].

Kirsh, D. (2000) 'A few thoughts on cognitive overload', *Intellectica. Revue de l'Association Pour La Recherche Cognitive*, 30: 19–51.

Lee, R.L. and Ashforth, B.E. (1996) 'A meta-analytic examination of the correlates of the three dimensions of job burnout', *Journal of Applied Psychology*, 81(2): 123–33.

Maslach, C., Schaufeli, W.B. and Leiter, M.P. (2000) 'Job burnout', *Annual Review of Psychology*, 52: 397–422.

SCVO (2020) *Supporting Scotland's Vibrant Voluntary Sector: Coronavirus and Its Impact on the Scottish Voluntary Sector – What Do We Know So Far?* [online], Available from: //storage.googleapis.com/scvo-documents-evidence/0693z00000AuvcFAAR-CoronavirusSurveys_May2020_8Jun.pdf [Accessed 25 February 2022].

19

Afterword

Margaret Harris

The chapters of this book provide a variety of perspectives on voluntary and community sector organisations (VCOs) during the period which began in March 2020 with the Westminster government's formal public response to the arrival of the COVID-19 virus in the UK (Prime Minister's Office, 2020). The period since then has been one of extraordinary turbulence for individuals, institutions and public policy. As this collection shows, VSOs too have been heavily impacted by the pandemic. They have also been an important part of the UK's response.

This Afterword chapter builds on research presented in the preceding chapters to consider two broad questions. First, what are the key themes which emerge from collected research to date on the behaviour of VCOs during the pandemic period? And, second, what are the pointers to the future for the sector as we stand in early 2022 (the time of writing) on the threshold of what we hope will be a period of 'recovery' from the pandemic?

As with the preceding chapters, the focus here is on non-governmental, nonprofit-seeking organisations. While this tight focus is necessary for building knowledge specifically about the VCS, it should not obscure the broader contextual picture, that the pandemic arrived in a UK already struggling to cope with some major economic, social and political challenges. These included differences in policy approaches between the four UK nations, the implementation of Brexit, the ongoing economic and social fallout from the 2008 global financial crisis and deep-seated public expectations of a freely available national healthcare system, one available for all in times of health need as well as free at the point of use (Light, 2003).

Thus, in March 2020, when the pandemic hit fully in the UK and infection rates were rising rapidly, many VCOs were already struggling with pressure to fill gaps in governmental health and welfare provision, gaps which were in part a legacy of the 'Big Society' policy agenda which basically *assumed* that the sector would fill gaps left by the retreat of public services provision (Alcock, 2010). Meeting the needs of refugees and asylum seekers, minority groups and low-income households was of special concern to VCOs at that point, as existing inequalities had been aggravated by public sector austerity measures over preceding years. These measures had not only increased the demands on voluntary sector welfare and healthcare providers, but had also diminished the resources available to the voluntary sector, especially from the sector's supporting infrastructure bodies (Clifford, 2017).

This context – a sector *already struggling* at the beginning of 2020 with the impact of rising demand for its services alongside diminished and uncertain future resources – needs to be borne in mind when taking an overview of the VCS during the COVID-19 period.

Voluntary and community organisations in the COVID-19 era

Initial response

One of the most outstanding features of the VCS response to the pandemic was what happened in the first few weeks of the crisis in March and April 2020. While national governments were consulting with specialists about how to respond to the emergency situation and what systems to set up in order to protect and support people deemed especially vulnerable for social or medical reasons, the immediate basic needs of those same people were in practice being met by the spontaneous voluntary efforts of individuals and informal, often newly formed, groupings operating at the street and neighbourhood level. In the first days and weeks of the pandemic, it was 'good neighbours' (many of whom were not able to attend their regular places of work and therefore had time to volunteer) who ensured that food and medicines were delivered to those confined to their homes and who ensured that social support and information was provided to people who simply could not comprehend the new situation in a country cast abruptly into 'lockdown' (Harris, 2021). The work of these community grassroots 'mutual aid' groups was supported after the first few surreal days by local 'networks' which facilitated sharing of advice about needs, available sources of help and good practice in volunteering; for example, how to mitigate risks to housebound people obliged to trust unknown volunteers with cash for shopping and how to coordinate individual requests for help.

Collaboration and networks

In fact, the formation of various kinds of collaborations and coordinating networks emerges from this book's chapters as a second notable theme. The aptly named 'mutual aid' network was one such. But it was also the case that many of the early and later voluntary efforts involved collaboration between pre-existing VCOs as well as between voluntary sector infrastructure organisations and local authorities. Many local authorities quickly reassigned staff to crisis tasks such as food distribution and, later, digital support. Often, local authorities worked in close cooperation with local voluntary organisations which had close (sometimes superior) local knowledge about needs and potential needs. It appears from research reports that these local-level, cross-sector collaborations between local governments and VCOs worked most effectively when they were able to build on cordial and trusting relationships that were well established prior to the pandemic.

As regards the links between the Westminster government and VCOs, these were largely 'behind the scenes' in the early weeks of the pandemic when cross-sector collaborations were most in evidence at the local community level. However, as shown in the preceding chapters, there were noticeable differences between the four nations in the speed and nature of collaborations established between national governments and voluntary organisations to respond to the pandemic.

Organisational adaptation

Although it seems that immediate spontaneous responses from individuals, small voluntary organisations and some local authorities ensured that basic needs were mostly met at the start of the pandemic, albeit in an unsystematic fashion, the strain on individual volunteers and paid staff in terms of dealing with highly stressful situations with little organisational support was overwhelming in the longer term. At the same time, the changes and increase in need occurred in the context of great concern from sector leaders and trustees about future availability of financial resources and community assets. Although many voluntary and community organisations started the pandemic period with some financial reserves, there were necessarily concerns about how the pandemic would impact on future funding streams. Would philanthropic support diminish, for example, if face-to-face appeals and fundraising events were no longer possible? Would charitable foundations have the resources to continue providing support? Those VCOs which were usually reliant on annual grants paid *after* service delivery had to make difficult choices about responding to urgent needs without being sure that they would be able to cover their expenditure in the future, a business model which would normally attract criticism of trustee behaviour (Charity Commission, 2022).

It was therefore fortunate that, as the immediate shock of the pandemic situation receded, established and larger voluntary organisations found ways to reprioritise or adapt their working systems so as to continue to meet needs but in modified or different ways. Some unofficially expanded their 'client base' and declared purposes. Volunteers who had formerly provided face-to-face services were not needed once social mixing was forbidden, but new volunteering opportunities emerged as different needs were identified (for example, the need for food deliveries to isolated and 'shielding' individuals, and for cooked meals and toiletries for medical staff working extended shifts on hospital COVID-19 wards).

Numerous examples are given in this book of such adaptations in working practices, practices additional to the networking mentioned earlier. Paid staff and volunteers used to delivering services face to face found new ways of remaining in touch with users, assessing their needs and providing practical and emotional support. Where service users did not have internet provision or computers or did not know how to access online communication systems, some voluntary organisations were able to provide digital mentoring or computer equipment – for school-age children and others who were 'digitally excluded'. Ways had to be found of training up volunteers at speed for pandemic-related tasks. In fact, research presented in this book tends to confirm the stereotype of smaller- and medium-size voluntary organisations being able to adapt quickly to changing circumstances and new needs, and to respond flexibly in times of crisis.

Conclusions about VCO behaviour

Chapters in this book suggest two key conclusions about the period following the initial arrival of the pandemic. One is that *local and small* VCOs were often able to work collaboratively and effectively – albeit informally – with other voluntary organisations and local authorities in responding to challenges thrown up by the pandemic, sharing information about needs and available resources, coordinating responses and involving volunteers alongside paid staff. Often, they were building on pre-existing local networks and trust-based relationships.

The second noteworthy point is how comparatively slow the response was to pandemic-related need from the Westminster government, leaving medium and smaller voluntary organisations to step in informally to identify and fill gaps in provision. Ironically perhaps, this was a playing out of the Big Society vision (of the third sector stepping up as the state retreats), but in crisis circumstances never envisaged by the framers of that public policy initiative.

Looking ahead and recovery from COVID-19

Change and challenge for individual VCOs

As the chapters collated in this volume show, the VCS encompasses a wide variety of nongovernmental, nonprofit-seeking organisations with a range of purposes, beneficiaries, legal statuses and organisational characteristics. Contributors also illustrate the truism that public policy impacts on VCOs in differing ways, depending largely on where they are located within the UK and the purposes they seek to fulfil. All the same, it does seem from the preceding chapters that VCOs serving some client groups have been particularly organizationally challenged during the pandemic by the combination of lack of resources with high demand for services. This point applies especially to BAME groups and to those responding to the needs of migrants. It follows that the generalisations made in the following paragraphs may not be applicable to all voluntary organisations or to all four nations of the UK.

With this proviso noted, we attempt in the following paragraphs to tease out from the book's chapters the key elements that have changed for individual VCOs during the period of the pandemic. In addition to the major shifts mentioned at the end of the preceding section – that needs changed, and mostly increased, at the same time as there was real concern about future funding streams – other important changes emerge from the research in this volume.

One point to note is that many VCOs have in practice changed their key organisational purposes in response to new needs and new demands, as well as increases in certain kinds of welfare needs (such as mental health, domestic violence, elderly people living alone and child poverty) exacerbated by the pandemic. Also, many VCOs have found new ways of meeting their main purposes, many of which are likely to endure after recovery from the pandemic; for example, moving face-to-face services to virtual format or planning with shorter time horizons. Many VCOs increased their advocacy activities during the pandemic, or changed the balance of their activities between service provision and advocacy. Many had to adapt and relax their approaches to 'risk' and use of 'reserves'.

The impact on paid staff, volunteers and board members of this need for constant adaptation to new needs and new regulations during the pandemic will no doubt be a subject for research in the future. Evidence presented in this volume suggests that some staff formerly committed to working in the sector will feel burnt out and will wish to move elsewhere. Others may feel that the COVID-19 pandemic was an event which gave meaning to their vocations and reinforced their commitment to the sector for the future.

Change and challenge for the sector

The chapters in this book have provided a range of perspectives on the behaviour of individual VCOs during the pandemic. The chapters also allow us to draw out some themes about what happened in the sector as a whole during the pandemic and the implications for the future of the sector.

One emergent theme is the need for sector organisations to reconsider access to resources; not simply 'getting in the money', but paying close attention to major sources of funding and how sustainable they are likely to be in times of crisis in the future. The long-established maxim that VCOs should aim to secure their sustainability as well as their independence by having a mix of funding sources is also confirmed by the experiences recounted in this book. Certainly, questions are raised about the advisability of relying on Westminster or national governments for funding when there is a sudden surge in demand. In the case of the COVID-19 crisis, Westminster politicians were fulsome in praise of the sector and 'civil society' but were slow to announce a (modest) funding initiative to help support the sector in the first period of the pandemic (DCMS, 2020). Politicians generally seemed to have little understanding of the distinctive operational realities for the sector. On the contrary, it can be said the Westminster government sought to 'co-opt' the public willingness to volunteer for good causes during the pandemic by setting up their own volunteering initiative in collaboration with just a few well-established, well-known charities (NHS, 2020) and later commissioning a report intended to provide proposals for sustaining the 'community spirit' evidenced during the lockdown phases of the pandemic (Kruger, 2020).

A second emergent theme relates to the long-standing speculation among policy commentators about the possible 'blurring of boundaries' between the governmental and voluntary sectors. The research collected in this book confirms that, at least in time of national emergency, there is a willingness and ability on the part of local authorities and their respective VCSs to work in such close cooperation that the usual barriers of differing working systems (Harris and Cairns, 2011) collapse, and it is 'all hands on deck in the public interest', irrespective of sector.

However, the 'blurred boundaries' idea does not fit well with what we now know happened at the Westminster government level during 2020. Civil servants and politicians made one-off arrangements with large, well-established charities, but did not work in a collaborative manner with them in a way which could be said to have blurred sector distinctions. The institutions of the two sectors worked within their own organisational traditions, with the links between them being on a formal and distant level. In an emergency and crisis situation, UK national governments remain focused, it seems, on continuing to do things their way.

Looking ahead

As we look ahead to a period beyond 2022 when, it is hoped, COVID-19 will be less of a social, economic and public health threat, what will be the legacies of the pandemic for VCOs that we might see? Some interesting trends to watch for emerge from a consideration of the chapters in this book.

One is that there will perhaps be more collaborations between community-level voluntary organisations and also between VCOs and their respective local authorities. The experience of successful cooperation during the pandemic may encourage organisations in both sectors to have confidence that cooperation can happen without co-optation of one sector by the other. The organisational self-confidence of VCOs might also have been boosted by their experiences of successful advocacy activity during the crisis. At the time of writing, there is some evidence of pandemic-generated interest in new forms of collaboration between organisations *within* the broader VCS (NCVO, 2021).

Second, it seems likely that the nature of volunteering will be changed for the long term by the experiences of the pandemic. Many who have not volunteered before may be attracted into one-off or 'episodic' volunteering which enables people to contribute to good causes without making regular or long-term commitments. Also, many volunteer-involving organisations may feel able to offer opportunities which do not require physical attendance but can be done long-distance or virtually. The pandemic has forced many volunteer managers to think in new ways about how they involve volunteers in their organisations and to think how new opportunities may be offered to volunteers.

Incentives to consider new ways of involving volunteers may be provided by a third possible trend, the turnover of paid staff in the sector occasioned by 'furloughing', redundancies and burnout during the pandemic period. Some who had thought they had a vocation to work solely in the sector may move into the business or governmental sectors as a means to refresh their career trajectories and recover from the emotional toll of the pandemic. Conversely, we can expect the churn in employment positions to result in more paid staff moving from other sectors *into* the VCS, as people reassess their life choices because of traumatic pandemic experiences. Such transfers could encourage the trend to more collaborative cross-sector working mentioned above.

We may also speculate, on the basis of chapters in this book, that many individual VCOs will emerge from the pandemic with a changed view of their purposes and goals. Many will wish to enlarge or modify the scope of their intended beneficiaries, having discovered new needs in new areas. Others will wish to continue to develop a close link in their work between service provision and advocacy on behalf of their beneficiaries. Others may be driven by resource concerns to narrow their purposes, change the ways they respond to needs, seek mergers or even dissolve entirely.

Finally, we may speculate about whether there is likely to be any change in the approach to the VCS by the Westminster government. Under the Conservative government in power at the time of writing, it seems that here is one area in which little change is likely. The Big Society idea that the third sector should pick up the slack as the state retreats from public service provision appears to have been fully justified by the research evidence provided in this book. When the country has its back to the wall, it seems, the sector can be relied on to respond flexibly to new needs and – literally – save lives. It seems that the Westminster government wants to preserve and encourage the 'community spirit' so much in evidence during the pandemic, but whether any governmental funding will follow to help VCOs contribute to the implementation of government policies (HM Government, 2022) remains to be seen. After the pandemic, VCOs will need not only direct financing and investment but also access to infrastructure organisations, many of which were weakened or disappeared during the years of austerity which preceded the COVID-19 crisis.

References

Alcock, P. (2010) 'Building the big society: a new policy environment for the third sector in England', *Voluntary Sector Review* 1(3): 379–89.

Charity Commission (2022) 'Charity inquiry: keeping kids company', [online], Available from: www.gov.uk/government/publications/charity-inquiry-keeping-kids-company/charity-inquiry-keeping-kids-company [Accessed 22 February 2022].

Clifford, D. (2017) 'Charitable organisations, the great recession and the age of austerity: longitudinal evidence for England and Wales', *Journal of Social Policy*, 46(1): 1–30.

DCMS (Department for Digital, Culture, Media and Sport) (2020) 'Financial support for voluntary, community and social enterprise (VCSE) organisations to respond to coronavirus (COVID-19)', [online], Available from: www.gov.uk/guidance/financial-support-for-voluntary-community-and-social-enterprise-vcse-organisations-to-respond-to-coronavirus-covid-19 [Accessed 5 February 2022].

Harris, M. (2020) 'Familiar patterns and new initiatives: UK civil society and government initial responses to the Covid-19 crisis', *Nonprofit Policy Forum*, 12(1): 25–44.

Harris, M. and Cairns, B. (2011) 'Local cross-sector partnerships: tackling the challenges collaboratively', *Nonprofit Management and Leadership*, 21(3): 311–24.

HM Government (2022) 'Levelling up the United Kingdom White Paper published February 2022', [online], Available from: www.gov.uk/government/publications/levelling-up-the-united-kingdom [Accessed 4 February 2022].

Kruger, D. (2020) *Levelling Up Our Communities: Proposals for a New Social Covenant*, [online], Available from: www.dannykruger.org.uk/new-social-covenant [Accessed 3 February 2022].

Light, D.W. (2003) 'Universal health care: lessons from the British experience', *American Journal of Public Health*, 93(1): 25–30.

NCVO (2021) *The Civil Society Group Launches to Increase Collaboration, Improve Efficiency, Effectiveness and Streamline Engagement*, [online], Available from: www.ncvo.org.uk/about-us/media-centre/press-releases/2834-the-civil-society-group-launches-to-increase-collaboration-between-charity-bodies-improve-efficiency-and-effectiveness-and-streamline-engagement-with-governments [Accessed 4 February 2022].

NHS (2020) *NHS Volunteer Responders*, [online], Available from: goodsamapp.org/NHS [Accessed 4 February 2022].

Prime Minister's Office (2020) 'Prime Minister's statement on coronavirus (Covid-19)', [online], Available from: www.gov.uk/government/speeches/pm-statement-on-coronavirus-12-march-2020 [Accessed 1 February 2022].

Index

References to figures appear in *italic* type; those in **bold** type refer to tables. References to endnotes show both the page number and the note number (197n3). As the COVID-19 pandemic is the major subject of this title, entries under this keyword have been kept to a minimum, and readers are advised to seek more specific headings.

A

Abbotsdale Community Centre 229
ABCD (Asset Based Community Development) 217–18, 219, 222
absorptive capacity
  BAME-led VSOs 104, 113
  community-led businesses 191
  definition of 197n7
  LNNs 11, 161, 163, 164, **164**, 167
ACOSVO (Association of Chief Officers of Scottish Voluntary Organisations) leadership study 12, 237, 246–7
  changing experiences, 2020–2021 239–41
  context 237–8
  early stage of the pandemic, 2020 238–9
  future fears 243–4
  future hopes 245–6
  impact on leaders 241–3
ACRE (Action for Communities in Rural England) 225, 226, 227, 229, 235
adaptive capacity
  BAME-led VSOs 104, 113
  community-led businesses 191
  definition of 197n7
  LNNs 11, 161, 163–4, **164**, 167
advocacy 122–3, 153
  advocacy work of VSOs in Wales 10, 126–8
  barriers to statutory services 123–4
  changing ways of working 124–5
  community advocacy 119, 123
  defining advocacy 122–3
  formal and informal 119–20
  individual advocacy 118–19, 124
  learning and innovation 125–6
  political advocacy 118, 124–5, 126
  study methodology 121–2
  nature of 118–21
affective emotions 174
  see also emotions
Age Better in Sheffield programme 106
Aiken, M. 133
Alakeson, V. 20
Allcock, Tyler, D. 238
Almog-Bar, M. 126
armed forces, and 'moral injury' 64

Asian women, online exercise class for 108
Asset Based Community Development (ABCD) 217–18, 219, 222
assets, physical
  disposal of by public bodies 132
  see also community buildings
Association of Chief Officers of Scottish Voluntary Organisations (ACOSVO) *see* ACOSVO (Association of Chief Officers of Scottish Voluntary Organisations) leadership study
asylum seekers *see* refugees, migrants and asylum seekers
austerity policies 31, 34, 35, 91, 92–3, 98, 99, 138, 147, 249–50, 256
Australia, charitable organisation formation and dissolution 48, *51*
Australian Charities and Not-for-profits Commission 48
autonomy, of TSOs 34–5
Aves, G. 212

B

BAME (Black, Asian and Minority Ethnic) communities 119, 249, 253
  disproportionate COVID-19 morbidity and mortality among 143–4, 145–6, 147–8
  inequalities 92, 104–5, 118, 146
  vaccine hesitancy in 113–14
  VSO advocacy services to 121, 122
BAME-led VSOs 10, 11, 104, 105–6, 113–15, 143–4, 151–2
  challenges and concerns 145–7
  demand issues 146, 148–9
  Ealing 104, 107, 111–13, 114
  financial resources and funding issues 10–11, 105–6, 109, 110, 112–13, 114–15, 144, 146–7, 149–51, 152
  implications for the future 150–1
  research approaches 144–5
  Salford 104, 107, 109–11, 114
  Sheffield 104, 106, 107–9, 114
  structural racism 147–8
  study methodology 106–7
BAOBAB Foundation 150
Barnes, M. 78

258

Index

Becaries, L. 146
Bell, A. 226
'Belle Isle Elderly Winter Aid' 157
Benton, E. 200, 201
Bevan Foundation 22
Beveridge, W.H.B. 199, 200–1
Bevy in Lockdown, The (Reid) **188**, 189, 191–2, 194
Big Society policies 31, 249, 252, 255
Black, Asian and Minority Ethnic (BAME) communities *see* BAME (Black, Asian and Minority Ethnic) communities; BAME-led VSOs
Black Lives Matter movement 174–5
Bolton, S. 175
bonding social capital
 and CSCs (community sports clubs) 205–6, 208
 see also social capital
'boundary-spanning' role of community-led businesses 195
Brett, W. 20
Brewis, G. 26
Brexit 2, 249
'bridging' role of VSOs between communities and statutory services 91, 96–7, 100
bridging social capital
 and CSCs (community sports clubs) 206, 208
 see also social capital
Brighton Aldridge Community Academy 194
British Red Cross 218, *220*
'building back better' 245
bureaucracy, as a barrier to collaborative working 87
burnout 9, 68
 employees 7, 22, 68, 173, 175, 179, 181–2
 leaders 237–8, 242, 243
 volunteers 7, 179

C

Camden, VAC (Voluntary Action Camden) 212, 215–17, *217*
Cameron, David 34
Canada, charitable organisation formation and dissolution 50, *51*
Canada Revenue Agency 48
capacity building 213
CCLORS (COVID-19 Community-Led Organisations Recovery Fund) 150, 151
CCT (Community Contact Tracing), Sheffield 109, 114
Centre for Ageing Better 157
ChangeUp programme 213
charitable organisations

formations and dissolutions 45–58, 227, 231–2
insolvencies 48–9, 55–6, *56*, 57
see also TSOs (third sector organisations); VCS (voluntary and community sector); VCSE (voluntary, community and social enterprise) sector; VSOs (voluntary sector organisations)
Charities Services, New Zealand 48
Charity Commission 227, 228
 NCVO *UK Civil Society Almanac* data 30, *31*, 32, 35, 39
Charity Commission for England and Wales 47, 48, 49
Charity Commission for Northern Ireland 48
charity insolvencies 48–9
#Charitysowhite 149–50
Chinese community, Wales 148
CiCs (community interest companies) 213
City Bridge Trust 149
Civil Contingencies Framework, Northern Ireland 24
Civil Society Strategy, England 20
Clifford, D. 46, 48
clinically extremely vulnerable (shielding) people 3, 81, 82, 97, 112, 149, 230, 251
 older people 161, 162–3, 166
coalition government 31, 34, 213
collaboration 8, 250–1, 254–5
 cross-sector collaborations between VCS and LAs 10, 78, 81–8
 as response to the pandemic 20–1, 22, 77
Collins, R. 174
Comic Relief 150, 151
Common Call (Do it Now Now) 150
Communities and Volunteering Circle, Scotland 24
community advocacy 119, 123
 see also advocacy
community buildings 10–11, 12, 130–1, 139–41, 225–7, 234–5
 changes in opportunity context 131, 134, 138–9, 140
 community-led businesses 189–90, 192, 196
 financial resources and funding issues 135–6, 141, 226, 229
 funding issues 135
 income-generating activities 133, 135–6
 management dilemmas during pandemic 134–6
 policy context and definitions 131–3
 remaking community 138–9, 140–1
 reopening, summer 2020 231–2, *232*
 response to lockdown 229–30
 sentiments, perceptions and challenges 136–8

study methodology 133–4, 227–8
urban-based 225, 235
volunteer numbers 232–3
Community Business Market in 2020 (Higton) 187, **188**, 188–9, 190, 191, 192–3, 195
Community Business Market in 2021 (Higton) **188**, 195, 196
Community Business Patchwork 194
Community Business Peer Networking before and during Coronavirus (Dobson) **188**, 194, 196
Community Contact Tracing (CCT), Sheffield 109, 114
community development work 119
community engagement programmes 84
community hubs 108–9, 211, 218, 221, 226
community interest companies (CiCs) 213
Community Matters research *see* community buildings
community ownership of physical assets *see* community buildings
community pubs 188, 189, 191, 192, 194
see also community buildings
Community Right to Bid 197n3
community shops 188
see also community buildings
community sports clubs (CSCs) *see* CSCs (community sports clubs)
community-led businesses 11–12, 186–7
changing workforce demands 191–2
community, trust and reputation 193–5
financial resources and funding issues 193, 194
future outlook for 195–6
research studies
Bevy in Lockdown, The (Reid) **188**, 189, 191–2, 194
Community Business Market in 2020 (Higton) 187, **188**, 188–9, 190, 191, 192–3, 195
Community Business Market in 2021 (Higton) **188**, 195, 196
Community Business Peer Networking before and during Coronavirus (Dobson) **188**, 194, 196
Helping Ensure Survival: Digitally Enhanced Services in Community Businesses (Gardner) **188**, 190, 192, 193, 195
Navigating Uncertainty and Remaining Resilient: The Experience of Community Businesses during Covid-19, Research Institute Report No. 28 (Avdoulos) **188**, 189, 190, 191, 192, 193–4, 194–5, 196
resilience 188–91
study methodology 187, **188**

support for 192–3
Companies House 48–9, 55
Conservative governments 31, 255
Conway, J. 246
Cook, J. 22
Coronavirus Job Retention Scheme (furlough) 3, 56, 57, 58, 66, 69, 202
community-led businesses 191–2
Corra Foundation 25
Councils for Social Services (CSSs) 212
councils for voluntary service (CVSs) *see* CVSs (councils for voluntary service)
County Voluntary Councils, Wales 81
Coutts, P. 20, 226
COVID-19 Community-Led Organisations Recovery Fund (CCLORS) 150, 151
COVID-19 pandemic
community initiatives to limit the local spread of 110–11
context and overview 2–5
misinformation 112
UK mortality and morbidity 3, 109
disproportionate effects among BAME communities 143–4, 145–6, 147–8
Crawford, L. 22
Cretu, C. 20
Croydon Voluntary Action (CVA) 217–19, 220, 221
CSCs (community sports clubs) 12, 199–200, 207–8
digital innovation 199, 206–7
financial resources and funding issues 202
meeting social needs 203–4
as mutual aid organisations 12, 199, 200–2, 207–8
and the needs of wider society 199, 205–6
study methodology 200
volunteer resilience 202–3
volunteers' responsibility for governance 201
CSSs (Councils for Social Services) 212
cultural awareness and understanding 112, 113–14
CVA (Croydon Voluntary Action) 217–19, 220, 221
CVSs (councils for voluntary service) 12, 211, 212, 214
see also voluntary sector infrastructure organisations

D

Dayson, C. 151, 173, 191
DCMSC (Digital, Culture, Media and Sport Select Committee) 146
demand, future implications of pandemic for VCS 7–8

Index

Digital, Culture, Media and Sport Select Committee (DCMSC) 146
digital exclusion 95, 107, 110, 120–1, 124, 127, 190, 207, 208, 252
digital inclusion 161, 163, 208
digital technology 21–2, 107, 108, 114, 120–1, 125–6, 127, 149, 239, 240–1, 242, 243, 245
  community-led businesses 190, 195–6
  CSCs (community sports clubs) 206–7, 208
dissolution of charitable organisations 45–8
  regulatory data study 48–50, *51*, 53–4, *54*, *55*, 56–8
distributed leadership 181
Do it Now Now (Common Call) 150
Doidge, M. 174
'doing good' during the pandemic, human costs of 9, 61–2, 71–2
  being a good employee 62, 65–8
  first response 63, 65–6
  organisational identity 63–5
  study methodology 62–3
  vignettes 63, 68–71
domestic violence survivors, VSO advocacy services to 121, 123

E

Ealing, BAME-led VSO response to pandemic 104, 107, 111–13, 114
Ecclesiatical 237–8
Economic and Social Research Council (ESRC) 18, 62
Ellis Paine, A. 21, 177, 212
Emergencies Leadership Group, Northern Ireland 24
Emergency Response Committee (ERC), London 218, 219, *220*, 221
emotions
  emotion management 175–6
  emotional labour 175
  motivational power of 174–5
  self-care 180–1, 181–2
  in the VCSE sector during the pandemic 11, 173
    context 177
    impact on workforce 177–9, 179–80, 182–3
    leaders' responses 179–83
    study methodology 175–6
  in the voluntary sector generally 173–5
employees
  burnout 7, 22, 68, 173, 175, 179, 181–2
  changing workforce demands in community-led businesses 191–2
  emotional impact on VCSE workforce during the pandemic 177–9, 179–80, 182–3
  future patterns of work 255

over-representation of BAME people in frontline/key worker staff 143–4, 145–6, 147–8
redeployment of 81–2
skills and emotional labour of VSO employees 99
vicarious trauma of VSO employees 97
see also furlough (Coronavirus Job Retention Scheme)
England
  charitable organisation formation and dissolution 46
  policy context 18, 20
  policy response to pandemic 23–4, 25
  volunteer mobilisation 78–9
  vulnerable migrants 94
England and Wales, charitable organisation formation and dissolution 46, 48–9, 50, *51*, *52*, 52–3, 54, *54*, 57
English language proficiency 96–7
English Village and Community Hall Survey 235
Equality Act 2010 145
ERC (Emergency Response Committee), London 218, 219, *220*, 221
ESRC (Economic and Social Research Council) 18, 62
Ethnic minority Youth Support Team (EYST), Wales 145, 148
Evers, A. 33
EYST (Ethnic minority Youth Support Team), Wales 145, 148

F

Facebook 107, 162, 230
Farah, A. 149
Filipino community 147–8
financial resources and funding issues 4–5, 61, 251
  advocacy VSOs in Wales 120, 124–5, 126, 127
  BAME-led VSOs 10–11, 105–6, 109, 110, 112–13, 114–15, 144, 146–7, 149–51, 152
  community buildings 135–6, 141, 226, 229
  community-led businesses 193, 194
  CSCs (community sports clubs) 202
  emotions in VCSE (voluntary, community and social enterprise) sector during the pandemic 177, 183
  future patterns and prospects 7, 253–4, 256
  LNN ('Leeds Neighbourhood Network') for older people and healthy ageing 157, 166–8
  refugees, migrants and asylum seekers 92, 93, 95, 96, 98, 99
Scotland 24–5

261

TSOs (third sector organisations) 36–7, 38, 39, 40–1, *41*
voluntary sector infrastructure organisations 213–14, 215, 219
flexibility
 community buildings 137
 TSOs (third sector organisations) 35–7, 36, *38*, 39–40
 VSO support for refugee and migrant families in Glasgow 91, 94–5
Floyd, George 174–5
food provision services during the pandemic 4, 6, 12, 81, 94–5, 99, 107, 111, 137, 148, 178, 189, 219, 221, 250, 251
food banks 82, 98, 194, 208, 218, 222
older people 159, 160, 163, 230
formal advocacy 119
 see also advocacy
formation of charitable organisations 45–8
 regulatory data study 48–50, *51*, *52*, 52–3, *53*, 56–8
Foundation Scotland 25
four nations comparative study 17–18, 25–6
 existing research publications findings 20–2
 policy divergence and adjustments 22–5
 study design 18–20
frontline staff
 emotional labour 175
 over-representation of BAME people as 143–4, 145–6, 147–8
functional ability, of older people 158, **159**, 160
funding *see* financial resources and funding issues
furlough (Coronavirus Job Retention Scheme) 3, 56, 57, 58, 202
 community-led businesses 191–2

G

gaps in provision 91, 92–3, 98–9
Gilchrist, A. 87
Glasgow, Scotland, VSO support for refugee and migrant families 91–2, 93–4, 99–100
 'bridging' role between communities and statutory services 91, 96–7, 100
 flexibility and adaptability 91, 94–5
 navigating and challenging policy 91, 93, 97–8
 trusted relationships 91, 93, 95–6
global financial crash 2008 32, 35, 41, 138, 147, 249
Good Friday Agreement, Northern Ireland 18
GoodGym 216, 217, *217*
GoodSAM Responders app 3, 79, 83
Goodwin, J. 174

governance, volunteers' responsibility for in CSCs (community sports clubs) 201
Granovetter, M. 211, 214, 216, 217, 219
Greater London Authority 218, *220*
Greene, A. 174
Grotz, J. 17

H

Haldane, A. 205
Hall, S. 143–4, 152
Hampstead Council for Social Welfare (CSS) 212, 215
Hancock, Matt 3
Haque, Z. 104, 105
Health and Social Community of Practice 194
healthy ageing *see* LNN ('Leeds Neighbourhood Network') for older people and healthy ageing
Helping Ensure Survival: Digitally Enhanced Services in Community Businesses (Gardner) **188**, 190, 192, 193, 195
Higher Education Innovation Fund 106
Hill, M. 212
Hochschild, A. 175
Hoggett, P. 173, 174
home schooling 71, 173, 238
 support for in Salford 110
homeless people, VSO advocacy services to 121
'hostile immigration environment' 147–8
Hustedde, R. 175–6

I

ICNARC (Intensive Care National Audit and Research Centre) 145
Immigration and Asylum Act (1999), Section 4 98
Inclusion London 149
Independent SAGE Report 146
individual advocacy 118–19, 124
 see also advocacy
informal advocacy 119–20
 see also advocacy
information sharing 86–7
Institute for Voluntary Action Research (IVAR) 176, 181, 182, 183
Intensive Care National Audit and Research Centre (ICNARC) 145
Internal Revenue Services, United States of America 48
internet access *see* digital inclusion
Interrupted Time Series Analysis (ITSA) 49, 50, 53, 54
ITSA (Interrupted Time Series Analysis) 49, 50, 53, 54
IVAR (Institute for Voluntary Action Research) 176, 181, 182, 183

Index

J
James, M. 203
Jasper, J.M. 174
Johnson, Boris 2, 5, 21

K
Kanlugan 147–8
Kaye, S. 4, 20, 21
Kearney, J. 17
key workers, over-representation of BAME people as 143–4, 145–6, 147–8
Kim, M. 46
King, B. 175–6

L
Labour Party 5
language barriers 110, 112, 118, 123–4
  see also translation services
LAs (local authorities) 34, 250–1, 254
  cross-sector collaborations with VCS (voluntary and community sector) 10, 78, 81–8
  policy response to pandemic 21, 77
Laville, J.L. 33
leadership 67
  ACOSVO (Association of Chief Officers of Scottish Voluntary Organisations) study 12, 237, 246–7
  changing experiences, 2020–2021 239–41
  context 237–8
  early stage of the pandemic, 2020 238–9
  future fears 243–4
  future hopes 245–6
  impact on leaders 241–3
  leaders' health and wellbeing 238, 239, 240, 241, 242–3, 246–7
  VCSE leaders' responses to emotions during the pandemic 179–83
Leeds see LNN ('Leeds Neighbourhood Network') for older people and healthy ageing
Leeds City Council 157, 167
'Levelling-Up White Paper,' 2022 8
LGBT+ Consortium 149
LGBTIQ (lesbian, gay, bisexual, trans, intersex and queer) people, Salford 111
LIOs (local infrastructure organisations) 4
Litz, B.T. 64
'Living with COVID' strategy 5
Lloyds Bank Foundation for England and Wales 107
LNN ('Leeds Neighbourhood Network') for older people and healthy ageing 11, 156–7, 167–8
  effectiveness and resilience characteristics 164–7
  financial resources and funding issues 157, 166–8
  implications of pandemic for 163–4, **164**
  pre-pandemic support services 158, **159**, 160
  resources 166–7
  response to pandemic 160–3
  study methodology 156–7
Local Area Coordination 84
local capacity building 213
local groups 4, 9, 20
  see also mutual aid organisations
local infrastructure organisations (LIOs) 4
Localism Act 2011 197n3
London Plus 214, 215, 218, 219, *220*
Lyons, M. 200

M
Macmillan, R. 4, 7, 18, 56, 85, 114, 147, 151
Majonzi Fund 150
Mali Enterprising Leadership (MEL) 151
Manchester Settlement 226
medicine provision services during the pandemic 3, 4, 6, 12, 83, 111, 161, 163, 250, 251
  VAC (Voluntary Action Camden) 215–16, 217, *217*
MEL (Mali Enterprising Leadership) 151
Mesarič, A. 93, 99
migrants see refugees, migrants and asylum seekers
Miller, C. 173, 174
'moral injury' 64
MoVE (Mobilising Volunteers Effectively) research project 78, 79
Murray, K. 105
Muslim community, Salford 110–11
mutual aid organisations 4, 9, 20, 81, 82–3, 87, 88, 148, 251
  CSCs (community sports clubs) as 12, 199, 200–2, 207–8
  see also volunteering

N
National Council for Voluntary Organisations (NCVO) see NCVO (National Council for Voluntary Organisations)
National Lottery Community Fund 150
National Trust, England 174, 201, 202
national volunteer schemes 78–81, 83
  NHS Volunteer Responders scheme 3, 21, 79–80, 83, 148

Navigating Uncertainty and Remaining Resilient: The Experience of Community Businesses during Covid-19, Research Institute Report No. 28 (Avdoulos) **188**, 189, 190, 191, 192, 193–4, 194–5, 196
Nazroo, J. 146, 151
NCVO (National Council for Voluntary Organisations) 4–5, 206–7, 226–7
  UK Civil Society Almanac 30, *31*, 32, 35, 39
NDPBs (non-departmental public bodies)/quangos 34
neighbourhood networks *see* LNN ('Leeds Neighbourhood Network') for older people and healthy ageing
NET (National Emergencies Trust) 25, 149–50
network diffusion 216, 217
New Labour governments 31, 213
New Public Management 31
New Zealand, charitable organisation formation and dissolution 48, *51*
NHS (National Health Service)
  'moral injury' 64
  NHS Volunteer Responders scheme 3, 21, 79–80, 83, 148
  North Central London Commissioning Group (NCL CCG) 215, 216, 217, *217*
Nichols, G. 203
NCL CCG (NHS North Central London Commissioning Group) 215, 216, 217, *217*
no recourse to public funds (NRPF) policy 92, 98
non-departmental public bodies (NDPBs)/quangos 34
'nonprofit density' literature 46
'nonprofit dissolution' literature 46
northern England *see* TSOs (third sector organisations)
Northern Ireland
  charitable organisation formation and dissolution 48, 50, *51*
  policy context 18, 20
  policy response to pandemic 23, 24
Northern Ireland Volunteering Strategy 17
Northern Rock Foundation 32
Nottingham Trent University 226–7
NRPF (no recourse to public funds) policy 92, 98

O

Office of the Scottish Charity Regulator 48
older people

digital inclusion and exclusion 161, 163, 207
see also LNN ('Leeds Neighbourhood Network') for older people and healthy ageing
online booking systems 206

P

PAR (participatory action research) 78
peer support *see* ACOSVO (Association of Chief Officers of Scottish Voluntary Organisations) leadership study
personal protection equipment (PPE) 105, 125
Phoenix Fund 150
Phoenix Way 150
physical assets
  disposal of by public bodies 132
  see also community buildings
Pierson, C. 26
political advocacy 118, 124–5, 126
PPE (personal protection equipment) 105, 125
prescription medication *see* medicine provision services during the pandemic
private sector organisations, difference from TSOs 33–4, 40
Public Accounts Committee 227
Public Health England 105
public sector organisations, difference from TSOs 34–5
Putnam, R.D. 222

Q

quangos/NDPBs (non-departmental public bodies) 34
Quinn, N. 100
'Quirk Review' 131

R

racism 91, 143–4, 152
  structural racism 147–8
  see also BAME (Black, Asian and Minority Ethnic) communities
reactive emotions 174
  see also emotions
Ready Scotland 79
refugees, migrants and asylum seekers 249, 253
  emotions, and VCSE social workers 175
  financial resources and funding issues 92, 93, 95, 96, 98, 99
  'hostile immigration environment' 147–8
  VSO advocacy services to 118, 120, 121, 122, 123

VSO support for refugee and migrant families in Glasgow 91–2, 93–4, 99–100
  'bridging' role between communities and statutory services 91, 96–7, 100
  flexibility and adaptability 91, 94–5
  navigating and challenging policy 91, 93, 97–8
  trusted relationships 91, 93, 95–6
remote working 66–7, 69–70, 178
  community-led businesses 190, 195–6
  see also digital technology; working from home
resilience
  of community-led businesses 188–91
  of CSC volunteers 202–3
  effectiveness and resilience characteristics of LNNs 164–7
  volunteer resilience in CSCs (community sports clubs) 202–3
  see also absorptive capacity; adaptive capacity; transformational capacity
Resilient Communities Team, Scotland 24
resources see financial resources and funding issues
Resourcing Racial Justice 150
'Respond, recover, reset: the voluntary sector and COVID-19' project, Nottingham Trent University 46
Robinson, K. 175, 181
Rochester, C. 212
Roma communities
  Glasgow, Scotland 92, 94, 95, 97
  Sheffield 107
  VSO advocacy services to 122
Rudnicka, E. 158

S

safeguarding issues 85, 89n2
Salford, BAME-led VSO response to pandemic 104, 107, 109–11, 114
Sandri, J. 174
SARS-CoV-2 see COVID-19 pandemic
Schmid, H. 126
Scotland
  charitable organisation formation and dissolution 48–9, 50, *51*, 52–3, *53*, 54, *55*
  COVID-19 relief funding 24–5
  financial resources and funding issues 24–5
  policy context 18, 20
  policy response to pandemic 5, 23, 24–5
  pre-pandemic inequalities 92
  volunteer mobilisation 78–9
  VSO support for refugee and migrant families in Glasgow 91–2, 93–4, 99–100
  'bridging' role between communities and statutory services 91, 96–7, 100
  flexibility and adaptability 91, 94–5
  navigating and challenging policy 91, 93, 97–8
  trusted relationships 91, 93, 95–6
  see also ACOSVO (Association of Chief Officers of Scottish Voluntary Organisations) leadership study
Scotland Cares 79
'Scotland Cares' campaign 24
Scottish Council for Voluntary Organisations (SCVO) 25
Scottish Emergency Funding Advisory Board 25
Scottish Third Sector Tracker 47
Scrub Hub 230
SCVO (Scottish Council for Voluntary Organisations) 25
secondary trauma, of VSO employees 97
Seebohm Report 212
self-care 180–1, 181–2, 246–7
Sharkey, P. 46
Sheffield, BAME-led VSO response to pandemic 104, 106, 107–9, 114
Sheffield Fraternal of Black Majority Churches 109
Sheffield Hallam University 226, 227
shielding (clinically extremely vulnerable) people 3, 81, 82, 97, 112, 149, 230, 251
  older people 161, 162–3, 166
SNP (Scottish National Party) 5
social capital 120, 222
  community-led businesses 194
  CSCs (community sports clubs) 205, 208
social networking platforms 107, 114
  see also Facebook; WhatsApp; Zoom
social prescribing 84, 215, 216, 222
Social Renewal Advisory Board, Scotland 24
Sport England 199, 200, 201, 202
sports facilities see community buildings; CSCs (community sports clubs)
state, retreat of 98–9
Stephenson, Helen 227
Sunak, Rishi 5

T

Taylor-Gooby, P. 25
Team Rubicon 218, *220*
Terry, V. 67
Tesco 218, *220*
Third Sector Support Wales 24
Tiratelli, L. 4, 20, 21
transformational capacity, community-led businesses 191

translation services 96, 97, 109, 112, 113, 120, 123–4
trust relationships, VSOs (voluntary sector organisations) 91, 93, 95–6, 120, 124, 127, 151
TSOs (third sector organisations) 9, 30, 31, 40–2, *41*
  adaptability and robustness of 31–2
  difference and distinctiveness of 33–5
  financial resources and funding issues 36–7, *38*, 39, 40–1, *41*
  flexibility and financial fluctuations 35–7, *36*, *38*, 39–40
  impact of COVID-19 pandemic on 39–40, 41–2
  see also charitable organisations; VCS (voluntary and community sector); VCSE (voluntary, community and social enterprise) sector; VSOs (voluntary sector organisations)
TSTS (Third Sector Trends Study) *see* TSOs (third sector organisations)

U

Ubele Initiative 146–7, 149
  MEL (Mali Enterprising Leadership) 151
Ubele Report 144–5, 147, 150
UK Civil Society Almanac, NCVO 30, *31*, 32, 35, 39
UK Data Service 62
UKRI (UK Research and Innovation) 2, 9, 18, 61
University of South Wales 122
USA (United States of America), charitable organisation formation and dissolution 46, 48, 50, *51*

V

VAC (Voluntary Action Camden) 212, 215–17, *217*
Vacchelli, E. 93, 99
vaccinations 5, 24, 163
  vaccine hesitancy in BAME (Black, Asian and Minority Ethnic) communities 113–14
VAs (voluntary actions) 12, 211
  see also voluntary sector infrastructure organisations
VCs (volunteer centres) 12, 211
  see also voluntary sector infrastructure organisations
VCS (voluntary and community sector) 77–8
  context and overview 3–5
  cross-sector collaborations with LAs (local authorities) 10, 78, 81–8
  experiences and knowledge 5–7
  four nations comparative study 17–26
  future implications of 7–8
  government support for 4–5
  infrastructure organisations 85
  initial response to pandemic 251
  organisational adaptation 251–2
  recovery and future prospects 252–6
  research response 6–7
  volunteer mobilisation 78, 88–9
    local responses 81–3
    national volunteer schemes 78–81, 83
  see also charitable organisations; TSOs (third sector organisations); VCSE (voluntary, community and social enterprise) sector; VSOs (voluntary sector organisations)
VCSE (voluntary, community and social enterprise) sector 61, 62, 190
  emotions in during the pandemic 11, 173–6
  context 177
  financial resources and funding issues 177, 183
  impact on workforce 177–9, 179–80, 182–3
  leaders' responses 179–83
  study methodology 175–6
  see also charitable organisations; TSOs (third sector organisations); VCS (voluntary and community sector); VSOs (voluntary sector organisations)
vicarious trauma, of VSO employees 97
village halls 130, 187, 225, 226, 227, 230, 233, 235
  see also community buildings
Voluntary Action Camden (VAC) 212, 215–17, *217*
voluntary action, definition of 17
Voluntary and Community Sector Resilience Advisory Group, Scotland 24
voluntary sector infrastructure organisations 12, 211–12, 221–2, 256
  bridging role between statutory and voluntary sectors 213–14, 216, *217*, 219, 222
  CVA (Croydon Voluntary Action) 217–19, *220*, 221
  embeddedness of 212, 214, 216–17, 218, 219, 221, 222
  financial resources and funding issues 213–14, 215, 219
  role of 212–14
  study methodology 214–15
  VAC (Voluntary Action Camden) 212, 215–17, *217*
volunteering 10, 21–2, 77–8, 88–9, 148–9, 211, 251
  burnout 7, 179
  changes over lifecourse 26
  community-led businesses 192

cross-sector collaborations between VCSs and LAs 10, 78, 81–8
future patterns of 255
importance of informal volunteering in pandemic response 9, 20
local schemes 81–3
national volunteer schemes 3, 21, 78–81, 83
TSOs *38*, 39, 40
volunteers' responsibility for governance in CSCs 201
see also mutual aid organisations
Volunteering for All: Our National Framework, Scotland 20
Volunteering Strategy, Northern Ireland 24
VSOs (voluntary sector organisations)
advocacy work of VSOs in Wales 10, 118–21, 126–8
barriers to statutory services 123–4
changing ways of working 124–5
financial resources and funding issues 120, 124–5, 126, 127
learning and innovation 125–6
nature of advocacy 118–21, 122–3
study methodology 121–2
collaboration and funding 97
and the retreat of the state 98–9
skills and emotional labour of employees 99
support for refugee and migrant families in Glasgow 91–2, 93–4, 99–100
'bridging' role between communities and statutory services 91, 96–7, 100
flexibility and adaptability 91, 94–5
navigating and challenging policy 91, 93, 97–8
trusted relationships 91, 93, 95–6
see also BAME-led VSOs; charitable organisations; TSOs (third sector organisations); VCS (voluntary and community sector); VCSE (voluntary, community and social enterprise) sector
VSSN (Voluntary Sector Studies Network) 1

W

Wales
advocacy work of VSOs 10, 118–21, 126–8
barriers to statutory services 123–4
changing ways of working 124–5
learning and innovation 125–6
nature of advocacy 118–21, 122–3
study methodology 121–2
BAME-led VSOs 145, 148
COVID-19 relief funding 24
England and Wales, charitable organisation formation and dissolution 46, 48–9, 50, *51*, *52*, 52–3, 54, *54*, 57
policy context 18, 20
policy response to pandemic 5, 23, 25
volunteer mobilisation 78, 80–1
Welsh government, and political advocacy by VSOs 124–5
Ward, J. 174
WCVA (Wales Council for Voluntary Action) 24, 121
weak ties 217, 219
Welsh Voluntary and Community Association 80
WhatsApp 83, 107, 112, 114, 126, 127, 162, 180, 204
WHO (World Health Organisation), healthy ageing definition 158
Wilding, Karl 146
Williamson, V. 64
Wolfenden Report 212–13
Women's Resource Centre 149
working from home 66–7, 69–70, 243
impact on leaders 238
work-life balance 66–8, 70–1, 178–9, 239
Wrixon, K. 67

Y

Yemeni community, Salford 110–11

Z

Zoom 6, 68, 94, 108, 125–6, 162, 180, 204

www.ingramcontent.com/pod-product-compliance
Lightning Source LLC
Chambersburg PA
CBHW071152070526
44584CB00019B/2756